THE
WINNER'S CURSE
Paradoxes
and Anomalies of
Economic Life

Richard H. Thaler

PRINCETON UNIVERSITY PRESS

PRINCETON, NEW JERSEY

Published by Princeton University Press, 41 William Street,
Princeton, New Jersey 08540
In the United Kingdom: Princeton University Press,
Chichester, West Sussex

Library of Congress Cataloging-in-Publication Data
Thaler, Richard H., 1945–
    The winner's curse: paradoxes and anomalies of economic life /
Richard H. Thaler.
        p.   cm.
    Originally published: New York: Free Press, © 1992.
    "A Russell Sage Foundation book."
    Includes bibliographical references and index.
    ISBN 0-691-01934-7 (paperback)
    1. Economics—Miscellanea. 2. Paradoxes. I. Title.
HB199.T47   1994
330—dc20   93-27713

First Princeton Paperback printing, 1994

Reprinted by arrangement with The Free Press,
a Division of Macmillan, Inc.

Princeton University Press books are printed on acid-free paper
and meet the guidelines for permanence and durability of the
Committee on Production Guidelines for Book Longevity of the
Council on Library Resources

10   9   8   7   6   5   4

Printed in the United States of America

http://pup.princeton.edu

To
Jessi, Maggie, and Greg
My Favorite Anomalies

Contents

Acknowledgments

This book required more than the usual amount of help to write. Versions of each of the chapters in this book were previously published by the *Journal of Economic Perspectives* in a special feature on "Anomalies." I owe thanks to the editors, Carl Shapiro and Joseph Stiglitz, for inviting me to write this series. (The idea for the Anomalies feature was hatched during a dinner conversation I had with Hal Varian, who then passed on the suggestion to the *Journal*.) Without those quarterly deadlines, there is no way I would have ever produced this book (see Chapter 8). Carl and Timothy Taylor also read, commented on, edited, and greatly improved all the columns. Their suggestions were always constructive, and often followed.

For more than half of the columns I solicited one or more collaborators. Their names appear in the Table of Contents and on the first page of the corresponding chapters. Many of the coauthored chapters would have been impossible for me to write alone, and none of them would have been as good (or as much fun to do) if I had done them by myself. I want to emphasize that every coauthor was a full partner, and I would request that academics who wish to cite a coauthored chapter of this book please either cite the original column or be sure to include the coauthor's name in the citation. (The original references to the published columns appear below.)

Writing four columns a year took a lot of time, and, as we know, time is money. I am grateful to Concord Capital Management and the Russell Sage Foundation for providing the money, and to the Johnson Graduate School of Management at Cornell for yielding the time. Eric Wanner at Russell Sage went well beyond the normal duties of a Foundation President by serving as my book agent. And Tom Dyckman has been very helpful and flexible in arranging my Cornell duties, though please don't tell him that.

I have also had the help of several patient friends who have read far more than their share of my first (and sometimes second and third) drafts. Those who have carried a special burden are Maya Bar-Hillel, Colin Camerer, Werner De Bondt, Pat Degraba, Bob Frank, Danny Kahneman, Ken Kasa, Jay Russo, and Tom Russell. All were cooperative well before they read Chapter 2. Dennis Regan, Charlotte Rosen, and Deborah Treisman all read the galley proofs and helped spot numerous typos. Finally, Peter Dougherty, my editor at The Free Press, helped me turn 13 columns into a book. Thanks.

The material in this book was previously published in the *Journal of Economic Perspectives* and is reprinted here with the permission of the American Economics Association. The articles were revised for this book. The original references are Robyn M. Dawes and Richard H. Thaler (1988), "Cooperation," *Journal of Economic Perspectives*, Vol. 2, No. 3, pp. 187–97; Werner F. M. DeBondt and Richard H. Thaler (1989), "A Mean-Reverting Walk Down Wall Street," *Journal of Economic Perspectives*, Vol. 3, No. 1, pp. 189–202; Kenneth A. Froot and Richard H. Thaler (1990), "Foreign Exchange," *Journal of Economic Perspectives*, Vol. 4, No. 3, pp. 179–92; Daniel Kahneman, Jack L. Knetsch, and Richard H. Thaler (1991), "The Endowment Effect, Loss Aversion, and Status Quo Bias," *Journal of Economic Perspectives*, Vol. 5, No. 1, pp. 193–206; Charles M. C. Lee, Andrei Shleifer, and Richard H. Thaler (1990), "Closed-End Mutual Funds," *Journal of Economic Perspectives*, Vol. 4, No. 4, pp. 153–64; George Loewenstein and Richard H. Thaler (1989), "Intemporal Choice," *Journal of Economic Perspectives*, Vol. 3, No. 4, pp. 181–93; Richard H. Thaler (1987), "The January Effect," *Journal of Economic Perspectives*, Vol. 1, No. 1, pp. 197–201; Richard H. Thaler (1987), "Seasonal Movements in Security Prices II: Weekend, Holiday, Turn of the Month, and Intraday Effects," *Journal of Economic Perspectives*, Vol. 1, No. 1, pp. 197–201; Richard H. Thaler (1988), "The Winner's Curse," *Journal of Economic Perspectives*, Vol. 2, No. 1, pp. 191–202; Richard H. Thaler (1988), "The Ultimatum Game," *Journal of Economic Perspectives*, Vol. 2, No. 4, pp. 195–206; Richard H. Thaler (1989), "Interindustry Wage Differentials," *Journal of Economic Perspec-*

tives, Vol. 3, No. 2, pp. 181–93; Richard H. Thaler (1990), ''Saving, Fungibility, and Mental Accounts,'' *Journal of Economic Perspectives,* Vol. 4, No. 1, pp. 193–205; Richard H. Thaler and William T. Ziemba (1988), ''Parimutuel Betting Markets: Racetracks and Lotteries,'' *Journal of Economic Perspectives,* Vol. 2, No. 2, pp. 161–74; Amos Tversky and Richard H. Thaler (1990), ''Preference Reversals,'' *Journal of Economic Perspectives,* Vol. 4, No. 2, pp. 201–11.

[1]

Introduction

A friend of yours is the Chairman of the Acme Oil Company. He occasionally calls with a problem and asks your advice. This time the problem is about bidding in an auction. It seems that another oil company has gone into bankruptcy and is forced to sell off some of the land it has acquired for future oil exploration. There is one plot in which Acme is interested. Until recently, it was expected that only three firms would bid for the plot, and Acme intended to bid $10 million. Now they have learned that seven more firms are bidding, bringing the total to ten. The question is, should Acme increase or decrease its bid? What advice do you give?

Did you advise bidding more or less? Most people's intuition in this problem is to bid more. After all, there are additional bidders, and if you don't bid more you won't get this land. However, there is another important consideration that is often ignored. Suppose that each participant in the auction is willing to bid just a little bit less than the amount he or she thinks the land is worth (leaving some room for profits). Of course, no one knows exactly how much oil is in the ground: some bidders will guess too high, others too low. Suppose, for the sake of argument, that the bidders have accurate estimates on average. Then, who will be the person who wins the auction? The winner will be the person who was the most optimistic about the amount of oil in the ground, and that person may well have bid more than the land is worth. This is the dreaded *winner's curse*. In an auction with many bidders, the winning bidder is often a loser. A key factor in avoiding the winner's curse is bidding more conservatively when there are more bidders. While this may seem counter-intuitive, it is the rational thing to do.

This book is about economics anomalies, of which the winner's curse is an example. An anomaly is a fact or observation that is inconsistent with the theory. Here, the theory of rational bidding advises bidding less when the number of bidders increases, yet most people would end up bidding more. Two ingredients are necessary to produce a convincing anomaly: a theory that makes crisp predictions and facts that contradict those predictions. In the case of economics anomalies, both ingredients can be difficult to obtain. While there is no shortage of economic theories, the theories are often extremely difficult to pin down. If we can't agree on what the theory predicts, then we can't agree on what constitutes an anomaly. In some cases, economists have in fact argued that some theories are simply not testable because they are true by definition. For example, the theory of utility maximization is said to be a tautology. If someone does something, no matter how odd it may seem, it must be utility maximizing, for otherwise the person wouldn't have done it. A theory is indeed not testable if no possible set of data could refute it. (In fact, it is not really a theory, more like a definition.) However, while many economists have taken comfort in the apparent irrefutability of their theories, others have been busy devising clever tests. And in economics the following natural law appears to hold: where there are tests there are anomalies.

What is economic theory? The same basic assumptions about behavior are used in all applications of economic analysis, be it the theory of the firm, financial markets, or consumer choice. The two key assumptions are rationality and self-interest. People are assumed to want to get as much for themselves as possible, and are assumed to be quite clever in figuring out how best to accomplish this aim. Indeed, an economist who spends a year finding a new solution to a nagging problem, such as the optimal way to search for a job when unemployed, is content to assume that the unemployed have already solved this problem and search accordingly. The assumption that everyone else can intuitively solve problems that an economist has to struggle to solve analytically reflects admirable modesty, but it does seem a bit puzzling. Surely another possibility is that people simply get it wrong. The possibility of cognitive error is of obvious importance in light of what Herbert Simon has called *bounded rationality*. Think of the human brain as a personal computer, with a very slow processor and a memory system that is both small and unreliable. I don't know about you, but the PC I carry between my ears has more disk failures than I care to think about.

What about the other tenet of economic theory, self-interest? Just how selfish are people? The trouble with the standard economic model is illustrated by the behavior exhibited by the drivers in Ithaca where I live. There is a creek that runs behind Cornell University. The two-way road that crosses this creek is served by a one-lane bridge. At busy times of the day, there can be several cars waiting to cross the bridge in either direction. What happens? Most of the time, four or five cars will cross the bridge in one direction, then the next car in line will stop and let a few cars go across the bridge in the other direction. This is a traffic plan that would not work in New York City nor in an economic model. In New York City a bridge operating under these rules would, in effect, become one-way, the direction determined by the historical accident of the direction being traveled by the first car to arrive at the bridge![1] In economic models, people are assumed to be more like New Yorkers than like Ithacans. Is this assumption valid? Fortunately, the cooperative behavior displayed by the Ithaca drivers is not unique. Most of us, even New Yorkers, also donate to charity, clean up camp grounds, and leave tips in restaurants—even those we never plan to visit again. Of course, many of us also cheat on our taxes (they will just waste the money anyway), overstate losses when making claims to insurance companies (well, just to recover the deductible), and improve the lie of our balls in golf (winter rules in August, if no one is looking). We are neither pure saints nor sinners—just human beings.

Unfortunately, there aren't many human beings populating the world of economic models. For example, the leading economic model of savings behavior, the life-cycle hypothesis, takes no account of the most important human factor entering savings decision making—self-control. In this model, if you receive a $1000 windfall you are expected to save almost all of it, since you wish to evenly divide the consumption of the windfall over all of the rest of your remaining years of life. Who needs windfalls if you have to spend them like that!

[1] Indeed, every once in a while two cars do meet in the middle of the bridge, with a resulting game of chicken. My suspicion is that these drivers are from big cities.

We human beings do other things economists think are weird. Consider this one: You have won two tickets to the Super Bowl, conveniently (for this example) being played in the city where you live. Not only that, but your favorite team is playing. (If you are not a football fan, substitute something else that will get you appropriately excited.) A week before the game, someone approaches you and asks whether you would be willing to sell your tickets. What is the least you would be willing to accept for them? (Assume selling tickets is legal at any price.) Now, instead, suppose you do not have two tickets to the Super Bowl, but you have an opportunity to buy them. What is the most you would be willing to pay? For most people, these two answers differ by at least a factor of 2. A typical answer is to say that I wouldn't sell the tickets for less than $400 each, but I wouldn't pay more than $200. This behavior may seem reasonable to you, but according to economic theory your two answers should be almost identical, so the behavior must be considered an anomaly. This is not to say that there is anything wrong with the theory as a theory or model of rational choice. Rationality *does* imply the near equality of buying and selling prices. The problem is in using the same model to *prescribe* rational choice and to *describe* actual choices. If people are not always rational, then we may need two different models for these two distinct tasks.

Of course, I am hardly the first to criticize economics for making unrealistic assumptions about behavior. What is new here? To understand how the anomalies illustrated here present a new type of critique of economics, it is useful to review what the prior defenses of economic theory have been. The most prominent defense of the rational model was offered by Milton Friedman (1953). Friedman argued that even though people can't make the calculations inherent in the economic model, they act *as if* they could make the calculations. He uses the analogy of an expert billiards player who doesn't know either physics or geometry, but makes shots as if he could make use of this knowledge. Basically, Friedman's position is that it doesn't matter if the assumptions are wrong if the theory still makes good predictions. In light of this argument, this book stresses the actual predictions of the theory. I find that, assumptions aside, the theory is vulnerable just on the quality of the predictions.

A defense in the same spirit as Friedman's is to admit that of course people make mistakes, but the mistakes are not a problem in explaining aggregate behavior as long as they tend to cancel out. Unfortunately, this line of defense is also weak because many of the departures from rational choice that have been observed are systematic—the errors tend to be in the same direction. If most individuals tend to err in the same direction, then a theory which assumes that they are rational also makes mistakes in predicting their behavior. This point, stressed by my psychologist collaborators Daniel Kahneman and Amos Tversky, makes the new behavioral critique of economics more substantive.

Another line of defense is to say that neither irrationality nor altruism will matter in markets where people have strong incentives to choose optimally. This argument is taken to be particularly strong in financial markets where the costs of transactions are very small. In financial markets, if you are prepared to do something stupid repeatedly, there are many professionals happy to take your money. For this reason, financial markets are thought to be the most "efficient" of all markets. Because of this presumption that financial markets work best, I have given them special attention in this book. Perhaps surprisingly, financial markets turn out to be brimming with anomalies.

But why a whole book of anomalies? I think there are two reasons to bring these anomalies together. First, it is impossible to evaluate empirical facts in isolation. One anomaly is a mere curiosity, but 13 anomalies suggest a pattern. Thomas Kuhn, a philosopher of science, commented that "discovery commences with the awareness of anomaly, i.e., with the recognition that nature has somehow violated the paradigm-induced expectations that govern normal science." In this book I hope to accomplish that first step—awareness of anomaly. Perhaps at that point we can start to see the development of the new, improved version of economic theory. The new theory will retain the idea that individuals try to do the best they can, but these individuals will also have the human strengths of kindness and cooperation, together with the limited human abilities to store and process information.

[2]

Cooperation

A Monty Python sketch[1] keeps coming back to you. The two characters are a banker (played by John Cleese) and a Mr. Ford (played by Terry Jones), who is collecting money for charity with a tin cup.

BANKER: How do you do. I'm a merchant banker.

FORD: How do you do Mr. . . .

BANKER: Er . . . I forgot my name for a moment but I *am* a merchant banker.

FORD: Oh. I wondered whether you'd like to contribute to the orphan's home. (*He rattles the tin.*)

BANKER: Well I don't want to show my hand too early, but actually here at Slater Nazi we are quite keen to get into orphans, you know, developing market and all that . . . what sort of sum did have in mind?

FORD: Well . . . er . . . you're a rich man.

BANKER: Yes, I am. Yes, very, very, very, very, very, very, very, very, very, very, very rich.

FORD: So er, how about a pound?

BANKER: A pound. Yes, I see. Now this loan would be secured by the . . .

FORD: It's not a *loan*, sir.

BANKER: What?

FORD: It's not a loan.

BANKER: Ah.

With Robyn M. Dawes.
[1]This sketch is reproduced with permission from *The Complete Monty Python's Flying Circus: All the Words, Vol.2* (New York: Pantheon Books, 1989), pp. 92–94. Copyright Python Productions 1989.

FORD: You get one of these, sir. (*He gives him a flag.*)

BANKER: It's a bit small for a share certificate isn't it? Look, I think I'd better run this over to our legal department. If you could possibly pop back on Friday.

FORD: Well, do you have to do that, couldn't you just give me the pound?

BANKER: Yes, but you see I don't know what it is *for*.

FORD: It's for the orphans.

BANKER: Yes?

FORD: It's a gift.

BANKER: A what?

FORD: A gift?

BANKER: Oh a *gift!*

FORD: Yes.

BANKER: A tax dodge.

FORD: No, no, no, no.

BANKER: No? Well, I'm awfully sorry I don't understand. Can you explain exactly what you want?

FORD: Well, I want you to give me a pound, and then I go away and give it to the orphans.

BANKER: Yes?

FORD: Well, that's it.

BANKER: No, no, no, I don't follow this at all, I mean, I don't want to seem stupid but it looks to me as though I'm a pound down on the whole deal.

FORD: Well, yes you are.

BANKER: I am! Well, what is my incentive to give you the pound?

FORD: Well, the incentive is—to make the orphans happy.

BANKER: (*genuinely puzzled*) Happy? . . . Are you quite sure you've got this right?

FORD: Yes, lots of people give me money.

BANKER: What, just like that?

FORD: Yes.

BANKER: Must be sick. I don't suppose you could give me a list of their names and addresses could you?

FORD: No, I just go up to them in the street and ask.

BANKER: Good lord! That's the most exciting new idea I've heard in years! It's so simple it's brilliant! Well, if that idea of yours isn't worth a pound I'd like to know what is. (*He takes the tin from Ford.*)

FORD: Oh, thank you sir.

BANKER: The only trouble is, you gave me the idea before I'd given you the pound. And that's not good business.

FORD: It isn't?

BANKER: No, I'm afraid it isn't. So, um, off you go. (*He pulls a lever opening a trap door under Ford's feet and Ford falls through with a yelp.*)
Nice to do business with you.

Much economic analysis—and virtually all game theory—starts with the assumption that people are both rational and selfish. An example is the analysis of the famous prisoner's dilemma (Rapoport and Chammah, 1965). A prisoner's dilemma game has the following structure. Two players must each select a strategy simultaneously and secretly. In the traditional story, the two players are prisoners who have jointly committed some crime and are being held separately. If each stays quiet (cooperates) they both are convicted of a minor charge and receive a one-year sentence. If just one confesses and agrees to testify against the other (defects), he goes free while the other receives a ten-year sentence. If both confess, they both receive a five-year sentence. The game is interesting because confessing is a dominating strategy—it pays to confess no matter what the other person does. If one player confesses and the other doesn't, he goes free rather than spend five years in jail. If, on the other hand, the other player also confesses, then confessing means a five-year sentence instead of ten. The assumptions of rationality and self-interest yield the prediction that people playing a game with this structure will defect. People are assumed to be clever enough to figure out that defection is the dominant strategy, and are assumed to care nothing for outcomes to other players; they will, moreover, have no qualms about their failure to do ''the right thing.''

A similar analysis applies to what economists call *public goods.*

A public good is one which has the following two properties: (1) once it is provided to one person, it is costless to provide to everyone else; (2) it is difficult to prevent someone who doesn't pay for the good from using it. The traditional example of a public good is national defense. Even if you pay no taxes, you are still protected by the Armed Forces. Another example is public radio and television. Even if you do not contribute, you can listen and watch. Again, economic theory predicts that when confronted with public goods, people will "free ride." That is, even if they enjoy listening to public radio, they will not make a contribution because there is no (selfish) reason to do so. (For a modern treatment of the theory of public goods, see Bergstrom, Blume, and Varian, 1986.)

The predictions derived from this assumption of rational selfishness are, however, violated in many familiar contexts. Public television in fact successfully raises enough money from viewers to continue to broadcast. The United Way and other charities receive contributions from many if not most citizens. Even when dining at a restaurant away from home in a place never likely to be visited again, most patrons tip the server. And people vote in presidential elections where the chance that a single vote will alter the outcome is vanishingly small. As summarized by Jack Hirshleifer (1985, p. 55), "the analytically uncomfortable (though humanly gratifying) fact remains: from the most primitive to the most advanced societies, a higher degree of cooperation takes place than can be explained as a merely pragmatic strategy for egoistic man." But why?

In this chapter and the next one, the evidence from laboratory experiments is examined to see what has been learned about when and why humans cooperate. This chapter considers the particularly important case of cooperation versus free riding in the context of public good provision.

SINGLE-TRIAL PUBLIC GOODS EXPERIMENTS

To investigate why people cooperate, it is necessary to examine behavior in both single-play and multiple-play environments. Does cooperation evolve, for instance, only as individuals repeatedly interacting with each other find it in their interests to cooperate? A typical public goods experiment uses the following procedures. A group of subjects (often, college students) is brought to the laboratory. Groups vary in size, but experiments usually have between four and ten subjects. Each subject is given a sum of money, for example, $5. The money can either be kept and taken home, or some or all of the money can be invested in a public good, often called a *group exchange*. Money invested in the group exchange for the n participants is multiplied by some factor k, where k is greater than one but less than n. The money invested, with its returns, is distributed equally among all group members. Thus, while the entire group's monetary resources are increased by each contribution (because k is greater than one), each individual's share of one such contribution is less than the amount she or he invests (because k is less than n). To take a concrete example, suppose k = 2 and n = 4. Then if everyone contributes all $5 to the public good, each ends up with $10. This is the unique Pareto efficient allocation: no other solution can make everyone better off. On the other hand, any one individual is always better off contributing nothing, because in exchange for a player's $5 contribution, that player receives only $2.50, while the rest of the payoff ($7.50) goes to the other players. In this game, the rational, selfish strategy is to contribute nothing and hope that the other players decide to invest their money in the group exchange. If one player contributes nothing while all the others contribute $5, then that player will end up with $12.50, while the other players end up with $7.50. These conditions constitute what is sometimes called a "social dilemma."

What does economic theory predict will happen in such a game? One prediction, called the *strong free rider hypothesis*, is that everyone will choose the dominant strategy, that is, nothing will be contributed to the public good. This is surely the outcome predicted by the selfish rational model. A less extreme prediction, called the *weak free rider hypothesis*, is that some people will free ride while others will not, yielding a suboptimal level of the public good, though not necessarily zero. The weak free rider hypothesis obviously does not yield very precise predictions.

The results of single play ("one shot") public goods experiments lend little support to the strong free rider hypothesis. While not everyone contributes, there is a substantial number of contributors, and the public good is typically provided at 40–60 percent of the optimal quantity. That is, on average, the subjects contribute 40–60 percent of their stake to the public good. In a study by Marwell and Ames (1981), these results held in many conditions: for subjects playing the game for the first time, or after a previous experience; for subjects who believed they were playing in groups of 4 or 80; and for subjects playing for a range of monetary stakes, though in the experiments with the highest stakes, contribution rates were somewhat lower. Indeed, Marwell and Ames found only one notable exception to this 40–60 percent contribution rate. When the subjects were a group of University of Wisconsin economics graduate students, the contribution rate fell to 20 percent, leading them to title their article "Economists Free Ride: Does Anyone Else?"[2] (Interestingly, economists told about the experiments predicted on the average a rate of about 20 percent—but for all participants, not just their students.)

MULTIPLE TRIAL EXPERIMENTS

A natural question to ask about the surprisingly high level of co-operation observed by Marwell and Ames is what would happen if the same players repeated the game several times. This question has been investigated by Kim and Walker (1984), Isaac, Walker, and Thomas (1984), and Isaac, McCue, and Plott (1985). The experimental design in these papers is similar to that of Marwell and Ames, except that there are usually ten repetitions of the game. Two major conclusions emerge from these papers. First, on the initial trial, cooperation is observed at rates similar to those obtained by Marwell and Ames. For example, across nine different experiments with varying designs, Isaac, McCue, and Plott obtained a 53 percent contribution rate to the public good. Second, within a few repetitions, cooperation declines sharply. After five trials, the contributions to the public good were only 16 percent of the optimum. The experiments by Isaac, Walker, and Thomas also obtained a decline in the contribution rate over time, though the decline was not as abrupt.[3]

Why does the contribution rate decline with repetition? One

[2]This result has never been replicated, and so should be treated as preliminary. We wonder, however, whether economists *are* different. Do economists as a group donate less to charity than other similar groups? Are they less likely to leave tips in out-of-town restaurants?

[3]For experiments with a high return to contributing to the public good, the initial contribution rate was 52 percent which fell to 32 percent on trial 10. In versions with low returns to contributing, the initial rate was 40 percent and the final rate was 8 percent.

reasonable conjecture is that subjects learn something during the experiment that induces them to adopt the dominant strategy of free riding. Perhaps the subjects did not understand the game in the first trial and only learned that free riding was dominant over time. This possibility, however, appears unlikely in light of other experimental evidence. For example, the usual cooperation rates of roughly 50% are observed on trial 1 even for *experienced* subjects, that is, subjects who have participated in other multiple trial public goods experiments (e.g., Isaac and Walker, forthcoming). Also, Andreoni (1987a) has investigated the learning hypothesis directly using the simple procedure of restarting the experiment. Subjects were told they would play a ten-period public goods game. When the ten periods were completed, the subjects were told they would play again for another ten rounds with the same other players. In the first ten trials Andreoni replicated the decaying contribution rate found by previous investigators, but upon restarting the game contributions went back up to virtually the same contribution rates observed on the initial trial in the first game (44 percent on trial 1 of the second game versus 48 percent in the first). Such results seem to rule out any explanation of cooperation based on subjects' misunderstanding the task.[4]

RECIPROCAL ALTRUISM

One currently popular explanation of why we observe so much cooperation in and outside of the laboratory invokes reciprocal altruism as the mechanism. This explanation, most explicitly developed by Axelrod (1984), is based on the observation that people tend to reciprocate—kindness with kindness, cooperation with cooperation, hostility with hostility, and defection with defection. Thus, being a free rider may actually be a less fruitful strategy when the chooser takes account of the probable future response of others to his or her cooperation or defection. A cooperative act itself—or a reputation for being a cooperative person—may with high probability be reciprocated with cooperation, to the ultimate benefit of the cooperator.

The most systematic strategy based on the principle of reciprocal altruism is a TIT-FOR-TAT one first suggested by Anatol Rapoport, in which a player begins by cooperating and then chooses

[4] A similar conclusion is reached by Goetze and Orbell (forthcoming).

the same response the other player has made on the previous trial. The real strength of this explanation lies in demonstrating, both analytically and by computer tournaments of interacting players (programs) in iterated social dilemmas, that any person or small group of people practicing such reciprocal altruism will have a statistical tendency to receive higher payoffs "in the long run" than those who don't practice it. In fact, TIT-FOR-TAT "won" two computer tournaments Axelrod conducted in which game theorists proposed various strategies that were compared to each other in pairwise encounters with repeated plays. Because evolution is concerned with such long-run probabilistic phenomena, it can be inferred that reciprocating people have greater "inclusive fitness" than do non-reciprocating ones. Hence, to the degree to which such a tendency has some genetic basis, it should evolve as an adaptation to the social world.

An implication of reciprocal altruism is that individuals will be uncooperative in dilemma situations when there is no possibility of future reciprocity from others, as in situations of anonymity or interacting with people on a "one-shot" basis. Yet we observe 50 percent cooperation rates even in single-trial experiments, so reciprocal altruism cannot be used directly to explain the experimental results described so far. Also, of course, it is very difficult to play TIT-FOR-TAT, or any other strategy based on reciprocal altruism, when more than two people are involved in the repeated dilemma situation. If some members of a group cooperate on trial t while others defect, what should a player attempting to implement a TIT-FOR-TAT type strategy choose on the subsequent trial?

A related hypothesis that appears consistent with the decaying contribution rates observed in the multiple-trial experiments is suggested by the theoretical work of Kreps, Milgrom, Roberts, and Wilson (1982). They investigate the optimal strategy in a repeated prisoner's dilemma game with a finite number of trials. If both players are rational then the dominant strategy for both is to defect on every trial. While TIT-FOR-TAT has been shown to be effective in infinitely repeated prisoner's dilemma games (or equivalently, games with a constant small probability of ending after any given trial), games with a known end point are different. In any finite game both players know that they should defect on the last trial, so there is no point in cooperating on the penultimate trial, and by backward induction, it is never in one's best interest to cooperate. What Kreps et al. show is that if you are playing against an opponent who you think may be irrational (i.e., might play TIT-FOR-TAT even in a game with finite trials), then it may be rational to cooperate early in the game (to induce your irrational opponent to cooperate too). Since the public goods games have a similar structure, it could be argued that players are behaving rationally in the Kreps et al. sense. Once again, however, the data rule out this explanation. Cooperation never falls to zero, even in one-trial games or in the last period of multi-trial games when it can never be selfishly rational to cooperate.

Additional evidence against the reciprocity hypothesis comes from another experiment designed by Andreoni (1988). One group of 15 subjects played repeated trials in groups of five as described above. Another group of 20 subjects played the same game in groups of five, but the composition of the group varied on each trial. Moreover, the subjects did not know which four of the other 19 subjects would constitute their group in any given round of the game. In this condition, there can be no strategic advantage to cooperation, since the players in the next round will be, in essence, strangers. If cooperation in early rounds of these experiments is observed, strategic cooperation can be ruled out. Indeed, Andreoni found that cooperation was actually a bit higher in the stranger condition than in a comparable condition where the groups remained intact. (This effect was statistically significant, though slight.)

One conclusion which emerges from these experiments is that people have a tendency to cooperate until experience shows that those with whom they're interacting are taking advantage of them. This *norm of cooperation* will resemble reciprocal altruism in infinite repeated games; but, the behavior, as we have seen, is also observed in cases when reciprocal altruism would be inappropriate. One explanation for this type of behavior is offered by Robert Frank (1987). Frank argues that people who adopt a norm of cooperation will do well by eliciting cooperation from others, and attracting interaction with other cooperators. The key to Frank's argument is that one cannot successfully fake being cooperative for an extended period of time—just as one cannot be successful getting people to believe too many lies.[5] Furthermore, be-

---

[5] As the late Senator Sam Ervin said: "The problem with lying is that you have to have a perfect memory for what you said." None of us do. It's easier to remember what actually happened, although that is not easy either.

cause cooperators are, by assumption, able to identify one another, they are able to interact selectively and exclude defectors.

ALTRUISM

There are other explanations of why people cooperate both in the lab and in the real world. One is that people are motivated by "taking pleasure in others' pleasure." Termed *pure altruism* by Andreoni (1987b), this motive has been eloquently stated by Adam Smith, in *The Theory of Moral Sentiments* (1759; 1976): "how selfish soever man may be supposed to be, there are evidently some principles in his nature, which interest him in the fate of others, and render their happiness necessary to him, though he derive nothing from it, except the pleasure of seeing it." While the pleasure involved in seeing it may be considered "selfish" (following the sophomoric argument that altruism is by definition impossible, because people do what they "want" to do), the passage captures the idea that people are motivated by positive payoffs for others as well as for themselves. Consequently, they may be motivated to produce such results through a cooperative act. One problem with postulating such pure altruism as a reason for contributing to public goods is that such contributions cannot be explained purely in terms of their effects. If they could, for example, then governmental contributions to the same goal should "crowd out" private contributions on a dollar-for-dollar basis, since the results are identical no matter where the funding comes from. Such crowding out does not appear to be nearly complete. In fact, econometric studies indicate that an increase in governmental contribution to such activities is associated with a decrease in private contribution of only 5–28 percent (Abrams and Schmitz, 1978, 1984; Clotfelter, 1985).

Another type of altruism that has been postulated to explain cooperation is that involved in the act of cooperating itself, as opposed to its results. "Doing the right (good, honorable, . . .) thing" is clearly a motive for many people. Sometimes termed *impure altruism*, it generally is described as satisfaction of conscience, or of noninstrumental ethical mandates.

The roles of pure and impure altruism, and other causes for cooperation (or the lack thereof) have been investigated over the last decade by the team of Robyn Dawes, John Orbell, and Alphons van de Kragt. In one set of experiments (Dawes et al., 1986), they examined the motives for free riding. The game used for these experiments had the following rules. Seven strangers were given $5 each. If enough people contributed their stake to the public good (either three or five depending on the experiment), then every person in the group would receive a $10 bonus whether or not they contributed. Thus, if enough subjects contribute, each contributor would leave with $10 and each noncontributor would leave with $15. If too few contributed then non-contributors would keep their $5 while contributors would leave with nothing. Subjects were not permitted to talk to one another (though this was modified in subsequent experiments). In this context two reasons for not contributing can be identified. First, subjects may be afraid that they will contribute but not enough others will, so their contribution will be futile. This motive for defecting was termed "fear." Second, subjects may hope that enough others will contribute and hope to receive $15 instead of $10. This motive was called "greed." The relative importance of fear and greed was examined by manipulating the rules of the game. In the "no greed" condition, payoffs were changed so that all subjects would receive $10 if the number of contributors was sufficient (rather than $10 for contributors and $15 for free riders). In the "no fear" condition contributors were given a "money back guarantee": if a subject contributed and not enough others did, the subject would receive the money back. (However, in this condition if the public good was provided, contributors would receive only $10 while free riders would get $15.) The results suggested that greed was more important than fear in causing free riding. In the standard game contribution rates averaged 51 percent. In the no fear (money back) game contributions rose to 58 percent, but in the no greed game contributions were 87 percent.[6]

Another possible interpretation is that the no greed condition can produce a stable equilibrium, while the no fear cannot. If subjects in the no greed condition believe that the mechanism of

[6] Notice that contributing could be selfishly rational if a subject thought that the probability his or her contribution would be critical (that is, exactly M-1 others will contribute) was greater than one-half. However, subjects who contributed did not generally believe that their contribution was necessary. Virtually no contributors believed they were critical to obtaining the public good with a probability greater than .5. In fact, pooling across all conditions, 67 percent of the contributors believed so many others would contribute that their own contributions would be redundant.

truncating payoffs works to motivate others to contribute, their motive will be enhanced as well, because the only negative result of contributing occurs if enough others *don't* contribute. In contrast, subjects in the no fear condition who conclude that the conditions will encourage others to contribute will be tempted to free ride themselves, leading to the conclusion that others will be tempted as well, leading to the conclusion that they should themselves contribute, etc.—an infinite loop.

One of the most powerful methods for inducing cooperation in these games is to permit the subjects to talk to one another. Twelve groups were run with the same payoffs described earlier, but under conditions in which discussions were allowed. The effect of this discussion was remarkable (van de Kragt et al., 1983). Every group used the discussion period to specify a group of people who were designated to cooperate. The most common means of making the distributional decision was by lottery, though volunteering was also observed. One group attempted interpersonal utility comparisons to determine relative "need." Whatever methods the groups used, they worked. All 12 groups provided the public good, and in three of the groups more than the required number of subjects contributed. These results are consistent with the earlier ones. Subjects designated as contributors cannot greedily expect more from free riding, because their contributions are (believed to be) crucial for their obtaining the bonus (and were in all but three groups). Moreover, belief that others in the designated set of contributors will be motivated to contribute by the designated contributor mechanism will enhance—rather than diminish—each designated contributor's motive to contribute.

One possible explanation for the value of discussion is that it "triggers" ethical concerns that yield a utility for doing the "right" thing (i.e., impure altruism). Elster (1986), for example, has argued that group discussions in such situations yield arguments for group-regarding behavior (it is hard to argue for selfishness), and that such arguments have an effect not only on the listener but on the person making them as well. To test this hypothesis, a new set of experiments was conducted (van de Kragt et al., 1986). In this set of experiments all seven subjects were given $6 each. They could either keep the money or contribute it to the public good in which case it would be worth $12 to the other six members of the group. In this case, keeping the $6 is a dominant strategy, because the person who does so receives both that $6 and $2 from each of the other six group members who gave away the money.

Subjects first met in groups of 14 in a waiting room in which they were not allowed to talk, and were then divided into the two groups on a clearly random basis. Half of these sub-groups were allowed to talk about the decision, half not. The experimenters told half of the groups that the $12 given away would go to the other six people in their own group, while the other half of the groups were told that the money would go to six people in the other group. There are thus four conditions—discussion or no discussion crossed with money goes to own group or other group. If discussion simply makes individuals' egoistic payoffs clear, then it should not increase cooperation rates in any of these conditions since free riding is dominant. If, however, discussion increases utility for the act of cooperation per se, then discussion should be equally effective whether the money given away goes to members of their own group or to the other group—consisting, after all, of very similar people who were indistinguishable prior to the random drawing (usually college students or poorer members of the community).

The results were clear. In the absence of discussion, only about 30 percent of the subjects gave away the money, and those who did so indicated that their motive was to "do the right thing," irrespective of the financial payoffs.[7] Discussion raises the cooperation rate to 70 percent, but only when the subjects believe the money is going to members of their own groups: otherwise, it is usually less than 30 percent. Indeed, in such groups it was common to hear comments that the "best" possible outcome would be for all group members to keep their money while those in the other group gave it away (again, people from whom the subjects have been randomly separated about ten minutes earlier).

Thus, group identity appears to be a crucial factor in eschewing the dominating strategy. That result is compatible with previous

[7] In a similar—but simulated—"one shot" experiment, Hofsteadter (1983) discovered a roughly identical cooperation rate among his eminent friends. Most defect, but some cooperate, and for reasons of impure altruism. As one cooperator, Professor Daniel C. Dennett of Tufts, put it: "I would rather be the person who bought the Brooklyn Bridge than the person who sold it. Similarly, I feel better spending $3 gained by cooperation than $10 gained by defection." (Hofsteadter terms that a "wrong reason" for cooperating in a dilemma situation; yet it is the one often given by the subjects who cooperate without discussion in the experiments described above, and similar ones.)

social-psychological research on the "minimal group" paradigm (e.g. Tajfel and Turner, 1979; and the papers contained in Turner and Giles, 1981), which has repeatedly demonstrated that allocative decisions can be sharply altered by manipulations substantially weaker than ten minutes of discussion. For example, a "common fate" group identity—where groups received differing levels of payoffs depending on a coin toss—led subjects to attempt to "compensate" for non-cooperators in their own group by increasing cooperation rates, while simultaneously decreasing cooperation when the non-cooperators were believed to be in the other group, even when the identities of the people involved were unknown (Kramer and Brewer, 1986).

In the groups in which discussion was permitted it was very common for people to make promises to contribute. In a second series of experiments, Orbell, Dawes, and van de Kragt (forthcoming) investigated whether these promises were important in generating cooperation. Perhaps people feel bound by their promises—or believe they will receive a "satisfactory" payoff if they give away the money when others promise to do so because others will be bound by such promises. The main result was that promise making was related to cooperation only when every member of the group promised to cooperate. In such groups with universal promising, the rate of cooperation was substantially higher than in other groups. In groups in which promising was not universal there was no relationship between each subject's choice to cooperate or defect and: (1) whether or not a subject made a promise to cooperate, and (2) the number of other people who promised to cooperate. Consequently, the number of promises made in the entire group and the group cooperation rate were unrelated. These data are consistent with the importance of group identity if (as seems reasonable) universal promising creates—or reflects—group identity.

COMMENTARY

In the rural areas around Ithaca it is common for farmers to put some fresh produce on a table by the road. There is a cash box on the table, and customers are expected to put money in the box in return for the vegetables they take. The box has just a small slit, so money can only be put in, not taken out. Also, the box is attached to the table, so no one can (easily) make off with the money. We think that the farmers who use this system have just about the right model of human nature. They feel that enough people will volunteer to pay for the fresh corn to make it worthwhile to put it out there. The farmers also know that if it were easy enough to take the money, someone would do so.

In contrast to these farmers, economists either avoid judgments of human nature, or make assumptions that appear excessively harsh. It is certainly true that there is a "free rider problem." Not all people can be expected to contribute voluntarily to a good cause, and any voluntary system is likely to produce too little of the public good (or too much of the public bad in the case of externalities). On the other hand, the strong free rider prediction is clearly wrong—not everyone free rides all of the time.

There is a big territory between universal free riding and universal contributing at the optimal rate. To understand the problems presented by public goods and other dilemmas it is important to begin to explore some issues that are normally ignored in economics. For example, what factors determine the rate of cooperation? It is encouraging to note that cooperation is positively related to the investment return on the public good. The more the group has to gain through cooperation, the more cooperation is observed—the supply of cooperation is upward sloping. The results involving the role of discussion and the establishment of group identity are, however, more difficult to incorporate into traditional economic analyses. (One economist attempting to do so proposed that group discussion simply confuses subjects to the point that they no longer understand it is in their best interests to be defectors.)

More generally, the role of selfish rationality in economic models needs careful scrutiny. Amartya Sen (1977) has described people who are always selfishly rational as "rational fools," because mutual choices based only on egoistic payoffs consistently lead to suboptimal outcomes for all involved. Perhaps we need to give more attention to "sensible cooperators."

[3]

The Ultimatum Game

Late one evening, your daughter Maggie, off at
college, calls you to ask for your sage advice. She rarely
wants your advice, but when she does it is always late.
This time it sounds interesting. She has agreed to
participate in a laboratory experiment being run in the
economics department at her college. The rules were
explained in advance so that the subjects could think
carefully about their choices. The experiment involves
two-player bargaining, with Maggie placed in the role of
Player 1. She is to be given $10, and will be asked to
divide it between herself and another student (Player 2)
whose identity is unknown to her. The rules stipulate
that she must make Player 2 an offer, and then Player 2
can either accept the offer, in which case he will receive
whatever Maggie offered him, or he can reject the offer,
in which case both players will receive nothing. Her
question to her wise economist parent: How much
should she offer?

Stalling, you say you have to check the literature
before you offer advice, and so the next morning you
head for the library. The relevant theory turns out to be
in a paper by Ariel Rubinstein (1982; see also Stahl,
1972). You immediately notice that Rubinstein starts his
article with the disclaimer that he is only theorizing
about what will happen in a bargaining situation if both
parties behave rationally. He explicitly distinguishes this
question from two others, namely: "(i) the positive
question—what is the agreement reached in practice; (ii)
the normative question—what is the just agreement"
(p.97).

After reading Rubinstein, including his opening disclaimer, you realize that the theory for the simple game Maggie has to play is rather obvious. Player 1 should offer Player 2 a penny. Player 2 will accept this offer, since a penny is better than nothing. However, you now realize why Rubinstein was so careful. Offering only a penny seems to be a risky strategy. If Player 2 views such a small offer as insulting, it would cost him only a penny to reject it. Maybe Maggie should offer more than a penny? But how much more? What advice should you give?

While mulling over what to tell Maggie, you get a phone call from a local merchant offering you a consulting job, an event even less frequent than your daughter asking for your advice. The merchant owns a local motel in the college town in which you reside. He is troubled by the fact that a few times a year, such as graduation and homecoming weekends, there is enormous excess demand for rooms. On graduation weekend, for example, some parents stay in hotels as much as 50 miles away. The usual price for a room in his motel is $65 a night. Normal practice in town is to retain the usual rates, but to insist on a three-night minimum stay. He estimates that he could easily fill the motel for graduation weekend at a rate of $150 a night, while retaining the three-night minimum stay. However, he is a bit uneasy about doing this. He is worried about being labeled a "gouger," and thinks this label might hurt his regular business. "You are an economist," he says. "What should I do?" While thinking over this problem, you realize that it has something in common with Maggie's dilemma, and that you may need more than economic theory to advise either of your new "clients." But what?

SIMPLE ULTIMATUM GAMES

The game described by Maggie is known as an Ultimatum Game. The first experiments to use this game were conducted by three

German economists, Güth, Schmittberger, and Schwarze (1982) (GSS). They divided their sample of 42 economics students in half. One group was designated to take the role of Player 1, the Allocator; the other group took the role of Player 2, the Recipient. Each Allocator was asked to divide c German Marks (DM) between himself and the Recipient. If the offer, x, was accepted then the Allocator received $c - x$ and the Recipient received x. If the offer was rejected, both players received nothing. The size of the stake to be divided, c, was varied between DM4 and DM10. Then, a week later, the same subjects were invited to play the game again.

If the Rubinstein model is a good positive model (in spite of his disclaimer) then two results should be observed:(1) Allocators should make offers approaching zero, and (2) Recipients should accept all positive offers. The data are inconsistent with both of these predictions. In the first experiment (with inexperienced subjects) the modal offer was a 50 percent split (7 of 21 cases). The mean offer was .37c. Two students did ask for all of c in games where $c = DM4$, with one of these offers being accepted,[1] the other rejected. All other offers were for at least DM1, and one positive offer of DM1.20 was rejected.

In the replication, after a week to think about it, the offers were somewhat less generous but still considerably greater than epsilon (i.e., the smallest unit of currency available). The mean offer was .32c, and only two players offered an even split. However, there was only one offer of less than DM1 and it was rejected. Also, three offers of DM1 were rejected, as was an offer of DM3. Thus 5 of the 21 offers were rejected.

Both the Allocators and the Recipients take actions inconsistent with the theory. The Recipients' actions, however, are easier to interpret. When a Recipient declines a positive offer, he signals that his utility function has non-monetary arguments. (In English, this means he is insulted.) The decline of an offer of .1c says, "I would rather sacrifice .1c than accept what I consider to be an unfair allocation of the stake." The extent of this willingness to decline positive but unfair offers is explored below. The actions of the Allocators could be explained by either of two motives (or some combination of both). Allocators who make significantly positive offers could either have a taste for fairness, and/or could

---

[1]We can't be sure whether the Recipient who accepted the zero offer was confused, generous, or simply had a deep understanding of bargaining theory.

be worried that unfair offers will be (rationally or mistakenly) rejected. Further experiments reveal that both explanations have some validity.

GSS investigated the behavior of Recipients in a second experiment using 37 new subjects. In this study, subjects were told they would play the game twice, once as Allocator and once as Recipient. In all games, c = DM7. They were asked to make an offer as Allocator, and to indicate the minimum payment they would accept when they played the role of Recipient. (Note that these are real contingent responses, not answers to hypothetical questions.) The Allocators' responses in this experiment were even more generous than those observed in the earlier experiments, the mean offer being .45c. Of greater interest are the responses of the subjects as Recipients. All but two of the subjects indicated a reservation demand of at least DM1, and the median reservation demand was DM2.50.

Two related experiments were conducted by Kahneman, Knetsch, and Thaler (1986b) (KKT). In the first, conducted at the University of British Columbia, the GSS study was replicated to determine whether the results might be caused by subjects being confused about the task. A simple ultimatum game was played, with c = $10 (Canadian). Again subjects were asked to say what they would do in both roles. Two steps were taken to be sure that the subjects understood the task. First, the subjects were asked two preliminary diagnostic questions. Of the 137 subjects who participated in the study, 22 were dropped because they did not answer both questions correctly. Second, rather than asking subjects to directly state their reservation demand, the subjects were asked a series of yes or no questions of the form: If the other player offers you $0.50, will you accept the offer or reject it? These questions were repeated in increments of 50 cents. In three different experiments, the mean minimum acceptable offer varied between $2.00 and $2.59, amounts similar to those obtained by GSS.[2]

[2]The three experiments had different groups of students as subjects. In all cases they were told that their partner would be someone in another class. The offers of the Allocators were similar to those obtained by Güth et al., with the mean amount offered ranging from $4.21 to $4.76. Of interest is the fact that the most generous offers were made by students in a psychology class making offers to students in another psychology class. The psychology students were less generous when making offers to students in a commerce class, but the least generous offers were made by commerce students to the psychology students. Similarly, the commerce students indicated the smallest minimum acceptable offer.

The second KKT experiment investigated two questions. First, will Allocators be fair even if their offers cannot be rejected, and, second, will subjects sacrifice money to punish an Allocator who behaved unfairly *to someone else*. In the first part students in a psychology class at Cornell University were asked to divide $20 between themselves and another anonymous member of the class. They were given only two choices of allocations: they could keep $18 for themselves and give their partner $2, or they could offer an even split of $10 each. (At these stakes it was not possible to have a large sample size and still pay everyone. Thus, the subjects were told that eight pairs of students would be selected at random and paid.) Unlike the previous experiments, the offers made by the Allocators could not be rejected by the Recipients. Nonetheless, offers were still very generous. Of the 161 subjects, 122 (76 percent) divided the $20 evenly. Therefore, part of the explanation for the generous offers observed in the ultimatum game does appear to be explained by a taste for fairness on the part of the Allocators.

After completing the first part of the study, the same students were given another question. They were told they would be matched with two students who had not been selected to be paid in the first part of the experiment. One of these students had taken the $18 (called U for uneven) while the other had taken $10 (E). A subject was then asked to choose between the following. He could take $6 for himself and give $6 to U, or he could take $5 for himself and give $5 to E. Thus the question came down to whether subjects would be willing to pay a dollar to split money with a stranger who had been generous, rather than split with a stranger who had been greedy. A clear majority, 74 percent, elected to take the smaller reward in order to split with E.

TWO-STAGE BARGAINING GAMES

GSS (1982, p.385) conclude that game theory is "of little help in explaining ultimatum bargaining behavior." With the honor of game theory at stake (or at least its descriptive validity), game theorists Binmore, Shaked, and Sutton (1985) (BSS) performed a pair of experiments. They revised the GSS design by adding a second stage to the bargaining game and had the players communicate via linked microcomputers. The two-stage game begins as before with Player 1 in the role of Allocator, Player 2 in the role of Recipient, and with c = 100 U.K. pence. The Allocator makes an offer of x (keeping c − x for himself). If this offer is refused, then the game moves to round 2, with the players reversing roles and the stake reduced to δc, where the discount factor, δ, in this case was set at 0.25. The second round is a simple ultimatum game with c = 25p and Player 2 in the role of Allocator. The (subgame perfect) equilibrium for this game is found through a trivial backward induction. If the game reaches round 2, then Player 2 can offer Player 1 just a penny, retaining 24p for himself. Therefore, Player 2 will accept anything more than 24 in round 1, so Player 1 should offer 25p on round 1.

This game was played twice. In the first game, offers by the Allocators were similar to those observed in earlier experiments. The modal offer was 50p, and only 10 percent were in the range 24–26p. Also, 15 percent of the first-round offers were rejected (whereas the theory predicts the game will never reach the second round). In the second game, the subjects who had played in the role of Player 2 in the first game were invited to play another game, this time in the role of Player 1. (Responses of their hypothetical partners were not collected.) This time the subjects behaved more in accordance with game theory. The modal offer was just below the equilibrium of 25p. The authors conclude considerations of fairness "are easily displaced by calculations of strategic advantage, once players fully appreciate the structure of the game" (p. 1180). However, three aspects of the BSS experiments raise questions about how to interpret their results.

First, the subjects were not informed of the existence of the replay until after the first game was played. If subjects thought that the game was now one where they would take turns being Player 1, they may have felt that alternatively taking the equilibrium .75c would average out to a fair distribution.

Second, in conducting their experiments, BSS took the unusual step of telling their subjects how to behave. Specifically, the written instructions included the following passage: *"How do we want you to play?* YOU WILL BE DOING US A FAVOUR IF YOU SIMPLY SET OUT TO MAXIMIZE YOUR WINNINGS" (Emphasis and all caps in the original). It is difficult to say what effect such instructions might have on the results without a controlled experiment (though it is reassuring that the first-round results are similar to those obtained by GSS). However, in another similar context instructions did prove to have a powerful effect. Hoffman and Spitzer (1982) ran an experiment which is very similar to the ultimatum game. The Allocator (who was given that role as a result of a coin flip) could choose between an outcome which gave him $12 and the recipient nothing, or, if both players agreed, they could divide $14. Of course, the theory predicts that the players will agree to divide the $14, with the Allocator getting no less than $12. Instead, all pairs agreed to split the $14 evenly, i.e., $7 each. In a second paper Hoffman and Spitzer (1985) tried to understand why this happened. Two manipulations were crossed with each other to produce four conditions. (1) The role of Allocator was determined either by a coin flip, or by playing a simple game with the winner becoming the Allocator. (2) Winners of the coin flip or game were told either that they had "earned" the right to be the Allocator, or that they were "designated" as Allocator. Of the two manipulations, the second was the more powerful. The difference between the game and the coin flip was not significant, but the subjects that had been told that they had "earned" the property right took significantly more of the money. Further research on this type of demand characteristic is clearly needed.

Third, the two-stage game devised by BSS differs from the simple ultimatum game in one key respect. The equilibrium offer of 25p is distinctly positive. This means that compared to the simple ultimatum game, it is more costly for a Recipient to reject the equilibrium offer, and the equilibrium offer is more fair. To see whether these factors are important, Güth and Tietz (1987) tried a two-stage game with a discount factor of .1 or .9. When $\delta = .1$ the equilibrium offer is a rather unfair .10c, while when $\delta = .9$ the equilibrium offer is a full .90c (hardly fair to oneself!). The games were played twice with players switching roles.[3] The stake was either DM5, DM15, or DM35.

The results of these experiments did not support the BSS conclusion that rationality will take over if the players have a chance to think about the game. In the trials where $\delta = .1$, offers increased

---

[3]One additional rule was put in place. Player 2 could not reject an offer and respond with a counteroffer that gave himself less than he had been offered. Such actions constituted disagreement, with both players receiving zero. Thus when $\delta = .1$, if Player 1 offered more than .1c this amounted to an ultimatum since if Player 2 rejected the offer disagreement was declared. The experiments by Ochs and Roth (1988) discussed below show that this rule was probably binding.

(moved away from equilibrium) from trial 1 to trial 2 (from .24c to .33c). For the cases where $\delta = .9$, the mean offers also increased on trial 2 (from .37c to .49c), which is toward the equilibrium value. Averaging across both trials and all levels of c, the mean offers when $\delta = .1$ were .28c, while when $\delta = .9$ the mean offers were .43c. Neither is close to their respective equilibrium values of .1c and .9c. The variation in the level of c also provides some evidence on the robustness of the phenomena under study. If we compare the games played with c=DM5 to those with c=DM35, we find that the offers move part way toward the equilibrium levels (from .33c to .24c) when $\delta = .1$, and slightly away from equilibrium (from .36c to .34c) for $\delta = .9$. Thus, raising the stakes does little to improve the descriptive value of game theory.[4]

MULTI-STAGE GAMES

The next contribution to the analysis of ultimatum games is Neelin, Sonnenschein, and Spiegel (1987) (NSS). Subjects in their experiments were Princeton undergraduates enrolled in an intermediate microeconomics class. Subjects played a series of games with the number of periods (announced in advance) varying between two and five, and c=$5. Player 1 makes an offer in odd-numbered rounds, and Player 2 in even-numbered rounds. If the final round offer is rejected then both players get nothing. The discount rates were varied in such a way that the equilibrium offer in the first period was always $1.25 + \epsilon$ (or $1.26). In the two-period game the second period c is $1.25; in the three-period game c falls first to $2.50 and then to $1.25; in the five-period game the values for c are $5.00, $1.70, $0.58, $0.20, and $0.07.[5]

---

[4]What would happen in an ultimatum game with c=$1000, or $100,000? None of us have the research funds to run this experiment, so we can only guess. My own guess is that Recipients' minimum acceptable offers would increase with c, but not linearly. When c=$10, the median minimum acceptable offer is about .2c. For c=$1000 I would guess it would fall in the range .05c–.1c($50–$100). The minimum acceptable offer probably also increases with wealth, implying that resisting unfair offers is a normal good.

[5]Notice that the backward induction necessary to derive the equilibrium first-round offer is a bit more complicated in the three- and five-round games. The analysis for the five-round game is: if the game reaches the fifth round, Player 1 is the allocator, and he can offer Player 2 a penny (which Player 2 will, by assumption, accept) so Player 1 can get 6 cents at this stage. This implies that at the fourth stage, Player 2 must offer Player 1 at least 6 cents, keeping 14 cents for himself, and so forth.

Subjects first played a practice (four-round) game, then played the two-, three-, and five-round games in that order, each with a different anonymous partner. Subjects retained the same role in each game.

The idea behind the NSS design is that the results of the various length games can be compared to avoid conclusions that are special to a particular game. The value of the design is quickly appreciated when the results are examined. In the two-round games, the game theoretic prediction did pretty well. Of the 50 Allocators (whom NSS call "sellers"), 33 made offers between $1.25 and $1.50 (the equilibrium value is $1.26). These results are similar to those obtained in the second BSS experiment. In the three-round game, however, the results are completely different. Here 28 out of the 50 players offered an even split of $2.50, with 9 others making offers within $0.50 of this amount. Remember that the equilibrium offer in this game is still $1.26.

The five-round game yielded yet another pattern of results. The modal (14) first-round offer was $1.70 and 33 of the 50 offers were in the range $1.50–$2.00. NSS note that the players seem to have adopted the strategy of offering Player 2 the stake to be played for in round 2. This *is* the equilibrium offer in the two-stage game, but not in the longer games. Such a strategy might be adopted if players are myopic, and only think one step ahead, or are just conservative, wishing to minimize the risk that their partner will reject their offer, for rational or irrational reasons.

NSS conducted a second experiment in which subjects played the five-round game four times with all the payoffs increased by a factor of 3 (c = $15). The results were essentially unchanged. Seventy percent of the offers were in the range $5.00–$5.10 (the second round stake is $5.10). No offer close to the equilibrium $3.76 was observed. There was also no evidence of any learning. That is, there was no apparent trend in the offers over the four trials.

By far the most ambitious set of experiments conducted to date is reported in Ochs and Roth (1988). They introduced the following innovations. First, subjects complete 10 bargains, one after another, with all parameters held constant (but with a different opponent each time).[6] This feature allows for a test of whether

---

[6] Subjects were told that at the completion of the experiment one of the rounds would be selected at random, and they would be paid based on their outcome in that round.

subjects learn to be proper economists with practice. Second, discount rates were varied separately for each subject. This was accomplished by having subjects bargain for 100 "chips." In the first round of any game the chips were worth $0.30 to each player (so $c = \$30$). In the second round the chips would be worth $\delta_1(\$0.30)$ to Player 1 and $\delta_2(\$0.30)$ to Player 2. In the third round, for three-round games, the discount rates were squared. The two discount rates were common knowledge, but were not necessarily equal. Four combinations for (δ_1, δ_2) were varied experimentally: (.4, .4), (.6, .4), (.6, .6), and (.4, .6). These four conditions were crossed with the number of periods to be played (either two or three) to produce a 4×2 experimental design.

The authors use this complicated experimental design to test two implications of bargaining theory. (1) Player 1's discount factor should only matter in games with three periods. (Work through the backward induction to see why.) (2) Holding the discount rates constant, Player 2 should receive less in three-period games than in two-period games. (This is true because in three-period games Player 1 gets to make both the first and the last offer.) Also, the theory yields predictions of all the 28 pairwise comparisons between the cells of the experiment.

The results of these experiments provide little support for the descriptive value of game theory, even on the last trials of the experiments. The theory performed well in only one of the eight cells. In the other seven cells, the theoretical mean offer was never within two standard deviations of the actual mean on any trial. Also, both of the additional predictions mentioned in the previous paragraph failed. The Player 1 discount rate mattered in games when it shouldn't, and the length of the game didn't matter when it should. As one simple measure of the ability of the theory to explain the data, Ochs and Roth regressed the observed mean offer on the theoretical offer for the last trials of each cell of the experiment. The R^2 for this equation was .065, and the coefficient on the theoretical offer less than one standard deviation away from zero.

Ochs and Roth also replicate the earlier findings by GSS and KKT regarding Recipients' willingness to decline positive but unfair offers. In these games, if players cared only about monetary payoffs, then Player 2 would never reject Player 1's initial offer and subsequently demand less for himself in his counter-offer. Yet Ochs and Roth find that for 81 percent of the counterproposals, Player 2 demands less cash than he was originally offered by Player 1. The conclusion that subjects' utility functions have arguments other than money is reconfirmed.

We have seen that game theory is unsatisfactory as a positive model of behavior. It is also lacking as a prescriptive tool. While none of the subjects in Ochs and Roth's experiments came very close to using the game-theoretic strategies, those who most closely approximated this strategy did not make the most money. In fact, in four of the eight cells, the player with the highest average demand (over the ten trials) had the *lowest* average earnings.

ULTIMATUMS IN THE MARKET

The willingness of people to resist what they consider to be unfair allocations has implications for economics that go well beyond bargaining theory. Any time a monopolist (or monopsonist) sets a price (or wage), it has the quality of an ultimatum. Just as the Recipient in an ultimatum game may reject a small but positive offer, a buyer may refrain from purchasing at a price that leaves a small bit of consumer surplus but is viewed as dividing the surplus in an unfair manner. Consider the following problem posed to two groups of participants in an executive education program. One group received a version with the passages in brackets, the other the passages in parentheses.

> You are lying on the beach on a hot day. All you have to drink is ice water. For the last hour you have been thinking about how much you would enjoy a nice cold bottle of your favorite brand of beer. A companion gets up to go make a phone call and offers to bring back a beer from the only nearby place where beer is sold (a fancy resort hotel) [a small run-down grocery store]. He says that the beer might be expensive and so asks how much you are willing to pay for the beer. He says that he will buy the beer if it costs as much or less than the price you state. But if it costs more than the price you state he will not buy it. You trust your friend, and there is no possibility of bargaining with the (bartender) [store owner]. What price do you tell him? (Thaler, 1985)

Notice that the scenario here is a simple ultimatum game, with the respondent in the role of the Recipient. The median response for the fancy hotel version was $2.65, while the median for the grocery store version was $1.50. Because of a difference in perceived costs, the price of $2.65 seems fair for a resort hotel, but a "rip-off" in a run-down grocery store.

In general, consumers may be unwilling to participate in an exchange in which the other party gets too large a share of the surplus. This may explain why some markets (e.g., Super Bowl tickets, reservations at the most popular restaurant in town on Saturday night, Bruce Springsteen concert tickets, etc.) fail to clear at the official price set by the seller. Whenever the seller has an ongoing relationship with the buyer and the market-clearing price would be considered unfairly high, the seller has an incentive to keep prices below the equilibrium in order to retain future business. (These issues are discussed in more detail in Thaler, 1985, and Kahneman, Knetsch, and Thaler, 1986a.)

COMMENTARY

Bell, Raiffa, and Tversky (1988) have suggested that it is useful to distinguish three kinds of theories of decision making under uncertainty. *Normative* theories tell us how a rational agent should behave. *Descriptive* theories tell us how agents do behave. *Prescriptive* theories offer advice as to how to behave when faced with our own cognitive or other limitations. The research on the bargaining games indicates that we need a similar triple of game theories. Game theory as it currently exists is a normative theory. It characterizes optimal behavior when selfishness and rationality are common knowledge. Experimental research is starting to provide the evidence necessary to formulate a good description of how people actually behave. However, as yet we have little research that would help develop prescriptive game theory. The analysis of Maggie's problem illustrates this gap in our repertoire. To solve for the income-maximizing offer, one would have to be able to characterize the acceptance function for the Recipient. For any given offer, what is the probability it will be rejected by the Recipient?

In multi-stage games, the optimal strategy is even less clear. Consider the five-stage game in NSS, where $c = \$15$. The values for c in the second through fifth stages of the game are: $5.10,

$1.74, $0.60, and $0.21. What is an optimal offer at stage 1? There are two important prescriptive game theoretic considerations. (1) What offer will Player 2 consider fair? (2) Does Player 2 understand the game? Both factors may be important. To get a sense of the possible role of the second factor, I arranged to have a question posed in the final exam for an MBA-level course on Pricing and Strategy at Cornell. The course has intermediate microeconomics as a prerequisite, and the students had discussed game theory, backward induction, and simple ultimatum games in class. The exam consisted of eight questions from which the students had to answer five. The question of interest began with a description of the five-round game played in NSS. The students were told to assume that both players are rational, and both wish to maximize the money they earn in this game. They were then asked: What is the smallest offer Player 1 can make in round 1 which will be accepted by Player 2?

Of the 30 students in the class, only 13 chose to answer this question, and only 9 answered it correctly. This implies that more than half the class were not sure they knew the answer to the question, and of those who did think they knew the answer, 30 percent got it wrong. Clearly, this is not a trivial question, and backward induction is not an intuitively obvious concept. To see the importance of this issue, consider a Player 1 who is thinking about making an offer of $4.00 to Player 2. While Player 1 may know that this is more than Player 2 can hope to get if he rejects the offer, if Player 2 thinks he can get $5.09, he may mistakenly turn the offer down.

So, if Maggie were playing this five-round game, before giving her any advice we would want to know how smart her opponent is. Has he studied game theory? Does it look like he can subtract, much less perform a backward induction? More generally, in order to develop prescriptive game theory, the assumption that rationality and wealth maximization are common knowledge will have to be modified. A rational, wealth-maximizing player must realize that his opponent may be neither, and make appropriate changes to his policies.[7] Notice that in developing prescriptive game theory, it is necessary to do both theory and empirical work.

---

[7]This sort of analysis is common in expert bridge. In tournament bridge, experts often play against non-experts, unlike in many other competitive events. Optimal strategy in a weak field depends in part on giving one's opponents numerous opportunities to make mistakes.

Theory alone cannot tell us what factors enter our opponent's utility function, nor what bounds must be placed on his rationality.

One conclusion which emerges clearly from this research is that notions of fairness can play a significant role in determining the outcomes of negotiations. However, a concern for fairness[8] does not preclude other factors, even greed, from affecting behavior. In their article, BSS pose the problem starkly as a contest between two extreme positions. People are thought either to be "fairmen" who divide everything equally, or "gamesmen" who behave like proper economic agents, i.e., selfishly and rationally. I think it is safe to say that most people are not well described by either extreme view. Rather, most people prefer more money to less, like to be treated fairly, and like to treat others fairly. To the extent that these objectives are contradictory, subjects make trade-offs.[9] Behavior also appears to depend greatly on context and other subtle features of the environment. In some experiments most Allocators choose even splits, in others most choose the game-theoretic allocation. Future research should investigate the factors that produce each kind of behavior, rather than attempt to demonstrate that one type of behavior or the other predominates.

Just as the characterization of the behavior of subjects as either fairmen or gamesmen is too simplistic, so is any distinction on a "hard" versus "soft" dimension. There is a tendency among economists to think of themselves, and the agents in their models, as having hard hearts (as well as heads, noses, and other extremities). *Homo economicus* is usually assumed to care about wealth more than such issues as fairness and justice. In contrast, many economists think of other social scientists (and the agents in *their* models) as "softies." The research on ultimatum games

---

[8]It must be emphasized that issues of fairness are complicated. Perceptions of fairness often diverge from those which seem natural to economists. For example Kahneman, Knetsch, and Thaler (1986a) found that most people believe a queue is fairer than a market, and Yaari and Bar-Hillel (1984) found that when making judgments of justice, people distinguish between "needs" and "wants." Fairness *arguments* are also quite common in negotiations. While bargainers use fairness arguments for self-serving reasons ("I think I should get more because that would be fair . . . "), such arguments can nonetheless be effective (see Roth, 1987).

[9]To illustrate, in the experiment conducted by Kahneman et al. (1986b) Allocators were permitted to choose between just two divisions of $20, either 18-2 or 10-10. Most chose the even allocation. However, had they been allowed to choose an intermediate allocation, such as 12-8, many might have selected that.

belies such easy characterizations. There is a "soft" tendency among the Allocators to choose 50-50 allocations, even when the risk of rejection is eliminated. Yet the behavior of the Recipients, while inconsistent with economic models, is remarkably hard-nosed. They say, in effect, "Take your offer of epsilon and shove it!"

[4]

Interindustry Wage Differentials

A few years ago we hired a new secretary in my department. She was smart and efficient and we were pleased to have her. Much to our dismay, after just a few months she was offered and accepted a job from an IBM facility in a nearby city. She told me that she had been on a waiting list there for a year or so, and would be a fool to turn IBM down since they paid so much more than any of the other local employers. I wondered at the time whether her value typing IBM interoffice memos could be that much higher than it would be typing manuscripts and referee reports, and/or why IBM should find it profitable to pay much more than the going wage.

One of the most important principles of microeconomics is the *law of one price*. The idea is that if markets are working well, and there are no substantial transactions costs or transportation costs, the same object cannot sell at two different prices, because otherwise all buyers would try to buy in the market with the lower price and all sellers would want to sell in the market with the higher price. Pretty soon, the differing prices must converge. In some markets, such as financial markets, the law holds quite precisely. At any one moment, the price of gold does not differ by more than a few pennies in the various places around the world in which it is traded. In the markets for goods, there is greater variation in prices (see Pratt, Wise, and Zeckhauser, 1979) though some of the variation is explained by differences in services provided. If you buy a food processor at Bloomingdales, you consume more atmosphere than if you buy it at K-Mart. If consumers are willing to pay for atmosphere or courteous and well-informed sales help, there is no anomaly in differing prices.

As the example of my former secretary suggests, however, there may be serious violations of the law of one price in labor markets. Indeed, a glance at the employment classified ads in the newspaper, or the listings at an employment agency will confirm that the story of my secretary is not unusual. Firms advertise widely varying wages for jobs that appear to be very similar, such as secretary, data entry clerk, or "tele-marketing representative." My students who graduate from Cornell's MBA program often receive offers from several firms in the same city with substantially different salaries. In fact, one recent graduate received two offers for similar finance jobs in New York City that differed in annual salary by $45,000! Such a big disparity seems clearly to violate the law of one salary. Furthermore, the impression created by these casual bits of data is confirmed by more careful investigations. Some industries appear to pay higher wages than others, even when (measurable) labor quality is held constant. These interindustry wage differentials apply across occupations (if one occupation in an industry is high paid, then all other occupations tend to be) and over time. Why?

THE FACTS

There is a simple way to demonstrate the existence and measure the importance of interindustry wage differentials. Take a large data set with decent information about worker characteristics and income such as the Current Population Survey (CPS). First run a regression with the (log of the) wage rate for each individual on the left-hand side and a host of individual characteristics on the right-hand side such as age, education, occupation, gender, race, union status, marital status, region, and so on. Now, add industry dummy variables to this regression and see what happens.

This exercise has been conducted using the CPS by Krueger and Summers (1988) and Dickens and Katz (1987a). Both teams find large industry effects (the amount by which the industry wages differ from the average, controlling for everything possible), most of which are highly significant. For example, Krueger and Summers find the following proportional industry effects for 1984: mining, + 24 percent; autos, + 24 percent; leather, − 8 percent; petroleum, + 38 percent; educational services, − 19 percent (ouch!). The weighted (by number of employed) standard deviation of the differentials is 15 percent. Similar results are obtained by Dickens and Katz, with little difference between a sample of union workers and non-union workers. Remember, these effects are observed after controlling for individual characteristics.

Interindustry differentials are neither a recent nor transitory phenomenon. Slichter's (1950) study found stable industry patterns between 1923 and 1946. Over this period he found the rank correlation of industry wages was .73. Krueger and Summers (1987, p.22) have updated this analysis by comparing the 1923 pattern with their 1984 data. They find ''that relatively high-wage industries in 1923 such as auto manufacturing continued to be high-wage industries in 1984, and low-wage industries such as boot and shoe manufacturing continued to be low-wage industries in 1984. The correlation of industry wages in 1984 and 1923 is .56. Since this correlation is probably an underestimate due to changes in industry definitions and sampling error, we consider this evidence that the wage structure has remained relatively stable for a very long time.''

The industry wage pattern is also internationally pervasive. Krueger and Summers (1987) report a correlation matrix for manufacturing industry wages in 1982 across 14 countries. The correlations are remarkably high, especially among the developed, capitalist countries. For example, the correlations between the industry wages in the U.S. and those of Canada, France, Japan, Germany, Korea, Sweden, and the U.K. all exceed .80. The correlations between U.S. wages and Poland and Yugoslavia are .70 and .79, respectively.

Perhaps the most remarkable fact regarding the interindustry wage pattern is its stability across occupations. Katz and Summers (forthcoming) calculate industry wage differentials for secretaries, janitors, and managers. They find significant industry differentials of roughly the same magnitude as for all workers. For example, secretaries in the mining industry are paid 23 percent above the mean while those in the leather industry are paid 15 percent below the mean. Explaining this occupational uniformity in wages is a key task for any theory of industry wage structure.

POSSIBLE ALIBIS

Before the interindustry wage differentials can be considered a legitimate anomaly, two simple explanations must be ruled out. First, it is possible that the high wages are simply compensating differences for some unmeasured, undesirable aspects of the working conditions in the high-wage industries. Surely the high wages in the mining industry, for example, are explained in part by the unpleasant and unsafe working environment in the mines. Second, the high-wage industries might be hiring better workers. The data on worker quality in the CPS are, after all, rather sparse. Before turning to the detailed analyses of these issues, it should be pointed out that the uniformity of wage differentials across occupations works against both hypotheses. While it is plausible that an industry might want to hire high-quality workers in some occupations because of the nature of the technology, why should that be true for all occupations? Similarly, while working conditions might be harsh for some occupations in high-wage industries, why should secretaries and managers be highly paid in these industries?

While compensating differences are undoubtedly an important determinant of industry wages (Rosen, 1986), this hypothesis clearly cannot explain the pattern of differentials described above. To test the importance of such factors, Krueger and Summers (1988) tried adding a set of ten job characteristic variables to a wage-estimating equation using the 1977 Quality of Employment Survey. These characteristics included weekly hours, job shift, whether the job was hazardous, and the nature of the working conditions. Adding these variables did not substantially alter the measured interindustry wage differentials.

A more telling argument against the compensating wage hypothesis comes from data on quit rates. If the high-wage industries are simply compensating workers for unsavory conditions, then there is no reason to expect that the employers are paying more than necessary to retain their workers. This can be tested by examining quit rates. If the apparent high-wage industries are really paying high wages, then their employees should be reluctant to leave their jobs. In fact, researchers have found that high-wage industries do tend to have low quit rates (Katz and Summers, forthcoming; Akerlof, Rose, and Yellen, forthcoming), suggesting that workers in such industries feel they are being paid wages in excess of their opportunity costs.

The unobserved quality explanation is more difficult to evaluate. Krueger and Summers (1988) use two methods to investigate this issue. First they compare the wage estimation regressions with and without labor quality controls. They argue that unmeasured labor quality is probably correlated with measured quality. If this premise is accepted, and industry wage differentials are due to differences in unmeasured labor quality, then adding labor quality variables to a wage regression should substantially reduce the industry wage effects. However, when they add education, tenure, and age (crude measures of human capital) to the wage regression, the standard deviation of industry wage differentials falls by only one percentage point. They conclude (p. 13) that "unless one believes that variation in unmeasured labor quality is vastly more important than variation in age, tenure, and schooling, this evidence makes it difficult to attribute interindustry wage differences to differences in labor quality." Proponents of the unobserved ability model such as Murphy and Topel (1987) take seriously precisely the view scoffed at in the preceding quote. They argue that wage equations explain a very small proportion of the variance, and presumably most of the unexplained variance is due to unobserved ability. Giving no ground, they point out that industry wage differentials *are* positively correlated with observed ability measures, and in all likelihood, unobserved quality is positively correlated with observed quality.

Another way to approach the unobserved quality issue is to look at workers who leave their job for one in another industry (since quality is held constant). This task is more difficult to carry out than it might seem. There are complex issues raised by measurement error and selectivity bias. The measurement errors come into play because some of the workers who appear to have switched industries may have instead been incorrectly assigned to the wrong industry by the interviewer for one (or both!) of the two jobs. Krueger and Summers use some direct data from other sources to try to correct for this misclassification problem. The selectivity bias is present because the workers who go from a low-paying industry to a high-paying industry might be the better workers. The selectivity bias presumably imparts a positive bias to the estimated differentials (relative to the true, quality-adjusted values) because the observed switchers probably have unmeasured quality differences that are positively correlated with the industry differentials.[1]

With the potential problems in full view, Krueger and Summers take a stab at measuring the longitudinal wage differentials using a 1984 CPS survey of displaced workers. Krueger and Summers use only the workers who were involuntarily displaced from their jobs, so selectivity bias is reduced, and correct for industry misclassifications as best they can. They find strong industry effects of roughly the same size as those found in the simple cross-sectional regression. They conclude that interindustry wage differentials are unlikely to be explained by unmeasured labor quality. Similar results are obtained by Gibbons and Katz (1987) and Blackburn and Neumark (1987). However, using a different CPS sample, and a different procedure to correct for possible misclassifications, Murphy and Topel estimate that workers who switch industries initially gain only about one-third of the difference between the industry wage rates. They cite these results to support their view that industry effects are primarily due to unobserved quality.

These conflicting studies make it difficult to evaluate the unobserved quality hypothesis. If the wage pattern does reflect unobserved ability, however, then it seems reasonable to think that the industry wage differentials would be positively correlated with other measures of ability such as intelligence. Blackburn and Neumark (1987) investigate this using the National Longitudinal Study Young Men's Cohort which reports an IQ test score for many of its respondents. They find that after controlling for the usual observed quality measures including education there is a negative relationship between an industry's wages and the average IQ score of its workers. Of course, it is possible that high-wage industries are buying quality that is uncorrelated with IQ, but if the results of this study are taken at face value then the ability hypothesis seems to have suffered a serious blow.

---

[1]However, one factor that works in the opposite direction is that a worker in a low-wage industry might be willing to accept a reduction in seniority to gain entry to the high-wage industry. For these movers, the industry differential would be understated.

WHICH INDUSTRIES PAY HIGH WAGES AND WHY?

To begin to unravel the mystery of these industry wage patterns, researchers have identified four industry characteristics that appear to be associated with the level of compensation: firm size, profits and monopoly power, capital intensity, and union density.

An empirical phenomenon as strong and perhaps as anomalous as interindustry wage differentials is the fact that large firms pay more than small firms. Brown and Medoff (forthcoming) find that both plant size and firm size have important positive influences on wage rates, even after controlling for the characteristics of the workers and the working conditions of the jobs. Therefore, it is not surprising that industries with large average plant sizes tend to be high-wage industries. However, firm size seems more powerful in explaining within industry wage differentials than across industry patterns.[2] Indeed, firm size seems to reinforce the industry effects.

A second factor that some investigators have found correlated with industry pay levels is "ability to pay" as measured either by the market power or profitability of the firms. One indicator of market power is the four-firm concentration ratio (the percentage of sales in an industry by the largest four firms). Presumably, more concentrated industries are more profitable, and can thus afford to pay higher wages. However, researchers examining the relationship between concentration and pay have found mixed results. Some have found that concentration increases wages, but others have found that the relationship becomes insignificant once controls for labor quality are included.

A more direct measure of ability to pay is profitability. However, this variable is not without drawbacks. The reported profits data available are those reported by the firms themselves. These profit measures are not the theoretically correct indicator of true economic profit, and are subject to some manipulation by the firm. Also, the profit rate obviously is negatively related to wages since, ceteris paribus, paying an extra dollar of wages necessarily reduces profits by a dollar. Nevertheless, the profit rate has been found to be a reliable predictor of industry wages, especially for non-union workers.

---

[2]Groshen (1988) also finds significant within-industry effects by establishment. Indeed, establishment effects appear to be roughly equal in magnitude to industry effects.

The relationship between capital intensity and wages was first investigated by Slichter (1950). He examined the association between wages and labor's share of costs in an industry. This turned out to be negative, even though higher wages must contribute to a higher labor share. Similarly, Lawrence and Lawrence (1985) and Dickens and Katz (1987a) found that industries with high capital labor ratios tend to pay higher wages. As usual, one must be careful in interpreting causality. Is there something about the technology of highly capital-intensive firms that induces them to pay more to their workers, or do firms that must pay high wages substitute capital for labor?

The final factor that has been shown to be correlated with industry wage rates is union density (the percentage of the workers in an industry who belong to a union). Most studies find that the unionization rate increases wages for both union members and nonunion members in an industry (though Freeman and Medoff [1984] find no effect on nonunion members). Once again interpretation is difficult. Do unions raise wages, or are unions attracted to high-wage industries? More on this later.

THEORETICAL EXPLANATIONS

The puzzle posed by the observed interindustry wage differentials is that some industries seem to be paying more per unit of labor quality than others. Why? As Krueger and Summers (1987) point out, there are only two classes of theoretical explanations that can logically be considered consistent with the alleged facts. Either firms are choosing not to maximize profits, or, for some reason, high-wage firms find that lowering wages would decrease profits. Models based on the first premise need to explain why managers choose to pay higher than profit-maximizing wages. The models in which high wages above opportunity costs are consistent with profit maximization either assume that higher wages can increase output ("efficiency wage" models) or be a rational response to the threat of collective action.

The suggestion that firms do not maximize profits was once considered heresy. In recent years, however, the old-fashioned notion of *managerial discretion* has been given the respectable term *agency theory,* and the suggestion that managers might not maximize the wealth of the shareholders is no longer considered immediate grounds for excommunication. Still, there does seem to be a preference among economists for agency theories in which managers sacrifice stockholder wealth in order to enrich *themselves*. The idea that managers would reduce profits to enrich their employees, especially the blue-collar workers far removed from the manager's milieu, is an enigma. Perhaps for this reason, I know of no formal attempt to explain interindustry wage differentials with an agency model in which managers have a taste for both profits and highly paid employees. Nevertheless, the facts described above do suggest that this hypothesis is plausible. As Krueger and Summers stress, high wages are observed in industries with high profits and low labor shares, precisely the industries in which one might expect such behavior to be manifested.

Much more attention has been given to the "efficiency wage models" in which higher than competitive wages can be profitable.[3] The basic idea of efficiency wage models is that output depends on worker effort and effort in turn depends positively on the wage rate. The more you pay, the more effort you get. Several versions of the model have been proposed, with the variations coming from the presumed source of the positive effort-wage relationship. The models can be categorized in four types:

1. *Shirking models.* In most jobs, workers have some discretion in how hard they work. Piece rates are often impractical because of the difficulty in counting the "pieces," and monitoring is costly. In the shirking efficiency wage model (e.g., Shapiro and Stiglitz, 1984) firms pay above market wages, engage in some monitoring, and fire those workers caught shirking. By paying above market wages, firms decrease the incentive to shirk, since detection then entails loss of rents. According to the shirking model, high-wage industries should be those with high monitoring costs and/or industries which bear a relatively high cost of employee shirking.

2. *Turnover models.* Firms may also wish to pay above market clearing wages to reduce turnover. Models based on this premise (e.g., Salop, 1979, Stiglitz, 1974) are similar to (indeed, formally identical to) the shirking model. Here the idea is to pay high wages to reduce quits. The turnover

---

[3] A brief introduction to this literature is contained in Janet Yellen (1984). For a more comprehensive review, with particular attention to interindustry wage differentials, see Katz (1986). Stiglitz (1987) provides another survey with a theoretical emphasis.

model predicts that the high-wage industries are those in which turnover costs are highest.

3. *Adverse selection models.* In these models, (e.g., Stiglitz, 1976; Weiss, 1980) employers cannot costlessly learn the ability of workers, either as applicants or on the job. It is assumed that the average quality of the applicant pool increases with the wage rate. These models imply that industries which are more sensitive to quality differences, or have higher costs of measuring quality will offer higher wages.

4. *Fair-wage models.* The premise of the fair-wage models (e.g., Akerlof, 1982, 1984; Akerlof and Yellen, 1988; Solow, 1979) is that workers will exert more effort if they think they are being paid fairly. This premise gives firms an incentive to pay wages above competitive levels whenever their workers' perceived fair wage exceeds the competitive wage. If workers believe that fairness requires a firm to share rents with employees (for supporting evidence see Kahneman, Knetsch and Thaler, 1986a), then fair-wage models predict that industries with high profits will be those which pay high wages. The model also predicts high wages in industries where teamwork and worker cooperation are particularly important.

It should be noted that this taxonomy of efficiency wage models should not be interpreted as suggesting that the models are mutually exclusive. Firms might well pay above competitive wages to reduce shirking and quits, attract high-quality applicants, and improve worker morale. All of these ideas make sense and probably have some validity. What is at issue here is the extent to which any of these models can explain the interindustry wage pattern. The key fact to explain is the uniformity of the industry wages across occupations. The models based on shirking, turnover, and adverse selection seem to offer few insights into why the high-wage industries should offer above the market salaries for secretaries and janitors. The fair-wage models do better on this score. If an industry has to pay some of its workers high wages for exogenous reasons (such as compensating differences to miners), then it may pay other workers high wages for "internal equity" reasons. The fair wage models are also consistent with the correlation of industry wages and profits (since sharing rents is fair) and with the persistence of the wage differentials over time (high wages become a norm). However, fairness seems to have little to offer to explain the strong international correlations, especially those for Eastern bloc countries.

The other logical explanation for a firm paying higher than competitive wages is based on the threat of collective action (e.g., Dickens, 1986). In Dickens' model, nonunion workers can benefit from the threat of unionization if employers raise wages to prevent collective action. The model predicts that industries will have high wages where the threat of union action is highest: where workers are predisposed toward unions, where laws favor union formation, and where firms have rents to share.

Some of the evidence on industry wage differentials is consistent with the union threat model. High wages in the U.S. are correlated with union density and with industry profits, as the model predicts. However, Krueger and Summers (1987, p. 36) offer a plausible alternative view:

> Historical evidence suggests that high-wage industries already paid relatively high wages before the advent of wide-scale unionization in manufacturing. For instance, the Big Three automobile manufacturers in the US were wage leaders prior to successful union organization of General Motors and Chrysler in 1937 and Ford in 1941. Furthermore, unions have tended to concentrate their organizing efforts in industries which have a greater ability to pay high wages, and these industries appear to share their rents with unorganized workers anyway. Lastly, international evidence shows that the industry wage structure is similar in countries where there is not a threat of unions and in countries where there is widespread collective bargaining. All this suggests that union density is a correlate of industry wage differentials, but probably not an underlying determinant of the industry wage structure.

COMMENTARY

1. How surprising are the empirical findings described above? Several readers of the first draft of this chapter constructed an example within the academic labor market in which "industry" wage differentials would not be considered anomalous. Suppose we divide colleges and universities into two broad "industries":

research universities and teaching colleges. Note that most of the faculty in both industries will have PhDs, and thus will be indistinguishable based on the sort of data usually available on research tapes. Now run a wage regression for all faculty members and include an "industry" variable. Will anyone be surprised if the industry variable explains a significant portion of the variance? Surely not. So why should the significance of other industry variables be considered evidence against a competitive labor market?

I do not find this analogy compelling. First, note that this division of the academic labor market into "industries" is hardly arbitrary. We have good reason to expect that this market does sort workers in part by ability (at least on the research dimension—teaching might well be a different story). There is no similar presumption that automobile workers should have more ability than leather workers. Also, the analogy doesn't address the uniformity of wage differentials across occupations. Would we expect janitors at research universities to be paid more? If so, do we think they are better janitors? Finally, there are what I think are more telling analogies to industry wage patterns within the academic labor market. Consider the salaries of economists in economics departments, business schools, and law schools. Business and law schools appear to pay a substantial quality-adjusted premium, one that seems to have increased in recent years. While it is possible to argue that this is a compensating differential, few economists in business or law schools request transfers to the economics department. Rather, I think that the high salaries are explained by internal equity considerations. It seems unfair to pay a full professor of economics less than a new assistant professor of accounting! Of course, the high salaries will tend to attract good people, so over time the average quality of the economists in the professional schools will improve. But the point is that the high wages came first, for fairness reasons. There is, as far as I know, no technological reason why business schools and law schools should want (or in fact get) higher-quality economists than departments of economics.

The debate as to whether the industry wage pattern can be explained by variations in ability strikes me as a debate over whether the pattern is an anomaly or a puzzle. If it is true that the high-wage industries get higher-quality janitors and secretaries, then the competitive theory of labor markets is intact, but we are left with a puzzle as to why it is profit maximizing for automobile industry managers to have cleaner offices and better typists than their colleagues in the leather industry.

2. In trying to evaluate the competing theories of interindustry wage differentials, I am struck by the relevance of what might be called "Herb Simon's Lament." For many years, Simon has been critical of the economics profession's aversion to direct observation of economic decision making. The absence of such direct observations makes evaluating many economic theories difficult. Consider the shirking model. Do employees work harder when they think they are in danger of losing a highly paid job? More to the point, do they work enough harder to justify the higher wages? Are the firms that pay high wages those who would gain the most from an increase in worker effort? As far as I know, we have virtually no empirical basis for evaluating the shirking model.

The situation is only slightly better for the turnover model. Since data on quit rates are published, it is possible to see whether paying high wages decreases quit rates (it does). But if we wish to know whether the observed pattern of wages and quit rates is consistent with profit maximization, we also must know how turnover costs vary by industry. Are the industries that pay high wages those with the highest turnover costs? Who knows?

While the fair wage model seems to fit the data best, it too has little direct empirical support. Are workers more productive if morale is high? Common sense and social psychological research on "equity theory" both suggest that the sign of the effect is right. But again we are not close to being able to test whether firms have found the true efficiency wage which sets the marginal gains from increased morale equal to marginal costs.[4]

To address any of these issues we need much more in the way of what might be called micro-micro (nano?) economics. Economists would have to get their hands dirty collecting data on the actual operation of organizations. Unless the profession is willing to reward this type of time-consuming research activity, many interesting questions will remain unresolved.

3. There is an interesting relationship between the fair-wage models of Akerlof and Yellen and the topics of the last two chap-

---

[4]One interesting effort along these lines is Raff and Summers' (1987) evaluation of Ford's decision in 1913 to double wages.

ters. In Chapter 2 on Cooperation the anomaly discussed was the fact that people often cooperate in public goods-prisoner's dilemma type situations in which a selfish action is dominant. Furthermore, cooperation is more common in situations where the participants can talk to one another and/or have some sense of group identity. Chapter 3 presented evidence on the Ultimatum Game. Two types of anomalous behavior were observed in these games. First, Allocators made generous offers, often close to a 50–50 split. Second, Recipients often rejected positive offers that were felt to be insultingly small.

What would happen if we combined these two research paradigms? Suppose two subjects first played an ultimatum game and then a one-trial prisoner's dilemma. It seems plausible to assume that Recipients who received what they considered to be an unfair offer in the ultimatum game would subsequently be less likely to cooperate in the prisoner's dilemma game. More generally, it is probably not a good strategy to offer a Recipient a penny in the ultimatum game and then ask her for a favor.

Now consider the case of two large firms with plants located in the same community. Both firms have clerical staffs that perform virtually identical services within the firms. Firm H is in a high-wage industry and pays its clerical staff W_H, while Firm L is in a low-wage industry and pays its clerical staff only $W_L < W_H$. Suppose that Firm H decides to save money by cutting the wage of its clerical workers to W_L. Is this action profitable? That depends on the reaction of the clerical workers. If the workers think of their old wage (equal to the wage the firm pays its clerical workers at other facilities) as a fair one (which seems likely) they may resist the wage cut in various ways that can be summarized as saying they become less *cooperative*. The reduction in worker cooperation could easily offset any gains from reducing the wage bill. One model that comes very close to this point of view is presented by Lindbeck and Snower (1988).

To sum up, I find the pattern of industry wages difficult to understand unless we assume that firms pay attention to perceived equity in setting wages, an assumption that only an economist would find controversial.

[5]

The Winner's Curse

Next time you find yourself a little short of cash for a night on the town, try the following experiment in your neighborhood tavern. Take a jar and fill it with coins, noting the total value of the coins. Now auction off the jar to the assembled masses at the bar (offering to pay the winning bidder in bills to control for penny aversion). Chances are very high that the following results will be obtained:

1. The average bid will be significantly less than the value of the coins. (Bidders are risk averse.)
2. The winning bid will exceed the value of the jar.

In conducting this demonstration, you will have simultaneously obtained the funding necessary for your evening's entertainment and enlightened the patrons of the tavern about the perils of the "winner's curse."

The winner's curse is a concept that was first discussed in the literature by three Atlantic Richfield engineers, Capen, Clapp, and Campbell (1971). The idea is simple. Suppose many oil companies are interested in purchasing the drilling rights to a particular parcel of land. Let's assume that the rights are worth the same amount to all bidders, that is, the auction is what is called a *common value* auction. Further, suppose that each bidding firm obtains an estimate of the value of the rights from its experts. Assume that the estimates are unbiased, so the mean of the estimates is equal to the common value of the tract. What is likely to happen in the auction? Given the difficulty of estimating the amount of oil in a given location, the estimates of the experts will vary substantially, some far too high and some too low. Even if companies bid somewhat less than the estimate their expert provided, the firms whose experts provided high estimates will tend to bid more than the firms whose experts guessed lower. Indeed, it may occur that the firm that wins the auction will be the one whose experts provided the highest estimates. If this happens, the winner of the auction is likely to be a loser. The winner can be said to be "cursed" in one of two ways: 1. the winning bid exceeds the value of the tract, so the firm loses money; or 2. the value of the tract is less than the expert's estimate so the winning firm is disappointed. Call these winner's curse versions 1 and 2, respectively. Notice that the milder version 2 can apply even if the winning bidder makes a profit, as long as the profit is less than expected at the time the bid was made. In either version the winner is unhappy about the outcome, so both definitions seem appropriate.

The winner's curse cannot occur if all the bidders are rational (see Cox and Isaac, 1984), so evidence of a winner's curse in market settings would constitute an anomaly. However, acting rationally in a common value auction can be difficult. Rational bidding requires first distinguishing between the expected value of the object for sale, conditioned only on the prior information available, and the expected value conditioned on winning the auction. However, even if a bidder grasps this basic concept, version 2 of the winner's curse can occur if the bidder underestimates the magnitude of the adjustment necessary to compensate for the presence of other bidders.

In a normal type of auction in which the high bidder wins and pays whatever he or she bid, there are two factors to consider, and they work in opposite directions. An increase in the number of other bidders implies that to win the auction you must bid more aggressively, but their presence also increases the chance that if you win, you will have overestimated the value of the object for sale—suggesting that you should bid less aggressively.[1] Solving for the optimal bid is not trivial. Thus, it is an empirical question whether bidders in various contexts get it right or are cursed. I will present some evidence, both from experimental and

[1]As Capen et al. (1971, p.645) put it:"If one wins a tract against two or three others he may feel fine about his good fortune. But how should he feel if he won against 50 others? Ill."

field studies, suggesting that the winner's curse may be a common phenomenon.

EXPERIMENTAL EVIDENCE

The jar of coins example cited above has in fact been conducted under experimental conditions by Max Bazerman and William Samuelson (1983). Their subjects were MBA students taking microeconomics classes at Boston University. The objects auctioned off were jars of coins or other objects such as paper clips valued at four cents each. Unknown to the subjects, each jar had a value of $8. Subjects submitted sealed bids and were told that the highest bidder would receive the defined value of the object less his or her bid. A total of 48 auctions were conducted, 4 in each of 12 classes. No feedback was provided until the entire experiment was completed. Subjects were also asked to estimate the value of each jar (point estimates and 90 percent confidence limits), and a $2 prize was offered for the best guess in each class.

The estimates of the actual values turned out to be biased downward. The mean estimate of the value of the jars was $5.13, well below the true value of $8.00. This bias, plus risk aversion, would tend to work against observing a winner's curse. Nevertheless, the mean winning bid was $10.01, producing an average loss to the winning bidder of $2.01. Clearly these experiments do not require large NSF grants!

Samuelson and Bazerman (1985) have run another series of experiments about the winner's curse in a different context. Try this problem (pp.131–33) yourself before continuing.

> In the following exercise, you will represent Company A (the acquirer) which is currently considering acquiring Company T (the target) by means of a tender offer. You plan to tender in cash for 100% of Company T's shares but are unsure how high a price to offer. The main complication is this: the value of the company depends directly on the outcome of a major oil exploration project it is currently undertaking.
>
> The very viability of Company T depends on the exploration outcome. In the worst case (if the exploration fails completely), the company under current management will be worth nothing—$0/share. In the best case (a complete success), the value

under current management could be as high as $100/share. Given the range of exploration outcomes, all share values between $0 and $100 per share are considered equally likely. By all estimates the company will be worth considerably more in the hands of Company A than under current management. In fact, whatever the value under current management, the company will be worth 50% more under the management of Company A than under Company T.

The board of directors of Company A has asked you to determine the price they should offer for Company T's shares. This offer must be made now, before the outcome of the drilling project is known.

Thus, you (Company A) will not know the results of the exploration project when submitting your offer, but Company T will know the results when deciding whether or not to accept your offer. In addition, Company T is expected to accept any offer by Company A that is greater than or equal to the (per share) value of the company under its own management.

As the representative of Company A, you are deliberating over price offers in the range $0/share to $150/share. What offer per share would you tender?

The typical subject thinks about this problem roughly as follows: The firm has an expected value of $50 to Company T, which makes it worth $75 to Company A. Therefore if I suggest a bid somewhere between 50 and 75, Company A should make some money. This analysis fails to take into consideration the asymmetric information that is built into the problem. A correct analysis must calculate the expected value of the firm conditioned on the bid being accepted. To see this, work through an example. Suppose you bid $60. If the bid is accepted, then the company must be worth no more than $60 under the current management. Since all of the values less than $60 are equally likely, this implies that the firm, on average, will be worth $30 to the current owners, or $45 to you. By bidding $60 you expect to lose $15. In fact, for any bid B that is greater than zero, you expect to lose .25B. Thus, this problem produces an extreme form of the winner's curse in which any positive bid yields an expected loss to the bidder.

This experiment was run in two conditions, one with monetary incentives and one without. The results, as shown in Table 5-1, are quite similar for the two conditions, with the bids in the condi-

Table 5-1

Bids	No incentives (N = 123)	Monetary incentives (N = 66)
0	9%	8%
1–49	16	29
50–59	37	26
60–69	15	13
70–79	22	20
80+	1	4

Source: Samuelson and Bazerman (1985).

tion with monetary incentives somewhat lower. In both conditions over 90 percent of the subjects make positive bids, and a majority are in the range between $50 and $75.

Economists often respond to examples like this by hypothesizing that although people can be fooled once or twice by such a problem, they will figure out the trap with experience. Sheryl Weiner, Max Bazerman, and John Carroll (1987) have investigated this hypothesis by giving the "buy-a-firm" problem to 69 Northwestern MBA students via a microcomputer. All subjects repeated the experiment 20 times with financial incentives and feedback after each trial. The feedback included the "true" value of the company, whether their bid was accepted, and how much money they made or lost. Of the 69 subjects, five learned to bid one dollar or less by the end of the experiment. For these five subjects, the average trial in which they began to bid one dollar or less was trial 8. There was no sign of any learning among the others; in fact the average bid drifted up over the last few trials. It may be possible to learn to avoid the winner's curse in this problem, but the learning is neither easy nor fast.

Another series of experiments has been conducted by John Kagel and his colleagues at the University of Houston. Many of the experiments have the following structure. An object is to be sold using a sealed-bid auction. The value of the object, X^*, varies from one trial to another but is always between X_L and X_H. Before the bidding, each bidder is given a clue about the value of the object on this trial. The clue is obtained by receiving one draw, X_i, from a uniform distribution $X^* \pm \epsilon$, with the width of the band around X^*, ϵ, varying from trial to trial. Subjects thus know the range of values that X^* could take and their one draw, X_i, which corresponds to the expert estimate in the oil bidding example. An auction is then conducted, the bids are posted, and the winner has a profit or loss credited to his or her account. (Bidders were given some capital to start with, usually about $10. Once their account reached zero they were no longer permitted to bid.) The experimental manipulations included varying ϵ, N (the number of bidders), and the type of auction (first price, second price, and low price[2]). Typically subjects first participated in small groups of three–five bidders, and then in "large" groups of six or seven. A nice feature of all the experiments is that for each trial the authors compute the outcome that would be predicted by a bidding model in which everyone bids rationally. They call this a risk-neutral Nash equilibrium or RNNE model.[3]

In Kagel and Levin (1986), which used first price auctions, the results varied with group size. In the small groups, there were typically profits which were, on average, 65.1 percent of the RNNE profits. However, in the large groups losses of $0.88 per auction period were observed, in contrast to the $4.68 profit predicted by the RNNE. The winner's curse emerged in the larger groups because the subjects bid more aggressively as the size of the group increased, while the RNNE bid function requires bidding more conservatively.

These results have been replicated in Kagel, Levin, and Harstad (1987) using a second price auction method. Again there were profits in the small group experiments, here 52.8 percent of RNNE profits, and losses of $2.15 per period in the large groups, compared to the RNNE prediction of $3.95 in profits.

Finally, Dyer, Kagel, and Levin (1987) report on a series of low price auctions. In these auctions there were losses in both the small groups and the larger groups. However, the most interesting and innovative feature of the paper is that they included an experiment with a group of construction firm managers. A common criticism of experimental economics, especially if the results of the experiment do not accord with economic theory, is that the subjects are "only college students working on toy problems, and

---

[2]In a first price auction, the item is awarded to the highest bidder who pays whatever she bid. In a second price auction, the item is given to the highest bidder, but she pays whatever was the second highest bid. In a low price auction, such as construction contract bidding, the winner is the one who submits the lowest bid. Low price auctions can use either first or second price rules.

[3]A Nash equilibrium is achieved if no bidder would want to change his strategy even if he knew all the other bidders' strategies.

in the real world, experts wouldn't make these silly mistakes." So how did the construction managers do? While the experimenters worried that the experts might take them to the cleaners, in fact the experts did no better or worse than the students. This is surprising, given that construction firms participate in low bid auctions all the time, and would soon go bankrupt if they fell prey to the winner's curse. Dyer et al. believe the result occurs because the managers have learned situation-specific rules of thumb rather than the relevant theory (pp. 23–24):

> We believe that in the field the executives have learned a set of situation specific rules of thumb which permit them to avoid the winner's curse in the field but could not be applied in the laboratory. . . . However, these rules of thumb do not translate into a structurally similar, but different environment which lacks familiar references. When placed in a new environment which does not contain the usual stimuli, the learning process must take place anew, since without theory absorption there is nothing to be carried over from previous experience.

FIELD DATA

The laboratory evidence demonstrates that avoiding the winner's curse is not easy. Even experienced subjects who are given significant learning opportunities fail to solve the buy-a-firm problem and fail to understand the need to become more conservative when the number of bidders increases. Do bidders in large stakes auctions in the "real world" make the same mistakes? There are numerous studies that claim to have found evidence of the winner's curse in market contexts. For example, in the field of book publishing, Dessauer (1981, p. 33) reports that: "The problem is, simply, that most of the auctioned books are not earning their advances. In fact, very often such books have turned out to be dismal failures whose value was more perceived than real."[4] Cassing and Douglas (1980) looked at the market for free agents in baseball and concluded that free agents were overpaid. The owners of major league baseball teams seem to have come to the same conclusion, and responded with the effective tactic of collu-

---

[4]Of course, the quoted statement could be true but not be evidence of a winner's curse if the sales distribution is sufficiently skewed.

sion.[5] Here I will review the evidence in two other contexts: off-shore oil and gas leases, and corporate takeovers.

It is appropriate to start with the evidence on bidding for oil and gas drilling rights, since that is the domain which prompted the marvelous article by Capen et al. (1971) that first mentioned the concept of a winner's curse. They began their discussion by noting (p. 641):

> In recent years, several major companies have taken a rather careful look at their record and those of the industry in areas where sealed competitive bidding is the method of acquiring leases. The most notable of these areas, and perhaps the most interesting, is the Gulf of Mexico. Most analysts turn up with the rather shocking result that, while there seems to be a lot of oil and gas in the region, the industry is not making as much return on its investment as it intended. In fact, if one ignores the era before 1950, when land was a good deal cheaper, he finds that the Gulf has paid off at something less than the local credit union.

The authors cite several studies to document their claims, and report some interesting data of their own regarding the dispersion of bids. They report that the ratio between the highest and lowest bids by what they call "serious competitors" is commonly as high as 5 to 10 and can be as high as 100. While this result might be explained by some firms submitting low bids in the hope that there will be no other bidders (as was true for 15 tracts in the sample analyzed by Capen et al.) the authors report some other interesting data. In the 1969 Alaska North Slope sale, the sum of the winning bids was $900 million, while the sum of the second-highest bids was only $370 million. The winning bid exceeded the second bid by a factor of 4 or more in 26 percent of the tracts, and by a factor of at least 2 for 77 percent of the tracts. While these figures don't actually prove that anyone was behaving irrationally, they certainly seem consistent with a winner's curse scenario.

The Capen, Clapp, and Campbell article was published in 1971, before all the information was in on the Gulf of Mexico leases

---

[5]It has also been suggested that the construction managers in Dyer et al.'s experiments would have done better in an experiment emphasizing cartel skills rather than optimal bidding strategy.

they discuss. However, Walter Mead, Asbjorn Moseidjord, and Philip Sorensen (1983) have examined how those leases turned out. They calculate before-tax rates of return on 1223 leases issued in the Gulf of Mexico between 1954 and 1969, the period directly preceding the publication of Capen et al. They report (p. 42):

> [F]or all 1223 leases, firms suffered an average present value loss of $192,128 per lease using a 12.5% discount rate. [6] . . . 62% of all leases in our data base were dry. Consequently, the lessees had no revenues whatsoever to offset their bonus and rent payments, or their exploration costs. Another 16% of the leases were unprofitable (on an after-tax basis) although some production occurred. Only 22% of the leases were profitable, and these leases earned only 18.74% in aggregate on the after-tax basis.

These results seem consistent at least with version 2 of the winner's curse; that is, they are surely lower than the bidders anticipated when they bid on the property. In addition, these returns are helped by the fact that nominal crude oil prices increased from $3 to $35 a barrel between 1970 and 1981, something that could not have been anticipated when the leases were purchased. As to why the returns were so low, the authors venture this (p. 45): "The low and negative rates of return for the initial five lease sales [from 10/13/54 through 8/11/59] appear to reflect excessive enthusiasm for the amount of oil likely to be found."

Another analysis of the same lease sales was conducted by Hendricks, Porter, and Boudreau (1987). They use a 5 percent real discount rate and real price sequences that did not assume that the oil companies could anticipate the OPEC price shocks. They also make several other assumptions that differ from those used by Mead et al. Their results, in contrast to Mead et al., indicate that firms would have made profits even if oil prices had remained constant in real terms. Nevertheless, their data do provide some support for the winner's curse. For the 18 individual firms or consortiums of firms that made a significant number of bids (the average number of bids was 225) Hendricks et al. calculated the profit each firm would have made ex post if it had multiplied all of its bids by a constant, θ, assuming all other firms had kept their bids the same. They then determined θ^*, the value of θ that would have maximized profits. If all firms chose their bids

---

[6]They use nominal values for costs and selling prices; thus this rate seems reasonable.

according to risk-neutral Nash equilibrium behavior, then θ^* would be equal to one. However, for 12 of the 18 firms θ^* was less than one, with the median value being .68. For Texaco, which seems to have been particularly cursed, θ^* was .15, indicating that they should have reduced their bids by a factor of nearly 7! For many of the firms, the difference between the actual profits earned and those that would have been earned with optimal bidding amounted to hundreds of millions of dollars. The authors conclude (p. 529): "This result suggests that some firms may have systematically overvalued the tracts and/or failed to fully anticipate the impact of the 'winner's curse.'"

Richard Roll (1986) applies the concept of the winner's curse to the puzzling phenomenon of corporate takeovers. The puzzle is to explain why firms are willing to pay substantial premiums above the market price to acquire another firm. The empirical evidence suggests that while the stockholders of target firms make significant profits when their firms are purchased, there is little or no gain to the buyer. Why then do takeovers occur? Roll offers what he calls the hubris hypothesis as one plausible answer. According to this view, bidding firms, typically flush with cash,[7] identify potential target firms, estimate the value of the target, then bid for the target if and only if the estimated value exceeds the market value. Since Roll takes the efficient market hypothesis[8] seriously, he believes that (in the absence of synergy or insider information) the belief by acquirers that they can estimate true value better than the market is likely to be mistaken. As Roll points out (1986, p. 201):

Most other explanations of the takeover phenomenon rely on strong-form market inefficiency of at least a temporary duration. Either financial markets are ignorant of the relevant information possessed by bidding firms, or product markets are inef-

---

[7]Asquith (1983) reports that successful bidders earned 14.3 percent above the market over the 460-day period ending 20 days before the merger. In light of this fact, I think that the hubris hypothesis may be partially a "hot hand" phenomenon. Most basketball players and fans believe that there is strong positive serial correlation in the shooting of basketball players, that is, the probability of making a shot increases after making the previous shot and vice versa. In contrast to this perception, psychologists Gilovich, Vallone, and Tversky (1985) have found no serial correlation using actual NBA data. So, according to the hot-hand-hubris hypothesis, firms that have been doing well lately, perhaps because of a run of good luck, mistakenly think that they are "hot" (i.e., good managers) and will be able to perform miracles with any firm they purchase.

[8]The efficient market hypothesis is discussed in Chapters 10–14.

ficiently organized so that potential synergies, monopolies, or tax savings are being ineffectively exploited (at least temporarily), or labor markets are inefficient because gains could be obtained by replacement of inferior managers.

To test the hubris hypothesis Roll reviews the data on stock prices of bidders and targets around the announcement date. The hubris hypothesis predicts that the combined value of the bidder and the target should fall slightly, representing transactions costs; the value of the target firm should increase; and the value of the bidder should fall.[9] He interprets the evidence as consistent with these predictions and concludes as follows (p. 213):

> The final impression one is obliged to draw from the currently available results is that they provide no really convincing evidence against even the extreme (hubris) hypothesis that all markets are operating perfectly efficiently and that individual bidders occasionally make mistakes. Bidders may indicate by their actions a belief in the existence of takeover gains, but systematic studies have provided little to show that such beliefs are well founded.

While Roll is careful to explain how difficult it is to evaluate these studies, it seems clear that bidding firms are making very little money (if any) through takeovers. Again, version 2 of the winner's curse seems consistent with these data.

COMMENTARY

If my reading of the literature on oil leases and takeovers is correct, namely that the winner's curse is present in these markets, how surprised should economists be? What challenge does the existence of the winner's curse pose to the economics paradigm?

---

[9]Of course, it is an article of faith that the stock prices are rational. Indeed, Miller (1977) argues that stock prices in general are afflicted by the winner's curse because the investors most optimistic about a stock will be the ones who own it. Thus, in the case of mergers, the investors most optimistic about the prospects of the merger will end up owning the shares of the acquiring firm. This argument must be tempered by the possibility that pessimists can sell the acquiring firm short. Nevertheless, it is true that many investors, both individual and institutional, do not sell short, and it remains an empirical question whether the existing quantity of short selling is sufficient to prevent a winner's curse from emerging.

McAfee and McMillan (1987, p. 721) in their survey of auctions and bidding say: "Statements about the winner's curse [such as the quote by Dessauer about book publishing that appears above] come close to asserting that bidders are repeatedly surprised by the outcomes of auctions, which would violate basic notions of rationality." What they are saying can be paraphrased as follows: "These statements about the winner's curse suggest that bidders make systematic errors. Economic theory precludes such errors. Therefore, the statements must be wrong." The logic of this position is questionable. It is important to keep in mind that rationality is an assumption in economics, not a demonstrated fact. Given the results of the experimental studies, isn't it possible that bidders make mistakes in these auctions?

It is also interesting to note a peculiar tendency among many economic theorists. A theorist will sweat long and hard on a problem, finally achieving a new insight previously unknown to economists. The theorist then assumes that the agents in a theoretical model act as if they also understood this new insight. In assuming that the agents in the economy intuitively grasp what it took so long to work out, the theorist is either showing uncharacteristic modesty and generosity, or is guilty of ascribing too much rationality to the agents in his model. As Kenneth Arrow (1986, p. 391) has said: "We have the curious situation that scientific analysis imputes scientific behavior to its subjects. This need not be a contradiction, but it does seem to lead to an infinite regress."

The possibility of suboptimal behavior by other participants in an auction raises an issue rarely discussed in economic theory, namely what to do when you realize that your competitors are making mistakes. Theoretical treatments of bidding typically assume that bidders are rational and that the rationality of other bidders is common knowledge.[10] Suppose you are Capen and his colleagues and you have figured out the winner's curse. You now have an advantage over other oil firms. How can you exploit your new competitive advantage? If you react by optimally reducing your bids, then you will avoid paying too much for leases, but you will also win very few auctions. In fact, you may decide not to bid at all! Unless you want to switch businesses, this solution

---

[10]If you and I are playing a game, and rationality is common knowledge, then I am rational, you are rational, I know you are rational, you know I know it, I know you know I know it, etc. Bidding theory is explored in Wilson (1977), Milgrom and Weber (1982), and the recent survey by McAfee and McMillan (1987).

is obviously unsatisfactory. You could let your competitors win all the auctions and try to make money by selling their shares short, but this strategy can be risky. In the oil drilling case, the price of oil skyrocketed, and the price of oil stocks went up too, even for those firms who bid badly. A better solution may be to share your new knowledge with your competitors, urging them to reduce their bids as well.[11] If they believe your analysis, then the game can be profitable for the bidders. This, of course, is exactly what Capen, Clapp, and Campbell did. More generally the study of optimal strategy for games in which one's opponents are less than fully rational deserves greater attention from economists.

Even once one is aware of the winner's curse, it is easy to fail to appreciate some of the subtle ways in which it can operate. For example, Harrison and March (1984) discuss the concept of post-decision surprise, a situation similar to the second version of the winner's curse in which decision makers systematically observe outcomes which are worse than expected. They show that post-decision surprise will occur for any decision with great uncertainty and/or with many alternatives. Thus, the following should be true: For any organization hiring a new employee, the more candidates interviewed, the better the candidate they hire will be, *and* the more likely that candidate will fail to live up to the organization's expectations. Similarly, Brown (1974) discusses the case of capital investment projects within a firm. If many such projects are considered, and only a few are selected, then actual net revenues will tend to be less than projected, even if the projections are unbiased for the complete set of projects considered.

The winner's curse is a prototype for the kind of problem that is amenable to investigation using modern behavioral economics, a combination of cognitive psychology and microeconomics. The key ingredient is the existence of a cognitive illusion, a mental task that induces a substantial majority of subjects to make a systematic error. The existence of the cognitive illusion was recognized by Capen et al. and demonstrated by Bazerman and Samuelson, and by Kagel and Levin. Whenever such an illusion can be demonstrated, the possibility that market outcomes will diverge from the predictions of economic theory is present.

I will close with a fortune cookie provided by Capen et al. "He who bids on a parcel what he thinks it is worth, will, in the long run, be taken for a cleaning."

---

[11]Thanks to Julia Grant for making this point to me.

[6]

The Endowment Effect, Loss Aversion, and Status Quo Bias

A wine-loving economist you know purchased some nice Bordeaux wines years ago at low prices. The wines have greatly appreciated in value, so that a bottle that cost less than $10 when purchased would now fetch $200 at auction. This economist now drinks some of this wine occasionally, but would neither be willing to sell the wine at the auction price nor buy an additional bottle at that price.

This pattern—the fact that people often demand much more to give up an object than they would be willing to pay to acquire it—is called the *endowment effect* (Thaler, 1980). The example also illustrates what Samuelson and Zeckhauser (1988) call a *status quo bias*, a preference for the current state that biases the economist against both buying *and* selling his wine. These anomalies are a manifestation of an asymmetry of value that Kahneman and Tversky (1984) call *loss aversion*—the disutility of giving up an object is greater than the utility associated with acquiring it. This chapter documents the evidence supporting endowment effects and status quo biases, and discusses their relation to loss aversion.

With Daniel Kahneman and Jack L. Knetsch.

THE ENDOWMENT EFFECT

An early laboratory demonstration of the endowment effect was offered by Knetsch and Sinden (1984). The participants in this study were endowed with either a lottery ticket or with $2.00. Some time later, each subject was offered an opportunity to trade the lottery ticket for the money, or vice versa. Very few subjects chose to switch. Those who were given lottery tickets seemed to like them better than those who were given money.

This demonstration and other similar ones (see Knetsch, 1989), while striking, did not settle the matter. Some economists felt that the behavior would disappear if subjects were exposed to a market environment with ample learning opportunities. For example, Knez, Smith, and Williams (1985) argued that the discrepancy between buying and selling prices might be produced by the thoughtless application of normally sensible bargaining habits, namely understating one's true willingness to pay (WTP) and overstating the minimum acceptable price at which one would sell (willingness to accept or WTA). Coursey, Hovis, and Schulze (1987) reported that the discrepancy between WTP and WTA diminished with experience in a market setting (although it was not eliminated, see Knetsch and Sinden, 1987). To clarify the issue, Kahneman, Knetsch, and Thaler (1990) ran a new series of experiments to determine whether the endowment effect survives when subjects face market discipline and have a chance to learn. We will report just two experiments from that series here.

In the first experiment, students in an advanced undergraduate economics class at Cornell University participated in a series of markets. The objects traded in the first three markets were ''induced value tokens.'' In such markets all subjects are told how much a token is worth to them, with the amounts varying across subjects. Half the subjects were made owners of tokens, the other half were not. In this way, supply and demand curves for tokens are created.

Subjects alternated between the buyer and seller role in the three successive markets, and were assigned a different individual redemption value in each trial. Experimenters collected the forms from all participants after each market period, and immediately calculated and announced the market-clearing price and the number of trades. Three buyers and three sellers were selected at random after each of the induced markets and were paid off according to the preferences stated on their forms and the market-clearing price for that period.

These markets contained no grist for the anomaly mill. On each trial, the market-clearing price was exactly equal to the intersection of the induced supply and demand curves, and the volume of trade was within one unit of the predicted quantity. These results demonstrate that the subjects understood the task, and that the market mechanism used did not impose high transactions costs.

Immediately after the three induced value markets, subjects in alternating seats were given Cornell coffee mugs, which sell for $6.00 each at the bookstore. The experimenter asked all participants to examine a mug, either their own or their neighbor's. The experimenter then informed the subjects that four markets for mugs would be conducted using the same procedures as the prior induced markets with two exceptions: (1) One of the four market trials would subsequently be selected at random and only the trades made on this trial would be executed. (2) On the binding market trial, *all* trades would be implemented, unlike the subset implemented in the induced value markets. The initial assignment of buyer and seller roles was maintained for all four trading periods. The clearing price and the number of trades were announced after each period. The market that "counted" was indicated after the fourth period, and transactions were executed immediately—all sellers who had indicated that they would give up their mug at the market-clearing price exchanged their mugs for cash, and successful buyers paid this same price and received their mug. This design was used to permit learning to take place over successive trials and yet make each trial potentially binding. The same procedure was then followed for four more successive markets using boxed ballpoint pens with a visible bookstore price tag of $3.98, which were distributed to the subjects who had been buyers in the mug markets.

What does economic theory predict will happen in these markets for mugs and pens? Since transactions costs have been shown to be insignificant in the induced value markets, and income effects are trivial, a clear prediction is available: When the market clears, the objects will be owned by those subjects who value them most. Call the half of the subjects who like mugs the most "mug lovers" and the half who like mugs least "mug haters." Then, since the mugs were assigned at random, on average half of the mug lovers will be given a mug, and half will not. This implies that in the market, half of the mugs should trade, with mug haters selling to mug lovers.

The 50% predicted volume of trade did not materialize. There were 22 mugs and pens distributed so the predicted number of trades was 11. In the four mug markets the number of trades was four, one, two, and two, respectively. In the pen markets the number of trades was either four or five. In neither market was there any evidence of a trend over the four trials. The reason for the low volume of trade is revealed by the reservation prices of buyers and sellers. For mugs, the median owner was unwilling to sell for less than $5.25, while the median buyer was unwilling to pay more than $2.25–$2.75. The market price varied between $4.25 and $4.75. In the market for pens the ratio of selling to buying prices was also about 2 to 1. The experiment was replicated several times, always with similar results: median selling prices are about twice median buying prices and volume is less than half of that expected.

Another experiment from this series allows us to investigate whether the low volume of trading is produced by a reluctance to buy or a reluctance to sell. In this experiment, 77 students at Simon Fraser University were randomly assigned to three conditions. One group, the Sellers, were given SFU coffee mugs and were asked whether they would be willing to sell the mugs at each of a series of prices ranging from $0.25 to $9.25. A second group of Buyers were asked whether they would be willing to buy a mug at the same set of prices. The third group, called Choosers, were not given a mug but were asked to choose, for each of the prices, between receiving a mug or that amount of money.

Notice that the Sellers and the Choosers are in objectively identical situations, deciding at each price between the mug and that amount of money. Nevertheless, the Choosers behaved more like Buyers than like Sellers. The median reservation prices were: Sellers, $7.12; Choosers, $3.12; Buyers, $2.87. This suggests that the low volume of trade is produced mainly by owners' reluctance to part with their endowment, rather than by buyers' unwillingness to part with their cash. This experiment also eliminates the trivial income effect present in the first experiment, since the Sellers and Choosers are in the same economic situation.

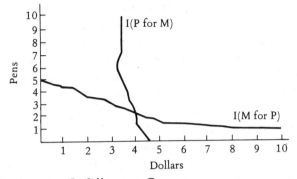

Figure 6–1. Crossing Indifference Curves

Crossing Indifference Curves

One of the first lessons in microeconomics is that two indifference curves can never intersect. This result depends on the implicit assumption that indifference curves are reversible. That is, if an individual owns x and is indifferent between keeping it and trading it for y, then when owning y the individual should be indifferent about trading it for x. If loss aversion is present, however, this reversibility will no longer hold. Knetsch (1990) has demonstrated this point experimentally. One group of subjects received five medium-priced ballpoint pens, while another group of subjects received $4.50. They were then made a series of offers which they could accept or reject. The offers were designed to identify an indifference curve. For example, someone who had been given the pens would be asked if she would give up one of the pens for a dollar. One of the accepted offers (including the original endowment) was selected at random at the end of the experiment to determine the subject's payment. By plotting the line between accepted and rejected offers, Knetsch was able to infer an indifference curve for each subject. Then he plotted the average indifference curve for each of the two groups (those who started with pens and those who started with money). These plots are shown in Figure 6–1. The curves are quite different: the pens were worth more money to those subjects who started with pens than to those who started with money. As a result, the curves intersect.[1]

What produces these "instant endowment effects"? Do sub-

---

[1]These curves were obtained from different individuals. Because subjects were randomly assigned to the two endowment groups, however, it is reasonable to attribute crossing indifference curves to the representative individual.

jects who receive a gift actually value it more than others who do not receive it? A recent study by Loewenstein and Kahneman (1991) investigated this issue. Half the students in a class (N = 63) were given pens, the others were given a token redeemable for an unspecified gift. All participants were then asked to rank the attractiveness of six gifts under consideration as prizes in subsequent experiments. Finally, all the subjects were then given a choice between a pen and two chocolate bars. As in previous experiments, there was a pronounced endowment effect. The pen was preferred by 56% of those endowed with it, but only 24% of the other subjects chose a pen. However, when making the attractiveness ratings, the subjects endowed with pens did not rate them as more attractive. This suggests that the main effect of endowment is not to enhance the appeal of the good one owns, only the pain of giving it up.

STATUS QUO BIAS

One implication of loss aversion is that individuals have a strong tendency to remain at the status quo, because the disadvantages of leaving it loom larger than the advantages. Samuelson and Zeckhauser (1988) have demonstrated this effect, which they term the *status quo bias*. In one experiment, some subjects were given a hypothetical choice task, such as the following, in a "neutral" version in which no status quo is defined (pp. 12–13):

> You are a serious reader of the financial pages but until recently have had few funds to invest. That is when you inherited a large sum of money from your great uncle. You are considering different portfolios. Your choices are to invest in: a moderate-risk company, a high-risk company, treasury bills, municipal bonds.

Other subjects were presented with the same problem but with one of the options designated as the status quo. In this case, after the same opening sentence the passage continues:

> . . . That is when you inherited a portfolio of cash and securities from your great uncle. A significant portion of this portfolio is invested in a moderate-risk company. . . . (The tax and broker commission consequences of any change are insignificant.)

Many different scenarios were investigated, all using the same basic experimental design. Aggregating across all the different questions, Samuelson and Zeckhauser are able to estimate the probability that an option is selected when it is the status quo, or when it is competing as an alternative to the status quo, as a function of how often it is selected in the neutral setting. Their results imply that an alternative becomes significantly more popular when it is designated as the status quo. Also, the advantage of the status quo increases with the number of alternatives.

A test of status quo bias in a field setting was performed by Hartman, Doane, and Woo (forthcoming) using a survey of California electric power consumers. The consumers were asked about their preferences regarding service reliability and rates. They were told that their answers would help determine the company policy in the future. The respondents fell into two groups, one with much more reliable service than the other. Each group was asked to state a preference among six combinations of service reliabilities and rates, with one of the combinations designated as the status quo. The results demonstrated a pronounced status quo bias. In the high reliability group, 60.2 percent selected their status quo as their first choice, while only 5.7 percent expressed a preference for the low reliability option currently being experienced by the other group, though it came with a 30 percent reduction in rates. The low reliability group, however, quite liked their status quo, 58.3 percent of them ranking it first. Only 5.8 percent of this group selected the high reliability option at a proposed 30 percent increase in rates.[2]

A large-scale experiment on status quo bias is now being conducted (inadvertently) by the states of New Jersey and Pennsylvania. Both states now offer a choice between two types of automobile insurance: a cheaper policy that restricts the right to sue, and a more expensive one that maintains the unrestricted right. Motorists in New Jersey are offered the cheaper policy as the default option, with an opportunity to acquire an unrestricted right to sue at a higher price. Since this option was made available in 1988, 83

---

[2]Differences in income and electricity consumption between the two groups were minor and did not appear to significantly influence the results. Could the results be explained by either learning or habituation? That is, might the low reliability group have learned to cope with frequent outages, or have found out that candlelight dinners are romantic? This cannot be ruled out, but it should be stressed that no similar explanation can be used for the mug experiments or the surveys conducted by Samuelson and Zeckhauser, so at least some of the effects observed are attributable to a pure status quo bias.

percent of the drivers have elected the default option. In Pennsylvania's 1990 law, however, the default option is the expensive policy, with an opportunity to opt for the cheaper kind. The potential effect of this legislative framing manipulation was studied by Hershey, Johnson, Meszaros, and Robinson (1990). They asked two groups to choose between alternative policies. One group was presented with the New Jersey plan while the other was presented with the Pennsylvania plan. Of those subjects offered the New Jersey plan, only 23 percent elected to buy the right to sue whereas 53 percent of the subjects offered the Pennsylvania plan retained that right. On the basis of this research, the authors predict that more Pennsylvanians will elect the right to sue than New Jerseyans. Time will tell.

One final example of a presumed status quo bias comes courtesy of the *Journal of Economic Perspectives* staff. Among Carl Shapiro's comments on this Anomalies column was this gem: "You may be interested to know that when the AEA was considering letting members elect to drop one of the three Association journals and get a credit, prominent economists involved in that decision clearly took the view that fewer members would choose to drop a journal if the default was presented as all three journals (rather than the default being two journals with an extra charge for getting all three). We're talking economists here."

LOSS AVERSION

These observations, and many others, can be explained by a notion of loss aversion. A central conclusion of the study of risky choice has been that such choices are best explained by assuming that the significant carriers of utility are not states of wealth or welfare, but changes relative to a neutral reference point. Another central result is that changes that make things worse (losses) loom larger than improvements or gains. The choice data imply an abrupt change of the slope of the value function at the origin. The existing evidence suggests that the ratio of the slopes of the value function in the two domains, for small or moderate gains and losses of money, is about 2 to 1 (Tversky and Kahneman, 1991). A schematic value function is shown in Figure 6-2.

The natural extension of this idea to riskless choice is that the attributes of options in trades and other transactions are also eval-

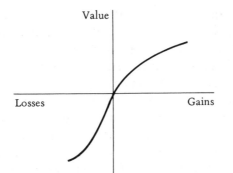

Figure 6–2. A Typical Value Function

Figure 6–3. Multiple Reference Points for the Choice Between A and D

uated as gains and losses relative to a neutral reference point. The approach is illustrated in Figure 6-3. The decision maker has a choice between state A, where she has more of good Y and less of good X, and state D, where she has more of good X and less of good Y. Four different reference points are indicated in the Figure. The individual faces a positive choice between two gains if the reference point is C, a negative choice between two losses if the reference point is B, and two different exchanges if the references are A or D, respectively. For example, if good Y is a mug and good X is money, the reference points for the Sellers and the Choosers in the mugs experiment are A and C. Loss aversion implies that the difference between the states of having a mug and not having one is larger from A than from C, which explains the different monetary values that subjects attach to the mug in these conditions.[3] (For a formal treatment that generalizes consumer theory by introducing the notions of reference and loss aversion, see Tversky and Kahneman, 1991).

In general, a given difference between two options will have greater impact if it is viewed as a difference between two disadvantages than if it is viewed as a difference between two advantages. The status quo bias is a natural consequence of this asymmetry: the disadvantages of a change loom larger than its advantages. However, the differential weighting of advantages and disadvantages can be demonstrated even when the retention of the status quo is not an option. For an example, consider the following question (from Tversky and Kahneman, 1991):

Imagine that as part of your professional training you were assigned to a part-time job. The training is now ending and you must look for employment. You consider two possibilities. They are like your training job in most respects except for the amount of social contact and the convenience of commuting to and from work. To compare the two jobs to each other and to the present one you have made up the following table:

Job	Contact with Others	Commute Time
Present job	isolated for long stretches	10 min.
Job A	limited contact with others	20 min.
Job D	moderately sociable	60 min.

The options A and D are evaluated from a reference job which is better on commute time and worse on personal contact (a point like A' in Figure 6–3). Another version of the problem presented the same options, but the reference job involved ''much pleasant social interaction and 80 minutes of daily commuting time,'' which corresponds to the point D'. The proportion of subjects choosing job A was 70 percent in the first version, 33 percent in the second. Subjects are more sensitive to the dimension in which they are losing relative to their reference point.

---

[3]Loss aversion does not affect all transactions. In a normal commercial transaction, the seller does not suffer a loss when trading a good. Furthermore, the evidence indicates that buyers do not value the money spent on normal purchases as a loss, so long as the price of the good is not thought to be unusually high. Loss aversion is expected to primarily affect owners of goods that had been bought for use rather than for eventual resale.

Enhanced Loss Aversion

Some asymmetries between buying and selling prices are much too large to be explained by garden-variety loss aversion. For example, Thaler (1980) told subjects that they had been exposed to a rare fatal disease and that they now face a .001 chance of painless death within two weeks. They must decide how much they would be willing to pay for a vaccine, to be purchased immediately. The same subjects were also asked for the compensation they would demand to participate in a medical experiment in which they faced a .001 chance of a quick and painless death. For most subjects the two prices differed by more than an order of magnitude.

A study by Viscusi, Magat and Huber (1987) documented a similar effect in a more realistic setting. Their respondents were recruited at a shopping mall and hardware store. The respondents were shown a can of fictitious insecticide, and were asked to examine it for their use. The current price of the can was said to be $10. Respondents were informed that all insecticides can cause injuries if misused, including inhalation and skin poisoning (in households with young children, child poisoning replaced skin poisoning). The current risk level was said to be 15 injuries of each type per 10,000 bottles sold. Respondents were asked to state their WTP to eliminate or reduce the risks. In households without children, the mean WTA to eliminate both risks was $3.78. The respondents were also asked to state the price reduction they would require to accept an increase of 1/10,000 in each of the two risks. The results were dramatic: 77 percent of respondents in this condition said they would refuse to buy the product at any positive price.

The striking difference between WTA and WTP in these studies probably reflects the large difference in the responsibility costs associated with voluntary assumption of additional risk, in contrast to a mere failure to reduce or eliminate existing risk. The asymmetry between omission and commission is familiar in legal doctrine, and its impact on judgments of responsibility has been confirmed by psychological research (Ritov and Baron, forthcoming). The asymmetry affects both blame and regret after a mishap, and the anticipation of blame and regret, in turn, could affect behavior.

A moral attitude is involved in another situation where huge discrepancies between buying and selling prices have been observed, the evaluation of environmental amenities in cost-benefit analyses. Suppose the Disney Corporation offers to buy the Grand Canyon and make it into a water park complete with the world's largest water slide. How do we know whether the benefits of this idea exceed its costs? As usual there are two ways to ask the question, depending on what is the status quo. If there is no theme park in the status quo, then people can be asked the minimum amount of money they would accept to agree to add one (WTA). Alternatively, if Disney currently owns the right, people could be asked how much they would be willing to pay to buy it back and prevent the theme park from being built (WTP). Several surveys have been conducted where the researchers asked both types of questions for such things as clean air and well-maintained public parks. Most studies find that the WTA responses greatly exceed the WTP answers (see Cummings, Brookshire, and Schulze, 1986). The difference in typical responses actually does not tell the entire story. As two close observers of this literature note (Mitchell and Carson, 1989, p. 34): "Studies using WTA questions have consistently received a large number of protest answers, such as 'I refuse to sell' or 'I want an extremely large or infinite amount of compensation for agreeing to this,' and have frequently experienced protest rates [outright refusals to answer the question] of 50 percent or more." These extreme responses reflect the feelings of outrage often seen when communities are faced with the prospect of accepting a new risk such as a nuclear power plant or waste disposal facility (Kunreuther et al. forthcoming, 1989). Offers of compensation to proposed communities often do not help, as they are typically perceived as bribes.[4]

JUDGMENTS OF FAIRNESS AND JUSTICE

An implication of the endowment effect is that people treat opportunity costs differently from "out-of-pocket" costs. Forgone

[4]This is a situation in which people loudly say one thing and the theory asserts another. It is of interest that the practitioners of contingent valuation elected to listen to the theory, rather than to the respondents (Cummings, Brookshire, and Schulze, 1986). The accepted procedure uses WTP questions to assess value even in a context of compensation, relying on the theoretical argument that WTP and WTA should not be far apart when income effects are small.

gains are less painful than perceived losses. This perception is strongly manifested in people's judgments about fair behavior. Kahneman, Knetsch, and Thaler (1986a) present survey evidence supporting this proposition. Samples of the residents of Toronto and Vancouver were asked a series of questions over the telephone about whether they thought a particular economic action was "fair." In some cases, alternative versions of the same questions were presented to different groups of respondents. For each question, respondents were asked to judge whether the action was completely fair, acceptable, somewhat unfair, or very unfair. In reporting the results the first two categories were combined and called "acceptable" and the last two combined and called "unfair." Perceptions of fairness strongly depended on whether the question was framed as a reduction in a gain or an actual loss. For example:

Question 1a. A shortage has developed for a popular model of automobile, and customers must now wait two months for delivery. A dealer has been selling these cars at list price. Now the dealer prices this model at $200 above list price.

N = 130   Acceptable 29 percent   Unfair 71 percent

Question 1b. A shortage has developed for a popular model of automobile, and customers must now wait two months for delivery. A dealer has been selling these cars at a discount of $200 below list price. Now the dealer sells this model only at list price.

N = 123   Acceptable 58 percent   Unfair 42 percent

Imposing a surcharge (which is likely to be judged a loss) is considered more unfair than eliminating a discount (a reduction of a gain). This distinction explains why firms that charge cash customers one price and credit card customers a higher price always refer to the cash price as a discount rather than to the credit card price as a surcharge (Thaler, 1980).

The different intensity of responses to losses and to forgone gains may help explain why it is easier to cut real wages during inflationary periods:

Question 2a. A company is making a small profit. It is located in a community experiencing a recession with substantial unemployment but no inflation. The company decides to decrease wages and salaries 7 percent this year.

N = 125   Acceptable 37 percent   Unfair 63 percent

Question 2b. A company is making a small profit. It is located in a community experiencing a recession with substantial unemployment and 12 percent inflation. The company decides to increase salaries only 5 percent this year.

N = 129   Acceptable 78 percent   Unfair 22 percent

In this case a 7 percent cut in real wages is judged reasonably fair when it is framed as a nominal wage increase, but quite unfair when it is posed as a nominal wage cut.

The attitudes of the lay public about fairness, which are represented in their answers to these fairness questions, also pervade the decisions made by judges in many fields of the law. Supreme Court Justice Oliver Wendell Holmes (1897) put the principle this way:

> It is in the nature of a man's mind. A thing which you enjoyed and used as your own for a long time, whether property or opinion, takes root in your being and cannot be torn away without your resenting the act and trying to defend yourself, however you came by it. The law can ask no better justification than the deepest instincts of man.

Cohen and Knetsch (1990) showed that this principle, embodied in the old expression that "possession is nine tenths of the law," is reflected in many judicial opinions. For example, in tort law judges make the distinction between "loss by way of expenditure and failure to make gain." In one case, several bales fell from the defendant's truck and hit a utility pole, cutting off power to the plaintiff's plant. The plaintiff was able to recover wages paid to employees which were considered "positive outlays" but could not recover lost profits which were merely "negative losses consisting of a mere deprivation of an opportunity to earn an income" (p. 18). A similar distinction is made in contract law. A party that breaches a contract is more likely to be held to the original terms if the action is taken to make an unforeseen gain than if it is taken to avoid a loss.

COMMENTARY

It is in the nature of economic anomalies that they violate standard theory. The next question is what to do about the problem. In many cases there is no obvious way to amend the theory to fit the facts, either because too little is known, or because the changes would greatly increase the complexity of the theory and reduce its predictive yield. The anomalies that have been described under the labels of the endowment effect, the status quo bias, and loss aversion may be an exceptional case, where the needed amendments in the theory are both obvious and tractable.

The amendments are not trivial: the important notion of a stable preference order must be abandoned in favor of a preference order that depends on the current reference level. A revised version of preference theory would assign a special role to the status quo, giving up some standard assumptions of stability, symmetry, and reversibility which the data have shown to be false. But the task is manageable. The generalization of preference theory to indifference curves that are indexed to reference level is straightforward (Tversky and Kahneman, 1991). The factors that determine the reference point in the evaluations of outcomes are reasonably well understood: the role of the status quo, and of entitlements and expectations are sufficiently well established to allow these factors to be used in locating the relevant reference levels for particular analyses.

As Samuelson and Zeckhauser noted, rational models that ignore the status quo tend to predict ''greater instability than is observed in the world'' (p. 47). It should be added that models that ignore loss aversion predict more symmetry and reversibility than are observed in the world, ignoring potentially large differences in the magnitude of responses to gains and to losses. Responses to increases and to decreases in prices, for example, might not always be mirror images of each other. The possibility of loss-aversion effects suggests, more generally, that treatments of responses to *changes* in economic variables should routinely separate the cases of favorable and unfavorable changes. Introducing such distinctions could improve the precision of predictions at a tolerable price in increased complexity.

After more than a decade of research on this topic we have become convinced that the endowment effect, status quo bias, and the aversion to losses are both robust and important. Then again, we admit that the idea is now part of our endowment, and we are naturally keener to retain it than others might be to acquire it.

[7]

Preference Reversals

In one of your more interesting assignments, you have been asked to advise the Minister of Transportation for a small Middle Eastern country regarding the choice of a highway safety program. At the current time, about 600 people per year are killed in traffic accidents in that country. Two programs designed to reduce the number of casualties are under consideration. Program A is expected to reduce the yearly number of casualties to 570; its annual cost is estimated at $12 million. Program B is expected to reduce the yearly number of casualties to 500; its annual cost is estimated at $55 million. The Minister tells you to find out which program would make the electorate happier.

You hire two polling organizations. The first firm asks a group of citizens which program they like better. It finds that about two-thirds of the respondents prefer Program B which saves more lives, though at a higher cost per life saved. The other firm uses a "matching" procedure. It presents respondents with the same information about the two programs except that the cost of Program B is not specified. These citizens are asked to state the cost that would make the two programs equally attractive. The polling firm reasons that respondents' preferences for the two programs can be inferred from their responses to this question. That is, a respondent who is indifferent between the two programs at a cost of less than $55 million should prefer A to B. On the other hand, someone who would be

With Amos Tversky.

willing to spend over $55 million should prefer B to A. This survey finds, however, that more than 90 percent of the respondents provided values smaller than $55 million indicating, in effect, that they prefer Program A over Program B.

This pattern is definitely puzzling. When people are asked to choose between a pair of options, a clear majority favors B over A. When asked to price these options, however, the overwhelming majority give values implying a preference for A over B. Indeed, the implicit value of human life derived from the simple choice presented by the first firm is more than twice that derived from the matching procedure used by the other firm.

What are you going to tell the Minister? You decide to call a staff meeting where various explanations for the results are offered. Perhaps one of the pollsters has made a mistake. Perhaps people cannot think straight about problems involving the value of a human life, especially in the Middle East. However, one staff member points out that there is a good reason to trust both surveys, since recent research by some psychologists[1] has produced exactly the same pattern using a wide range of problems such as selecting job applicants, consumer products, and savings plans. The psychologists conclude that the notion of preference that underlies modern decision theory is more problematic than economists normally assume because different methods of elicitation often give rise to systematically different orderings. Well? The Minister is waiting.

For almost two decades, economists and psychologists have been intrigued by a similar inconsistency involving risky prospects. Subjects are first asked to choose between two gambles with nearly the same expected values. One gamble, called the H bet (for high chance of winning) has a high chance of winning a relatively small prize (e.g., 8/9 chance to win $4), while the other

---

[1]See Tversky, Sattath, and Slovic (1988). The data regarding the two highway safety programs are taken from this paper.

gamble, the L bet, offers a lower chance to win a larger prize (e.g., a 1/9 chance to win $40). Most subjects choose the H bet. Subjects are then asked to price each of the gambles. Specifically, they are asked to state the lowest price at which they would be willing to sell each gamble if they owned it. Surprisingly, most subjects put a higher price on the L bet. (In a recent study that used this particular pair of bets, for example, 71 percent of the subjects chose the H bet, while 67 percent priced L above H.) This pattern is called a *preference reversal*. Sarah Lichtenstein and Paul Slovic (1971, 1973) first demonstrated such reversals in a series of studies, one of which was conducted for real money with gamblers on the floor of the Four Queens Casino in Las Vegas.

Lichtenstein and Slovic did not come upon this result by chance. In an earlier study (Slovic and Lichtenstein, 1968), they observed that both buying and selling prices of gambles were more highly correlated with payoffs than with chances of winning, whereas choices between gambles (and ratings of their attractiveness) were more highly correlated with the probabilities of winning and losing than with the payoffs. The authors reasoned that if the method used to elicit preferences affected the weighting of the gamble's components, it should be possible to construct pairs of gambles such that the same individual would choose one member of the pair but set a higher price for the other. Experimental tests supported this conjecture.

The preference reversal phenomenon raises an issue rarely discussed in economics: How is the notion of preference to be operationalized? We say that option A is preferred to option B if A is selected when B is available *or* if A has a higher reservation price than B. The standard analysis of choice assumes that these procedures give rise to the same ordering. This requirement—called procedure invariance—seldom appears as an explicit axiom, but it is needed to ensure that the preference relation is well defined. The assumption of procedure invariance is not unique to the study of preference. When measuring mass, for example, we can use either a pan balance or a spring to determine which of the objects is heavier, and we expect the two measurement procedures to yield the same ordering. Unlike the measurement of physical attributes such as mass or length, however, different methods of eliciting preference often give rise to systematically different orderings.

Economists were introduced to the preference reversal phe-

nomenon by David Grether and Charles Plott (1979) who designed a series of experiments ''to discredit the psychologists'
work as applied to economics'' (p. 623). These authors began by
generating a list of 13 objections and potential artifacts that would
render the preference reversal phenomenon irrelevant to economic theory. Their list included poor motivation, income effects,
strategic responding, and the fact that the experimenters were
psychologists (thereby creating suspicions leading to peculiar
behavior). Grether and Plott attempted to eliminate preference
reversals by various means (e.g., by offering a special incentive
system), but to no avail. Indeed, preference reversals were somewhat more common among subjects responding under financial
incentives than in a control group facing purely hypothetical
questions. Subsequent studies by both psychologists and economists, using a wide range of procedural variations, led to similar
conclusions. (See Slovic and Lichtenstein, 1983, for a review of
the early literature and Tversky, Slovic, and Kahneman, 1990, for
later references.)

Although these experimental studies have established the validity and the robustness of the preference reversal phenomenon,
its interpretation and explanation have remained unclear. To formulate the problem, we must introduce some notation. Let CH
and CL denote the cash equivalents (or minimum selling price) of
H and L (the gambles with high and low chances of winning,
respectively). Let $\succ$ and $\approx$ denote strict preference and indifference, respectively. Recall that a preference reversal occurs when
H is preferred to L but L is priced higher than H; that is, $H \succ L$
and $C_L > C_H$. Note that $\succ$ refers to preference between options,
whereas $>$ refers to the ordering of cash amounts.[2] It is not difficult to see that a preference reversal implies either the intransitivity of the preference relation, $\succ$, or a failure of procedure invariance, or both. Now, recall that if procedure invariance holds, a
decision maker will be indifferent when choosing between a bet
B and some cash amount X, if and only if the cash equivalent for
B is equal to X, that is $C_B = X$. So, if procedure invariance holds,
then a preference reversal implies the following intransitive pattern of preferences:

$$C_H \approx H \succ L \approx C_L > C_H$$

[2]We assume that for sure outcomes measured in dollars $X > Y$ implies $X \succ Y$; i.e., more
money is preferred to less.

where the two inequalities are implied by the assumed preference reversal and the two equivalences follow from procedure invariance.

Because procedure invariance is commonly taken for granted, many authors have interpreted preference reversals as intransitivities, and some have proposed nontransitive choice models to account for this phenomenon (see Loomes and Sugden, 1983; Fishburn, 1985). A preference reversal, however, does not imply cyclic choice; it can be consistent with transitivity if procedure invariance does not hold. Two types of discrepancies between choice and pricing could produce the standard pattern of preference reversal,[3] that is preferring H but assigning a higher value to L: either overpricing of L or underpricing of H. Overpricing of L is evident if the decision maker prefers her reservation price for the bet over the bet itself when offered a choice between them on another occasion (i.e., $C_L > L$). Underpricing of H is evident if the decision maker prefers the bet over its price in a direct choice on another occasion (i.e., $H > C_H$). (The terms overpricing and underpricing merely identify the sign of the discrepancy between pricing and choice; the labels are not meant to imply that the choice represents one's "true" preference and the bias resides in pricing.)

A third possible explanation of the preference reversal implicates the payoff scheme used to elicit cash equivalence. To encourage subjects to produce careful and truthful responses, several investigators have employed a payoff scheme called the BDM procedure after its originators Becker, DeGroot, and Marschak (1964). After the subject states a selling price for a gamble, an offer is generated by some random process. The subject receives the offer if it exceeds the stated selling price, and plays the gamble if the stated price exceeds the offer. The price stated by the subject, therefore, serves only to determine whether the subject will play the bet or receive the cash, but it does not determine the actual amount. As long as the subject is an expected utility maximizer, this procedure is incentive compatible: the decision maker has no incentive to state a selling price that departs from his or her actual cash equivalent. However, as noted by Holt (1968), Karni and Safra (1987), and Segal (1988), if the decision

---

[3]This is the standard preference reversal pattern. The other possible preference reversal, choosing L but assigning a higher value to H, is rarely observed. We use the term *preference reversal* to refer to this standard pattern.

maker does not obey the independence[4] (or reduction) axiom of expected utility theory, the BDM procedure no longer ensures that the stated price will correspond to the cash equivalent of the gamble. Indeed, Karni and Safra have shown that preference reversals observed under the BDM scheme are consistent with a generalized version of expected utility theory with non-linear probabilities.

So we now have three alternative interpretations of preference reversals. They can arise from violations of transitivity, procedure invariance, or the independence axiom. To determine which interpretation is correct we need to solve two problems. First, we need an experimental procedure that can distinguish between failures of transitivity and failures of procedure invariance. Second, we need an incentive-compatible payoff scheme that does not rely on the expectation principle. Both requirements have been met in a recent study of Tversky, Slovic, and Kahneman (1990).

To discriminate between the intransitivity and procedure invariance explanations, these investigators extended the original design to include, in addition to the standard H and L bets, a cash amount X that was compared to both of them. That is, subjects indicated their preferences between each of the pairs in the triple {H, L, X}. Using a method described below, subjects also produced cash equivalents, C_L and C_H, for both of the bets. By focusing on standard preference reversal patterns in which the pre-specified cash amount X has been set to lie between the values of C_L and C_H generated by this subject (i.e., H≻L and $C_L > X > C_H$), it is possible to diagnose each preference reversal pattern according to whether it was produced by an intransitivity, by an overpricing of L, by an underpricing of H, or by both. For example, if subjects indicated that L≻X, and that X≻H, then their preferences are intransitive since we are confining our attention to those cases in which H≻L. Alternatively, if subjects overprice the L bet, then their pattern of responses will be X≻L and X≻H. (The subjects produce a price for L that is greater than X, but when offered a choice between X and L, they choose X.) This pattern is transitive, though it is a preference reversal.

---

[4] Roughly speaking, the independence axiom amounts to this: If you prefer A to B then you should prefer a chance to win A with probability p to an equal chance to win B. While the axiom is appealing in the abstract, and is obeyed when its application is obvious, there are many circumstances in which people make choices that violate this principle.

The results of this study were very clear. Using 18 triples of the form {H, L, X} that cover a wide range of payoffs, the experiment yielded the usual rate of preference reversal (between 40 and 50 percent), but only 10 percent of preference reversal patterns were intransitive, and the remaining 90 percent violated procedure invariance. By far the major source of preference reversal was the overpricing of the L bet, which accounted for nearly two-thirds of the observed patterns. (Note that if subjects were choosing at random, the expected rate of the standard preference reversal is 25 percent.)

Having eliminated intransitivity as the major cause of preference reversal, let us turn now to the effect of the payoff scheme. Karni and Safra (1987) have shown that it is exceedingly difficult, if not impossible, to devise an incentive-compatible payoff scheme for the elicitation of cash equivalence that does not rely on expected utility theory. Fortunately, to demonstrate preference reversal, it is not necessary to elicit the actual selling prices; it is sufficient to establish their order—which can be obtained under much weaker conditions. Suppose the subject is presented with two tasks: pricing each bet separately and choosing between pairs of bets. The subjects are told that one of these pairs will be selected at random at the end of the session, and that they will play one of these bets. To determine which bet they will play, first a random device will be used to select either choices or prices as the criterion for selection. If the choice data are used, then the subject plays the bet chosen. If the pricing data are used, then the subject will play whichever gamble was priced higher.

In this latter procedure, called the *ordinal payoff scheme*, the prices offered by the subjects are only used to order the bets within each pair. Consistency, therefore, requires that the price orderings and choice orderings should agree, whether or not the subjects are expected utility maximizers. Thus, if the previously observed reversals were caused by a failure of expected utility theory, then they should not occur under the ordinal payoff scheme. This prediction was clearly refuted. The incidence of reversals was roughly the same (40 to 50 percent) whether the experiment employed the BDM scheme, the above ordinal scheme, or even no payoff scheme at all. This finding shows that preference reversal is not caused by the BDM procedure, hence it cannot be explained as a violation of the independence or reduction axioms of expected utility theory.

The conclusions of the Tversky, Slovic, and Kahneman study may be summarized as follows. First, intransitivity alone accounts for only a small portion of preference reversal patterns. Second, preference reversals are hardly affected by the payoff scheme, hence they are not attributable to the failure of expected utility theory. Third, the major cause of preference reversal is the failure of procedure invariance and, more specifically, the overpricing of the L bets. That is, the minimum selling prices associated with L bets (but not with H bets) are too high in comparison to the choices between the bets and cash amounts. These conclusions are further supported by a recent study of Bostic, Herrnstein, and Luce (1989) using a somewhat different design.

This analysis raises a new question: Why do people overprice the low-probability high-payoff bets? Why do people who prefer, say, $10 for sure over a one-third chance to win $40, assign to this bet a cash equivalent that exceeds $10? Research suggests that this counterintuitive finding is a consequence of a general principle of compatibility that appears to play an important role in human judgment and choice.

THE COMPATIBILITY HYPOTHESIS

The concept of stimulus-response compatibility has been introduced by students of human factors who studied perceptual and motor performance. For example, a square array of four burners on a stove is easier to control with a matching square array of knobs than with a linear array. Slovic, Griffin, and Tversky (1990) have extended this concept and proposed that the weight of a stimulus attribute in judgment or in choice is enhanced by its compatibility with the response scale. The rationale for this scale *compatibility hypothesis* is two-fold. First, if the stimulus and the response do not match, additional mental operations are needed to map one into the other. This increases effort and error and may reduce the impact of the stimulus. Second, a response mode tends to focus attention on the compatible features of the stimulus. Because there is neither a formal definition of compatibility nor an independent measurement procedure, the analysis is both informal and incomplete. Nevertheless, in many contexts the compatibility order is sufficiently clear for it to be investigated experimentally.

A simple study by Slovic, Griffin, and Tversky illustrates a case in which the compatibility hypothesis makes a clear prediction. Subjects were given two pieces of information about each of 12 large companies taken from *Business Week's* Top 100: the company's 1986 *market value* (in billions of dollars), and the company's *rank* (among the Top 100) with respect to 1987 *profits*. Half of the subjects were then asked to predict the 1987 market value in billions of dollars, whereas the other half were asked to predict the company's rank with respect to its 1987 market value. Thus each subject has one predictor measured on the same scale (that is, money or rank) as the dependent variable, and one predictor measured on a different scale. As implied by compatibility, each predictor was given more weight when the predicted variable was expressed on the same scale. As a consequence, the relative weight of the 1986 market value was twice as high for those who predicted in dollars than for those who predicted the corresponding rank. This effect produced many reversals in which one company was ranked above another but the order of their predicted values was reversed.

Because the cash equivalence of a bet is expressed in dollars, compatibility implies that the payoffs, which are expressed in the same units, will be weighted more heavily in pricing bets than in choosing between bets. Furthermore, since the payoffs of L bets are much larger than the payoffs of H bets, the major consequence of a compatibility bias is the overpricing of the L bet. The compatibility hypothesis, therefore, explains the major source of preference reversal, namely the overpricing of the low-probability high-payoff bets. This account has been supported by several additional findings. Slovic, Griffin, and Tversky presented subjects with H and L bets involving non-monetary outcomes, such as a one-week pass for all movie theaters in town, or a dinner for two at a good restaurant. If preference reversals are due primarily to the compatibility of prices and payoffs, which are both expressed in dollars, their incidence should be substantially reduced by the use of non-monetary outcomes. This is precisely what happened. The prevalence of preference reversals was reduced by nearly 50 percent. Schkade and Johnson (1989) found additional support for the role of compatibility in preference reversals in a computer-controlled experiment which allowed subjects to see only one component of each bet at a time. The percentage of time spent looking at the payoff was significantly greater in a pricing task than in a choice task. This pattern was pronounced when the subject produced a preference reversal, but not when the subject produced consistent responses. The finding that subjects attend to the payoffs more in pricing than in choice supports the hypothesis that people focus their attention on the stimulus components that are most compatible with the response mode.

Although the compatibility hypothesis can explain preference reversals between pairs of bets, the explanation does not depend on the presence of risk. Indeed, this hypothesis implies a similar discrepancy between choice and pricing for riskless options with a monetary component, such as delayed payments. Let (X, T) be a prospect that offers a payment of $X, T years from now. Consider a long-term prospect L ($2500, 5 years from now) and a short-term prospect S ($1600, 1.5 years from now). Suppose that subjects (i) choose between L and S, and (ii) price both prospects by stating the smallest immediate cash payment for which they would be willing to exchange the delayed payment. According to the compatibility hypothesis, the monetary component X would loom larger in pricing than in choice. As a consequence, subjects should produce preference reversals in which the short-term option is preferred over the long-term option in a direct choice, but the latter is priced higher than the former (i.e., $S > L$ and $C_L > C_S$). This was precisely the pattern observed by Tversky, Slovic, and Kahneman (1990). These investigators presented a large group of subjects with pairs of S and L options with comparable present values. The subjects chose between pairs of options, and also priced each option separately. Subjects exhibited the predicted pattern of preference. Overall, subjects chose the short-term option 74 percent of the time but priced the long-term option above the short-term option 75 percent of the time, and the rate of reversals exceeded 50 percent. The incidence of the non-predicted reversals was less than 10 percent. Further analysis revealed that—as in the risky case—the major source of preference reversal was the overpricing of the long-term option, as entailed by compatibility. These findings indicate that the preference reversal phenomenon is an example of a general phenomenon, rather than a peculiar characteristic of choice between bets.

Indeed, the preference reversal phenomenon is not the only example of a failure of procedure invariance. As illustrated by the life-saving example discussed in the introduction to this chapter, Tversky, Sattath, and Slovic (1988) have demonstrated a related discrepancy between choice and matching. These investigators observed that the more prominent dimension looms larger in choice than in matching. In the highway safety problem, for example, human lives are valued much higher in a direct choice than in the price matching procedure. Recall that in this study subjects selected the program that saved more lives when making a direct choice, but their stated prices favored the less expensive program. As a consequence, choice is more lexicographic than matching—the most important dimension is weighted more heavily in choice. Other violations of procedure invariance in the context of risky choice have been documented by Hershey and Schoemaker (1985). They first asked subjects to provide a certainty equivalent for some gamble, such as a 50 percent chance to win $100. Suppose the subject said $40. Later the subject was asked to indicate what probability of winning $100 would make the gamble just as attractive as a sure $40. If procedure invariance holds, then subjects should have responded with .5. However, subjects did not reproduce the probability they started with, and their departures were systematic rather than random. Other violations of procedural invariance involving choice and ratings of gambles are presented by Goldstein and Einhorn (1987).

COMMENTARY

Taken at face value the data [showing preference reversals] are simply inconsistent with preference theory and have broad implications about research priorities within economics. The inconsistency is deeper than the mere lack of transitivity or even stochastic transitivity. It suggests that no optimization principles of any sort lie behind the simplest of human choices and that the uniformities in human choice behavior which lie behind market behavior may result from principles which are of a completely different sort from those generally accepted. (Grether and Plott, 1979, p. 623)

The preference reversal phenomenon has been established in numerous studies during the last two decades, but its causes have only recently been uncovered. It appears that preference reversals cannot be attributed solely to intransitivities or to violations of the independence axiom of expected utility theory. Rather, they seem to be driven primarily by the discrepancy between choice and pricing, which in turn is induced by scale compatibility. This account is supported by several new experiments, and it gives rise to a new type of reversal in the domain of time preference. What are the implications of preference reversals for economics and decision theory? This phenomenon, or cluster of phenomena, challenges the traditional assumption that the decision maker has a fixed preference order that is captured accurately by any reliable elicitation procedure. If option A is priced higher than option B, we cannot always assume that A is preferred to B in a direct comparison. The evidence shows that different methods of elicitation could change the relative weighting of the attributes and give rise to different orderings.

These findings are in contrast to the standard economic formulation of choice which assumes that, in the presence of complete information, people act as if they could look up their preferences in a book, and respond to situations accordingly. Choose the item most preferred; pay up to the value of an item to obtain it; sell an item if offered more than its value; etc. The principle of procedure invariance is likely to hold under two conditions. First, people could have pre-established preferences. If you prefer football to opera, then this preference will emerge whether you are choosing between activities or bidding for tickets. However, procedure invariance could also hold even if people do not have pre-established preferences. We do not immediately know the value of $7(8+9)$, but we have an algorithm for computing it that yields the same answer whether we do the addition before or after the multiplication. The results of the experiments reported here indicate that neither condition holds. First, people do not possess a set of pre-defined preferences for every contingency. Rather, preferences are constructed in the process of making a choice or judgment. Second, the context and procedures involved in making choices or judgments influence the preferences that are implied by the elicited responses. In practical terms, this implies that behavior is likely to vary across situations that economists consider identical. For example, alternative auction mechanisms which are equivalent in theory might produce different outcomes if the auction procedures themselves influence bidding behavior.

The discussion of the meaning of preference and the status of value may be illuminated by the well-known exchange among three baseball umpires. "I call them as I see them," said the first.

"I call them as they are," claimed the second. The third disagreed, "They ain't nothing till I call them." Analogously, we can describe three different views regarding the nature of values. First, values exist—like body temperature—and people perceive and report them as best they can, possibly with bias (I call them as I see them). Second, people know their values and preferences directly—as they know the multiplication table (I call them as they are). Third, values or preferences are commonly constructed in the process of elicitation (They ain't nothing till I call them). The research reviewed in this chapter is most compatible with the third view of preference as a constructive, context-dependent process.

[8]

Intertemporal Choice

For a change, you get a phone call with good news. You have just won $100 in a lottery held at your local credit union. You now have a choice: you can take the money now, or you can wait and have more money later. What is the least you would be willing to accept to wait one month? one year? 10 years? (Assume that there are no risks or costs involved in waiting.) How would your answers change if the amount were $5000? Decide your answers before going on.

Are your answers to the questions involving $5000 equal to your answers for $100 multiplied by 50? Are your answers to both questions equal to the amount of interest you could earn on that amount of money for the given period of time? If not, you are not behaving according to the economic theory of intertemporal choice.

Intertemporal choices, decisions in which costs and benefits are spread out over time, are both common and important. How much schooling to obtain, whom to marry, whether to have children, how much to save for retirement, how to invest, whether to buy a house, and if so which house to buy—all these vital decisions have strong intertemporal components. As examples of individual decision making, intertemporal choices are also interesting because the relevant economic theory makes unusually testable predictions. In many contexts, economic theories of indi-

With George Loewenstein.

vidual behavior are untestable because the predictions are too vague. Almost any choice, no matter how bizarre, can be rationalized by finding some utility function for which the choice represents an optimal solution. In contrast, for decisions involving choices between time streams of money (receipts and payments), economic theory makes a precise and testable prediction, namely that (at the margin) people should discount money streams at the (after-tax) market rate of interest (r).

The existence of capital markets creates what amounts to an internal arbitrage opportunity for the consumer. Suppose the rate of interest is 10 percent, and a consumer can borrow and lend at this rate. If presented with an investment option that pays off at a rate of 12 percent, the consumer can enjoy greater consumption in every period by making the investment, and borrowing to finance it. Options that pay less than 10 percent should be rejected since they are dominated by lending in the capital market (i.e., saving). The implication is that consumers should make intertemporal trade-offs so that their marginal rate of time preference equals the interest rate. Furthermore, consumers should be consistent in their intertemporal choices. The discount rate used should be constant across situations and over time. However, research shows that, depending on the context examined, the implied discount rates of observed behavior can vary from negative to several hundred percent per year.

A well-known example of apparent negative discount rates is the fact that a large majority of U.S. taxpayers receive refunds every year from the Internal Revenue Service. These interest-free loans to the government are easily avoidable by adjusting the withholding rate. Similarly, many school teachers are given the choice between being paid in 9 monthly installments (September-June) or 12 (September–August). Most of those given this choice elect the latter option. Finally, studies of life-cycle consumption choices reveal that consumption tends to increase over time until retirement. In the absence of binding borrowing constraints, this pattern can only be consistent with the life-cycle theory if people have negative discount rates (more on this in Chapter 9).

Examples of extremely high discount rates are also easy to find. A recent change in West Virginia law provides an example. Students under the age of 18 who drop out of school lose their driving permits. The first-year results indicate that this law has reduced the drop-out rate by one-third. It seems implausible that one-third of the high school dropouts were so close to the margin that the loss of driving privileges for a year or two (or more precisely, the expected costs of driving illegally for this period) could tip a rational human capital investment decision toward completing high school. Rather, the behavior seems to reveal extremely myopic preferences. A similar myopia is evident in the lament of a dermatologist that her warnings about the risk of skin cancer have little effect, but "my patients are much more compliant about avoiding the sun when I tell them that it can cause large pores and blackheads."

It is not just teenagers and sun lovers who display high discount rates. Most homeowners have too little insulation in their attics and walls, and fail to buy more expensive energy-efficient appliances even when the pay-back period for the extra expense is less than a year. Hausman's (1979) study of air conditioner purchases, which examined consumer trade-offs between purchase price and delayed energy payments, estimated an average consumer discount rate of about 25 percent. A subsequent study by Gately (1980) comparing pairs of refrigerators differing only in energy use and initial purchase price revealed that the implicit discount rates associated with purchasing the cheaper models were incredibly high: from 45 to 130 percent assuming an electricity cost of 3.8 cents per kilowatt hour, and from 120 to 300 percent at 10 cents per kilowatt hour. Most recently, Ruderman, Levine, and McMahon (1986) computed the discount rates implicit in several different kinds of appliances (for the average model on the market, relative to the most efficient): space heaters, air conditioners, water heaters, refrigerators, and freezers. They found that the implicit discount rate for room air conditioners was 17 percent, somewhat lower than Hausman's estimate. However, the discount rates for other appliances was much higher, e.g., gas water heater, 102 percent; electric water heater, 243 percent; and freezer, 138 percent. Economic theory has a clear prediction about these inefficient appliances—they will not be produced. But they are produced, and purchased.[1]

[1] Two other explanations might be offered for the purchase of inefficient appliances: ignorance and illiquidity. According to the ignorance hypothesis, customers do not know, or bother to find out, the advantages of buying a more efficient model even though that information is plainly displayed on government-mandated labels. According to the illiquidity argument, customers are so short of cash that they cannot afford to buy the more efficient model. (Of course, these are precisely the customers who cannot afford to buy the cheaper model!) Since most appliances are probably purchased on credit, and since the

So, as usual, where there are testable predictions, there are anomalies. The remainder of this chapter examines a number of situations in which people do not appear to discount money flows at the market rate of interest or any other single discount rate. Discount rates observed in both laboratory and field decision-making environments are shown to depend on the magnitude and sign of what is being discounted, on the time delay, on whether the choice is cast in terms of speed-up or delay, on the way in which a choice is framed, and on whether future benefits or costs induce savoring or dread.

VARIATIONS IN THE DISCOUNT RATE
FOR AN INDIVIDUAL

One early experiment that investigated the first three of these effects was published in Thaler (1981). Subjects (mostly students) were asked to imagine that they had won some money in a lottery conducted by their bank. They could take the money now or wait until later. They were asked how much they would need to be paid to make waiting as attractive as immediate payment. Each subject received a 3×3 table to fill in with amounts of money varied along one dimension and length of time along the other. Four versions of the questionnaires were used, three involving gains, and one involving losses. In the losses version, subjects were asked to imagine that they had been issued a traffic fine that could either be paid at face value now or at an increased price later. In all cases subjects were asked to assume that there was no risk of not getting the reward (or of avoiding the fine) if they waited. All amounts were to be received (or paid) by mail.[2] The experiment

extra cost of the energy-efficient model is relatively small, it seems unlikely that borrowing constraints are really the answer.

[2]In this study, and some others described here, the questions asked were hypothetical. Of course, all things being equal it would be better to study actual choices. However, there are serious trade-offs between hypothetical and real money methods. Using hypothetical questions one can ask subjects to consider options that incorporate large amounts of money, both gains and losses, and delays of a year or more. In studies using real choices, the experimenter must reduce the size of the stakes and the length of the delay, and it is difficult to investigate actual losses. Also, in a hypothetical question, one can ask the subject to assume that there is no risk associated with future payments, while in experiments using real stakes, subjects must assess the experimenter's credibility. It is reassuring that in this domain, as well as many others, the phenomena discovered using hypothetical choices have been reproduced in studies using actual choices; see for example, Horowitz (1988), and Holcomb and Nelson (1989).

thus manipulates the three variables of interest: the length of time to be waited; the magnitude of the outcome; and whether the outcome is a gain or loss.

Three strong patterns emerged from the subjects' responses. First, discount rates declined sharply with the length of time to be waited, consistent with earlier findings for animals (Herrnstein, 1961; Ainslie, 1975). Second, discount rates also declined with the size of the reward. Discount rates for small amounts (under $100) were very high, while those for larger amounts were more reasonable. Third, discount rates for gains were much higher than for losses. Subjects needed to be paid a lot to wait for a reward, but were unwilling to pay very much to delay a fine.

These three findings have been replicated in a much larger study by Benzion, Rapoport, and Yagil (1989). They used a $4 \times 4 \times 4$ design which manipulated the time delay (0.5, 1, 2, and 4 years), the amount of money ($40, $200, $1000, and $5,000), and the scenario (postponing a gain; postponing a loss; expediting a gain; and expediting a loss). The subjects were undergraduate and graduate students in economics and finance at two Israeli universities, a sophisticated subject pool. Their results are shown in Figure 8–1 (averaging across the four scenarios). As the Figure clearly shows, discount rates again decline sharply with the length of time to be waited and the size of the prize.[3]

We will discuss each of these three strong patterns of discount rate variations in turn.

Dynamic Inconsistency

The negative relationship between discount rates and time delay has important consequences for the dynamic consistency of behavior. Suppose, as illustrated in Figure 8–2, that an individual

---

[3]It is obvious that whatever pattern of choices subjects indicate in these experiments, market interest rates do not depend (greatly) on either magnitude or time delay, but this does not imply that the experimental evidence is irrelevant for economics. Economics is concerned with predicting both market prices and individual behavior. Though arbitrageurs may insure that one cannot earn (much) more interest from buying and selling a series of 12 one-month Treasury bills than a single one-year bond, this does not guarantee that predictions at the individual level will be accurate. If car customers elect financing over more attractive rebates, no (costless) arbitrage opportunity exists for anyone else. A bank could try to convince car buyers that they would be better off taking the rebate and financing the purchase at their bank, but such campaigns are expensive, and consumers may be skeptical regarding the impartiality of the advice they are being given.

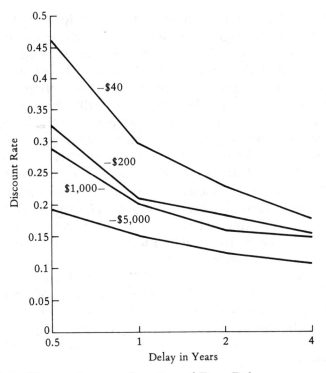

Figure 8–1. Discounting as a Function of Time Delay and Money Amount

Source: Benzion et al. (1989).

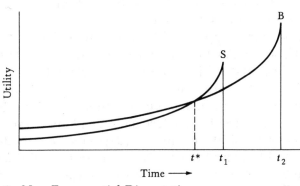

Figure 8–2. Non-Exponential Discounting

Source: Ainslie (1975).

must choose between two rewards, a small early reward S, which occurs at t_1, and a bigger later reward B, which occurs at t_2.[4] The lines represent the present utility of the rewards as perceived by the individual at different points in time. If the individual discounts the future at a constant rate (i.e., if discounting is constant for different time delays) then the curves will never cross. However if discounting decreases as a function of time delay, as the empirical research suggests, then the curves may cross, leading to a reversal of preference. When both rewards are sufficiently distant the individual prefers B, but as S becomes more proximate, its relative value increases until at t^*, S abruptly comes to dominate B in terms of present utility. The significance of the crossing curves is that behavior will not generally be consistent over time. In the morning, when temptation is remote, we vow to go to bed early, stick to our diet, and not have too much to drink. That night we stay out until 3:00 A.M., have two helpings of chocolate decadence, and sample every variety of Aquavit at a Norwegian restaurant. Applied to saving, as Strotz (1955) demonstrated, if the discount rate declines over time, then people will always consume more in the present than called for by their previous plans.

The problem of dynamic inconsistency raises questions about consumer sovereignty. Who is sovereign, the self who sets the alarm clock to rise early, or the self who shuts it off the next morning and goes back to sleep? It is instructive that we normally see the far-sighted self take actions which constrain or alter the behavior of the myopic self. Dieters pay money to stay on "fat farms" whose main appeal is that they guarantee to underfeed their guests; alcoholics take antabuse which causes nausea and vomiting if they take a drink; smokers buy cigarettes by the pack (rather than by the carton which is cheaper). And, though no longer fashionable, for many years Christmas clubs were extremely popular in the U.S. These savings plans offered the unusual combination of inconvenience (deposits were made in person every week), illiquidity (funds could not be withdrawn until late November), and low interest (in some cases, zero interest). Of course, illiquidity was the Christmas club's raison d'être since customers wanted to assure themselves of funds to pay for Christmas presents. Recognizing the limited ability of conven-

---

[4]This analysis is based on Ainslie (1975).

tional decision models to account for self-binding behavior and other forms of intrapersonal conflict, a number of authors have proposed models that view economic behavior as an internal struggle between multiple selves with conflicting preferences (Ainslie, 1975, forthcoming; Elster, 1979; Schelling, 1984; Thaler and Shefrin, 1981; Winston, 1980).

Magnitude Effects

The effect of magnitude on the discount rate is as strong as the effect of time delay. In both the Thaler and Benzion et al. studies using hypothetical questions, the implicit discount rates declined sharply with the size of the purchase. A similar result has been observed by Holcomb and Nelson (1989) over a small range of actual payoffs, $5–$17. Also, the very high discount rates observed for relatively small hypothetical rewards were obtained by Horowitz (1988) for an actual payoff of $50.

There are two plausible behavioral explanations for the magnitude effect. The first is based on the psychology of perception (psychophysics): people are sensitive not only to relative differences in money amounts, but also to absolute differences (Loewenstein and Prelec, 1989b). The perceptual difference between $100 now and $150 in a year, for example, appears greater than the difference between $10 now and $15 in one year, so that many people are willing to wait for the extra $50 in the first instance, but not for the $5 in the second. The second explanation relies on notions of mental accounting (Shefrin and Thaler, 1988). Suppose that small windfalls are entered into a mental checking account and are largely consumed, while larger amounts are entered into a mental savings account, with a much smaller propensity to consume. Then the cost of waiting for a small windfall may be perceived to be forgone consumption, while in contrast, the opportunity cost of waiting for a large windfall is perceived as simply forgone interest. If forgone consumption is more tempting than forgone interest, the magnitude effect will be observed.[5] (These issues are discussed at greater length in Chapter 9.)

[5]It seems likely that there are also differential discount rates by type of consumption good. One might be more impatient to receive a new car than a new (energy-efficient) furnace, as long as the old furnace works. More research is needed on this question.

Sign Effects

The third strong empirical regularity in the discounting surveys is that the discount rate for gains is much greater than for losses. People are quite anxious to receive a positive reward, especially a small one, but are less anxious to postpone a loss. Part of this preference comes from a simple "debt aversion." Many people pay off mortgages and student loans quicker than they have to, even when the rate they are paying is less than they earn on safe investments.

REFERENCE POINTS

As discussed in Chapter 6, the distinction between gains and losses has received considerable attention in descriptive theories of decision making under uncertainty. Decision makers do not appear to integrate outcomes with their wealth or existing consumption level, as normally assumed in expected utility theory. Rather, individuals appear to react to events as changes, relative to some natural reference point. This observation was first made by Markowitz (1952), and more recently by Kahneman and Tversky (1979).

Reference points are also important in intertemporal choice (Loewenstein and Prelec, 1989a). Loewenstein (1988) offers the following demonstration of a reference point effect. An experiment was conducted using 105 high school sophomores and juniors. All subjects received a $7 gift certificate for a local record shop. The expected time at which the students would receive the certificates was varied among one, four, and eight weeks. The students were then given a series of binary choices between keeping their certificates at the originally appointed times, or trading them either for smaller certificates to be received earlier, or for larger certificates to be received later. For example, subjects who expected to receive a four-week certificate were asked whether they would trade it for an 8-week certificate, the value of which was varied between $7.10 and $10.00. They were told that the experimenter would select and implement one of their choices at random.

The design of this experiment allows the role of the reference point to be empirically tested. Some subjects were asked to make a trade-off between the size of the reward and its *delay* from week

Table 8-1 Mean Amounts to Speed-Up and Delay Consumption ($7 Record Store Gift Certificate)

Time interval	Delay	Speed-up	Significance
1 week versus 4 weeks	$1.09	$.25	.001
4 weeks versus 8 weeks	$ .84	$.37	.005
1 week versus 8 weeks	$1.76	$.52	.001

Source: Loewenstein (1988).

1 to week 4, while other subjects were making a trade-off between the size of the reward and its *speed-up* from week 4 to week 1. If subjects were not influenced by reference points, then this manipulation would have no effect. The results of the experiment are shown in Table 8-1. The figures shown are the mean minimum amounts to speed up or delay consumption, depending on the condition. For all three comparisons, the mean delay premium is at least twice the mean speed-up cost, with all differences being statistically significant. Subjects demand more to wait past the expected arrival date than they are willing to pay to speed up its expected arrival. (Similar results are obtained by Benzion et al., 1989.) The result is compatible with Kahneman and Tversky's notion of *loss aversion* (discussed in Chapter 6), the idea that the disutility of losing a given amount of money is significantly greater in absolute value than the utility of gaining the same amount.

Loss aversion also induces preferences for particular patterns of consumption over time. In situations when past consumption levels set reference points for future consumption, individuals may prefer an increasing consumption profile. For example, Loewenstein and Prelec (1989a) asked 95 Harvard undergraduates three questions. First, the students were asked to choose between two free dinners to be consumed on a Friday night in one month: a dinner at a fancy French restaurant, or a dinner at a local Greek restaurant. Most had the good sense to prefer the French dinner. Then, they were asked whether they would rather have the French dinner in one month or two months. Of those who selected the French dinner originally, 80 percent preferred to have it in one month rather than two, implying a positive discount rate. The third question offered subjects two hypothetical meals, the first in one month, the second in two months. Subjects were asked which order they preferred: Greek in one month, and French in two months; or French in one month, and Greek in two months. Here, 57 percent of the French food lovers elected to have the Greek meal first. In a standard utility framework, this latter response implies a negative rate of time preference, inconsistent with the answer to the second question. There is no inconsistency, however, if people evaluate current consumption relative to past consumption and are loss averse. They simply prefer a pattern of increasing utility over time.

The preference for a rising consumption profile helps explain an anomaly in labor markets, namely that wages rise with age even when productivity does not (Medoff and Abraham, 1980). In many academic departments, for example, the highest paid faculty are the oldest, even if they are no longer the most productive. The two most important standard explanations for this pattern involve specific human capital and agency costs. The human capital argument is that firms offer the increasing age-earnings profile to encourage workers to stay in the firm long enough to make firm-specific training pay off. The agency cost argument, due to Lazear (1981), suggests that firms offer wages above marginal product for older workers to prevent workers from cheating and shirking. (A worker who gets caught risks losing the present value of the difference between pay and productivity.) While both of these explanations have merit in some occupations, Frank and Hutchens (1990) show that the same pattern of wages is observed for two occupations in which neither traditional explanation is plausible, namely airline pilots and intercity bus drivers. In the case of pilots, Frank and Hutchens show that wages increase sharply with age while productivity does not. Yet, virtually all the training pilots receive is general, and pilots who shirk on (say) safety are amply punished by nature. Rather, in this case, it seems that the upward sloping age-earnings profile must be due to a preference for income growth, per se.

Evidence for such a pattern of preferences comes from a survey of 100 adults polled at the Museum of Science and Industry in Chicago (Loewenstein and Sicherman, 1989). Respondents were asked to choose between several hypothetical jobs which lasted six years and were identical except in the wage profile they offered. All jobs paid the same total *undiscounted* wages but differed in slope. For one job, wages decreased yearly. For another, they remained constant, and for the remaining five they increased at varying rates. In addition to interest, virtually every economic consideration favored the job with declining wages. For example, if the subject didn't like the job and quit, or was fired before the end of the six years, the declining wage option would provide greater total payments. Despite the incentives for selecting the decreasing wage profile, only 12 percent of the subjects liked it best. Another 12 percent preferred the flat profile, with all other subjects selecting one of the increasing profiles as their favorite.

A result such as this one always makes an economist wonder whether the subjects were just confused. Certainly, if the subjects had the logic of the economic argument explained to them (that the downward sloping wage profile plus saving dominates the others) they would come to their senses, right? To check on this, subjects were asked their preferences again, but after they had been presented with the economic argument favoring the declining profile, and with psychological arguments in favor of increasing profiles. The effect of these arguments was minimal. The number of subjects preferring the increasing profile fell from 76 to 69 percent.

The preference for an increasing income stream can be understood by using two concepts discussed above: loss aversion and self-control. Loss aversion explains why workers prefer an increasing *consumption* profile (since the utility of current consumption will depend on previous consumption). Costly self-control explains why workers want an increasing *income* profile, because they cannot rely on themselves to save enough from a flat income (or declining) profile to produce the desired increasing consumption profile.

SAVORING AND DREAD

The standard discounted utility model assumes that the discount rate is constant and, normally, positive. Are there any circumstances in which people prefer to have gains postponed or losses expedited? Marshall (1891, p. 178) suggested one negative influence on the discount rate for gains: "When calculating the rate at which a future benefit is discounted, we must be careful to make allowance for the pleasures of expectation." We will use the terms *savoring* to refer to the positive utility derived from anticipating future pleasant outcomes and *dread* to refer to the negative contemplation of unpleasant outcomes.

The influence of both savoring and dread is demonstrated in

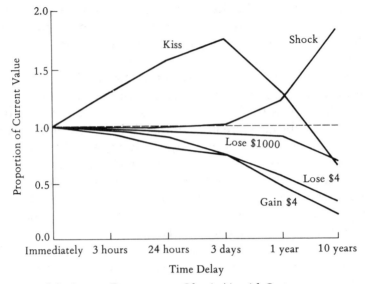

Figure 8–3. Maximum Payment to Obtain/Avoid Outcomes
at Selected Times*

*Proportion of current value ($N = 30$).

Source: Loewenstein (1987).

the following experiment conducted by Loewenstein (1987). Subjects were asked to specify "the most you would pay now" to obtain (avoid) each of five outcomes, immediately, and following delays of: three hours, one day, three days, one year, and ten years. The five outcomes were: gain $4; lose $4; lose $1000; receive a (non-lethal) 110 volt shock; receive a kiss from the movie star of your choice. The results are plotted in Figure 8–3.

Discounted utility predicts that the value of a gain and the aversiveness of a loss should decline with the delay before the event occurs. People should want to consume gains as soon as possible and postpone losses as long as possible. As can be seen, the two non-monetary outcomes yielded quite different patterns of time preference. For the kiss from the movie star, subjects preferred to delay the outcome for three days, presumably to savor its anticipation. For the electric shock, subjects were willing to pay substantially more to avoid a shock to be received in one or ten years than one in the immediate future. In this case subjects seemed to be willing to pay to avoid having to worry about the event over an extended period of time.

While a kiss from a movie star and an electric shock are rather exotic experiences, Loewenstein has also obtained similar results for more mundane items. In a demonstration of the utility of savoring, 84 percent of his subjects indicated that they would prefer to receive a dinner at a fancy French restaurant on the second of three weekends rather than the first. To demonstrate dread, subjects were asked: "What is the least amount of money you would accept for cleaning 100 hamster cages at the Psychology Department's animal laboratory. You will be paid immediately. . . . The job is unpleasant but takes only three hours. How much would you need to be paid to clean the cages: (1) once during the next seven days; (2) once during the week beginning one year form now?" (p. 674) The mean reservation wage for cleaning the cages next week was $30 while the reservation wage for doing the task in a year was $37. In fact, only 2 of 37 subjects gave a smaller response to question (2) than question (1).

COMMENTARY

1. The policy implications of this line of research are both interesting and treacherous. At a micro level, the high discount rates observed in some contexts (such as appliance purchases) and by some groups (such as teenagers) raise serious questions about consumer rationality. (As mentioned above, in many intertemporal situations involving self-control, individuals question *their own* ability to make rational, long-term choices.) How can it be rational for a consumer to choose a refrigerator that costs $50 less than another equivalent model but consumes $50 more in electricity every year? While such cases do not establish a presumption for government intervention, the presumption that consumers choose best for themselves is rather weakened.

At a macro level, the psychology of intertemporal choice complicates the already complicated question of selecting the proper social rate of discount (the rate at which the government should discount future costs and benefits). The standard view is that the market rate of interest, corrected for tax distortions, represents an aggregation of individual time preferences, and is the appropriate social rate of time discounting. However, correcting for tax distortions is far from trivial, and the situation is further complicated by the internationalization of capital markets, which obscures the relationship between time preferences and interest rates in a par-

ticular country. Lind (forthcoming) argues that, given these complications, the only reasonable way to determine the social rate of
time preference is to elicit time preferences at the individual level.
But, if individuals do not discount everything at a single rate,
then which rate is the one that is appropriate for social discounting? Suppose that an individual's freezer purchase implies a discount rate of 50 percent, but that the same person is indifferent
between saving 10 lives this year and 10 lives in 20 years? How
then should we decide between building another power plant
and improving highway safety?

2. Many economists view the research on the psychology of
decision making as a nuisance. The research often provides evidence that individuals violate certain assumptions of rational
choice without offering alternative assumptions that can easily be
incorporated into economic models. However, psychology can be
constructive as well as destructive. For example, in the case of
increasing wage profiles, the psychologists' observation that
people care about changes in as well as absolute levels of income
and consumption (which should be non-controversial since economists don't argue about tastes) can reconcile the preference for
increasing wage profiles with the standard economic assumption
that people discount the future. The advantage of drawing on
empirical research to suggest modifications in the utility function
is that the proposed modifications are less ad hoc. A good example of this kind of reasoning is offered by Constantinides (1988)
in his paper on the "equity premium puzzle" (why are returns
on stocks so much higher than on bonds?). Constaninides bases
his explanation on the assumption that the utility of current consumption depends on past levels of consumption, or, as he calls
it, habit formation. A cynic might argue that if you try enough
utility functions, you can explain anything. However, here that
criticism would be misplaced. The habit formation assumption
seems to fit intuitions about behavior, and is consistent with a
great deal of empirical research. It is even testable. Explanations
that rely on assumptions that are testable (or even better, true!)
are more attractive than others based on assumptions which are
untestable or implausible, for example those that depend on time-
varying changes in the unobservable risk of economic catas-
trophe.

[9]

Savings, Fungibility, and Mental Accounts

On New Year's Day, after a long evening of rooting the right team to victory in the Orange Bowl, you are lucky enough to win $300 in a college football betting pool. You then turn to the important matter of splurging the proceeds wisely. Would a case of champagne be better than dinner and a play in New York? At this point your son Greg comes in and congratulates you. He says: "Gee Dad, you should be pretty happy. With that win you can increase your lifetime consumption by $20 a year!" Greg, it seems, has studied the life-cycle theory of savings.

The standard model of saving in economics, for which Franco Modigliani won a Nobel Prize, is called the *life-cycle theory*.[1] It is a classic bit of economic theorizing. First, it specifies and solves an optimization problem. Then it assumes that people act as if they had solved the same problem. Here it is assumed that an individual has no interest in leaving any bequests, and values consumption equally in every period. How much should such a person consume in a given year? The answer is this: in any year, compute the present value of financial wealth, including current income, net assets, and the expected value of future income; fig-

[1]To get a sense of Modigliani's current views on the life-cycle theory, see Modigliani (1988). A similar theory was proposed by another Nobel winner, Milton Friedman. His (1957) theory is called the *permanent income hypothesis*. The distinctions between the two theories are not particularly important for the points raised in this chapter.

ure out the level annuity that could be purchased with that money; then consume the amount that would be received from such an annuity. The theory is simple, elegant, and rational—qualities highly valued by economists. Unfortunately, as Courant, Gramlich, and Laitner observe (1986, pp. 279–80), ''for all its elegance and rationality, the life-cycle model has not tested out very well.''

The anomalous empirical evidence on consumption falls into roughly two categories. First, consumption appears to be excessively sensitive to income. Over the life cycle, the young and the old appear to consume too little, and the middle-aged consume too much. Also, year-to-year consumption rates are too highly correlated with income to be consistent with the model. Second, various forms of wealth do not appear to be such close substitutes as the theory would suggest. In particular, households appear to have very low marginal propensities to consume[2] either pension wealth or home equity, compared to other assets. Several potential explanations of the empirical difficulties have been identified. Maybe people aren't rational enough to calculate present values and annuity payments. Then again, maybe people are hyperrational and altruistic, leading them to calculate not just the present value of their own wealth, but also the wealth of their heirs. Or perhaps credit markets are to blame, with liquidity constraints preventing people from achieving the life-cycle plan they would otherwise choose to adopt. These and other explanations have all received some support and criticism in the voluminous savings literature. In this chapter, however, I focus on an assumption of the life-cycle model that has not received very much attention, but which, if modified, allows the theory to explain many of the savings anomalies that have been observed. The key assumption is *fungibility*.

Fungibility, of course, is the notion that money has no labels. In the context of the life-cycle theory, the fungibility assumption is what permits all the components of wealth to be collapsed into a single number. According to the life-cycle hypothesis, the effect on current consumption (say, within the year) of winning the $300 football pool should be the same as having a stock in which I own 100 shares increase by $3 a share, or having the value of

---

[2]The marginal propensity to consume, or MPC, is the fraction of an incremental dollar that is spent rather than saved. If an individual receives a windfall of $100 and spends $95, saving $5, then the MPC is .95.

my pension increase by $300. The marginal propensity to consume (MPC) all types of wealth is supposed to be equal.

A simple way of thinking about how people actually behave with respect to various types of wealth is to assume households have a system of mental accounts. One simple formulation is to consider three broad accounts, a current income account C, an asset account A, and a future income account F. It is reasonable to think of the C account as corresponding to the household checking account, and the A account as the savings account. Roughly speaking, the MPC from C is close to unity, the MPC from F is close to zero, and the MPC from A is somewhere in between. Since the null hypothesis is that all three MPCs are equal, these predictions are quite strong.

Along with the system of mental accounts with varying MPCs, two other modifications to the standard life-cycle theory are in order, both of which were discussed in the previous chapter on intertemporal choice. First, people are impatient. Especially over the short run, people act as if their discount rate exceeds the interest rate. The presence of high short-run discount rates creates the second problem, self-control. The life-cycle theory assumes that individuals solve for the optimal consumption plan, and then execute it with will of steel. In real life, people realize that self-control is difficult, and so they take steps to constrain their future behavior. One method is to take irreversible actions, such as joining a pension plan or buying whole life insurance. The Social Security system, perhaps the most popular social policy of this century, is an example of legislated self-control. The other method is to adopt internally enforced *rules of thumb*. Examples of such rules are: keep two months' income in the assets account; do not borrow except to make durable goods purchases such as a house, car, or major appliance. Note that households following the latter rule might appear to be liquidity constrained, *unable* to borrow, whereas they are actually *unwilling* to borrow. This issue will be discussed in detail below.

To summarize, the household being described can be thought of as following the following prudent rules.[3] (1) Live within your means. Do not borrow from F or A to increase current consumption, except during well-defined emergencies, such as spells of

[3]This chapter draws heavily on my joint work with Hersh Shefrin, Thaler and Shefrin (1981) and Shefrin and Thaler (1988). Details of a model of savings behavior based on mental accounting and self-control are available in the latter paper.

unemployment. Even then, cut consumption as much as possible. (2) Keep a rainy day account equal to some fraction of income. Do not invade this account except in emergencies. (3) Save for retirement in ways that require little self-control. These rules are sensible solutions to the saving for retirement problems that humans face.

This chapter will review a small portion of the empirical savings literature, with the objective of showing how violations of fungibility, and more generally the role of self-control, strongly influence saving behavior.

THE CURRENT INCOME ACCOUNT:
CONSUMPTION TRACKS INCOME

A consensus seems to be emerging among economists that consumption is too sensitive to current income to be consistent with a lifetime conception of permanent income. The evidence in support of this view comes from a wide variety of sources, and the conclusion is the same whether one studies so-called low-frequency decisions (the shape of the lifetime consumption profile) or high-frequency decisions (the smoothing of year-to-year consumption).

Lifetime Consumption Profiles

The heart of the life-cycle theory of saving is a hump-shaped age-saving profile. The young, whose incomes are below their permanent income, borrow to finance consumption; the middle-aged save for retirement; the old dissave. Numerous authors have studied the shape of consumption profiles over the life cycle and have concluded that they resemble income profiles too much to be consistent with both the life-cycle theory and rational expectations unless there are important liquidity constraints (Kotlikoff and Summers, 1981; Courant, Gramlich, and Laitner, 1986).

In a recent look at this question, Carroll and Summers (1989) have evaluated the life-cycle theory from an international perspective. The permanent income savings model predicts that the consumption growth rate in a country depends primarily on the interest rate. Thus, if interest rates around the world are equalized, then so should long-term consumption growth rates (assuming "tastes"—the degree of impatience—are the same in all countries). Instead, what Carroll and Summers found is that consumption growth rates are highly correlated with income growth rates. They investigated and dismissed the idea that the former result is due to surprises in country growth rates, capital market imperfections across countries, or variations in tastes.

Another prediction of the life-cycle theory is that the shape of consumption profiles should be independent of the shape of income profiles, holding levels constant. Casual empiricism suggests that this is not true, since most graduate students, even those with high income expectations such as medical students, consume much less than their permanent income while they are in school. Hard data give the same impression. Carroll and Summers looked at the consumption and income profiles for various occupation and education groups in the U.S. They found that the age-consumption profile is strongly influenced by the income profile. This result is due in part to liquidity constraints, discussed below.

Short-Term Saving

Both the life-cycle theory and the permanent income hypothesis imply that year-to-year variations in income will be smoothed so that consumption is a constant proportion of permanent rather than current income. Hall and Mishkin (1982) showed that this prediction is violated systematically. Specifically, annual consumption appears to be excessively sensitive to current income. Although this result was described in terms of a modern, rational expectations model of permanent income, the empirical results are quite similar to those obtained by Milton Friedman (1957) in his original work on the consumption function. He estimated the discount rate of consumers to be between .33 and .40, implying a planning horizon of three years or less, and thus a consumption function that depends strongly on current income.[4]

---

[4] In a provocative paper, Deaton (1987) has argued that consumption is actually too smooth, rather than too variable. However, Deaton does not dispute the fact that consumption depends too much on current income. Rather, he argues that innovations in labor income are *underestimates* of changes in permanent income, so consumption changes should be *greater* than income changes. The correct interpretation depends on the stochastic properties of income.

One way of estimating the importance of income-sensitive behavior is to consider the possibility that there are two types of consumers: one type satisfies the permanent income hypothesis, the other type follows the rule of thumb "spend what you make." Campbell and Mankiw (1989) consider such a model, and estimate the relative proportions to be about 50-50.[5] The permanent income model does not appear to be a good characterization of the representative consumer. (Also, see Flavin, 1981.)

Interpreting the evidence on the time-series properties of consumption is tricky business. However, the excess sensitivity to income point has been demonstrated in a cleverly simple paper by Wilcox (1989). Wilcox studied the effect of changes in Social Security benefits on consumer spending, using monthly data between 1965 and 1985. Over this period there were 17 increases in benefits, all of which were announced at least six–eight weeks in advance of when they took place. The standard life-cycle prediction for these increases is that consumption should respond to the new (higher) level of permanent income at least by the time the changes are announced.[6] What Wilcox found is that consumer spending does increase, but only after the benefits start arriving, rather than when they are announced. The effect is particularly strong for durable goods sales.

Sources of Income, Bonuses, and Windfalls

Do all changes in wealth produce a similar short-term change in consumption? The mental accounting prediction for the MPC out of windfall gains depends on the size of the gains. Small gains, relative to income, will be coded as current income, and spent. Larger gains will enter the assets account, where the MPC is lower (though still higher than the annuity value). The source of a change in wealth can also matter. Some windfalls, such as unrealized capital gains, are naturally treated as changes in the assets account. Others, such as the sale of a security, could be treated as income. Empirical evidence confirms the reality of this distinction. For example, Summers and Carroll (1987) reported

[5]It is worth noting that even the permanent income consumers in their model have an intertemporal elasticity of consumption of close to zero. A similar result in the context of a permanent income model is obtained by Hall (1988).

[6]Actually, since 1975 the benefit levels were indexed to the CPI, so the changes were quite predictable months before the announcement date.

that the marginal propensity to save capital gains in the stock market is close to unity. But Hatsopoulos, Krugman, and Poterba (1989) found that when takeovers generate *cash* to the stockholders, consumption does increase. They estimated the MPC from the after-tax cash receipts from takeovers to be .59 (though with high standard error) compared to .83 for disposable income and .03 for household net worth. Also, as discussed below, increases in housing wealth and pension wealth have, if anything, the perverse effects of increasing other saving.

Even cash receipts can enter the assets account if the inflow is in a large enough lump, and not considered regular income. Interesting cases to consider are bonuses and windfall gains. Define a bonus to be a fully anticipated but lumpy payment. One example is the academic institution of summer salary, when it is received with certainty. Consider two professors. John earns $55,000, paid in monthly installments. Joan earns a base salary of $45,000 paid over twelve months, and a guaranteed extra $10,000 paid during the summer months. The standard theory predicts that the two professors will make identical saving decisions. The mental accounting formulation predicts that Joan will save more for two related reasons. First, since her "regular" income is lower, she will gear her life-style to this level. Second, when the summer salary comes in a lump, it will be entered into the assets account, with its lower MPC. One test of this prediction comes from the analysis of the effect of bonuses on savings in Japan,[7] where workers receive semi-annual bonuses which are quite predictable. Ishikawa and Ueda (1984) estimated the MPC from regular income and bonus income. In non-recession years they found that the MPC from regular income was .685 while the MPC from bonus income was only .437.[8] During the recession-oil shock period 1974–1976 the MPC from bonus income jumped to over 1.0, suggesting that the bonuses were used to spread consumption during emergencies.

The best data on consumption from windfalls is in Landsberg-

---

[7]It is frustratingly difficult to test the idea that the timing of income flows within the year might influence consumption behavior. Perhaps because of the prediction of economic theory that such matters are irrelevant, no standard data set includes questions about the magnitude and size of irregular income flows such as bonuses.

[8]The authors argue strongly that the bonuses should not be considered transitory income since they are well anticipated. They also use expectations data to test the hypothesis that workers spend unanticipated bonuses differently than expected bonuses, but find no evidence to support this view.

er's (1966) examination of the Israeli recipients of German restitution payments after World War II. He studied 297 families who received payments that varied over a wide range. He found that the group that received the largest windfalls (about 66 percent of annual income) had a MPC from the windfall of only 23 percent, while the group that received the smallest windfalls (about 7 percent of annual income) had MPCs from the windfall in excess of 2.0. Small windfalls were actually spent twice, a phenomenon familiar to all two-spender families.

IS WEALTH FUNGIBLE?

The life-cycle is powerful because it makes predictions about which variables should have an effect on saving and which should not. To a first approximation, the only factors that should affect a household's saving rate are the age of the family members, the family lifetime wealth, and the interest rate. The *composition* of wealth, holding the present value constant, should not have any effect. For most households, wealth consists almost exclusively of three components: future income, pension and Social Security wealth, and home equity.[9] Abstracting from liquidity considerations, these three types of wealth should be nearly perfect substitutes.

Pension Wealth

Consider two people with identical lifetime earnings profiles. One has $100,000 in pension wealth,[10] the other has no pension. The life-cycle prediction is that the person without the pension

[9]Most households have little in the way of liquid assets, even when they first reach retirement age. This fact, in and of itself, supports the view that self-control issues are paramount in studying saving. The vast majority of households do virtually no long-term "discretionary" saving.

[10]There are two important components of pension wealth in the U.S., Social Security benefits and private pensions. There is a large literature in each domain estimating this savings offset. The estimation problems are much more difficult for Social Security wealth because an individual's Social Security wealth is so highly correlated with age and prior earnings. After controlling for these two factors, there is essentially no cross-sectional variation in Social Security wealth. I will therefore just summarize the literature on private pensions. However, see Barro (1978) (which contains a reply from Feldstein) for a review of Social Security-savings literature.

should have $100,000 more in other savings. That is, there should be a one-for-one offset. The null hypothesis is that if one estimates the change in discretionary savings with respect to a change in pension wealth, it should be -1.0.

The earliest work on the effect of private pensions on other saving was done by Cagan (1965) and Katona (1965). Both obtained the surprising result that the effect of pension wealth on other saving was not close to -1.0—it was positive! Adding a dollar of pension wealth slightly increased other saving. Could this result be explained by selectivity bias? That is, do people with a taste for saving tend to work for companies that offer pension plans? This hypothesis was tested indirectly by Green (1981). He estimated the pension offset for a sub-sample that contained only people who had a pension, and again found the offset to be slightly positive. For this result to be explained by selectivity bias people would have to perfectly match themselves (on average) to firms based on pension benefits and saving preferences, which seems implausible. In a life-cycle framework, why shouldn't someone with a taste for saving simply take the best job overall and then adjust his discretionary saving to the optimum level given the firm's pension policy? Other estimates for the pension-saving offset have obtained the "right" negative sign, but none were close to -1.0. (See Shefrin and Thaler, 1988, for a summary and references.) People do not appear to treat pension wealth as a close substitute for other wealth.

Similar issues arise with regard to Individual Retirement Accounts, IRAs. The central issue is whether IRAs really generated "new" saving, or whether they just represented "reshuffling" of saving from other (taxable) forms to the new sheltered account. As Venti and Wise (1987, p. 6) put it: "It may be tempting to think of IRAs and conventional saving accounts as equivalent assets, or goods, simply with different prices, in which case one might think of IRAs as only a price subsidy of conventional saving with a limit on the quantity that can be had at the subsidized price. . . . But, . . . the analysis indicates quite strongly that the two are not treated as equivalent by consumers." Venti and Wise used the Consumer Expenditure Survey to analyze the IRA experience, and concluded that "the vast majority of IRA saving represents new saving, not accompanied by reduction in other saving" (p. 38). They also found that most IRA contributors had not done much saving before IRAs were introduced.

Feenberg and Skinner (1989) also examined the "new" saving versus reshuffling hypothesis using a sample of tax returns. If IRAs are primarily reshuffled savings, then IRA users should have lower taxable interest income than non-users (since the users will have "shuffled" some of their other savings into the IRAs, and will thus have lower taxable interest income). However, they found that within each wealth class, the IRA users had higher taxable interest income, suggesting a positive offset similar to that found in the pension studies.

Some other facts about IRA usage suggest that mental accounting and self-control factors are important. Since IRAs sheltered interest income, a rational person would purchase an IRA at the earliest possible date, so that the income would be sheltered as long as possible. This would be particularly true for someone who was just shifting assets from a taxable account to an IRA. According to the law, however, taxpayers could make tax deductible purchases for a given year up until April 15 of the following year. Summers (1986a) reported that for the 1985 tax year, nearly half of the IRA purchases were made in 1986. Also, Feenberg and Skinner found that, holding everything else constant, an important predictor of whether a household would purchase an IRA was whether they would otherwise have to write a check to the IRS on April 15. Those who owed money were more likely to buy an IRA than those who were getting refunds. This result begs for a mental accounting interpretation. ("I would rather put $2000 in an IRA than pay the government $800.") Feenberg and Skinner also found that wealth was a more important predictor of purchase than was income, suggesting that those households with liquid assets were more likely to buy IRAs.

If IRA purchases often come out of liquid assets, why do IRA purchases increase total saving? One reason is that money in the IRA account becomes both less liquid (it is subject to a special 10 percent tax surcharge if withdrawn before the purchaser reaches 59 1/2 years old) and less tempting. Funds in an IRA are regarded as "off-limits" except for the most dire of emergencies. As Venti and Wise (1989, p. 11) note, "Some persons of course may consider the illiquidity of IRAs an advantage: it may help insure behavior that would not otherwise be followed. It may be a means of self-control."[11] Also, if households have a desired level of their

---

[11]The experience with 401-k tax-deferred retirement plans illustrates that people may value illiquidity for retirement saving. Some plans permit withdrawals for "hardships," while

A account, then the purchase of the IRA will only decrease the account temporarily. Similarly, those who borrow to purchase an IRA will normally pay the loan off fairly quickly (certainly before they reach retirement age) and thereby increase net saving.

Housing Wealth

As in the case of pension wealth, the life-cycle theory assumes that home equity is fungible and therefore is a good substitute for other forms of wealth. To evaluate this part of the theory, it is useful to begin with some simple facts. Krumm and Miller (1986) used the Panel Survey of Income Dynamics between 1970–79 to study the effect of homeownership on other savings. They find the following pattern. Young households accumulate liquid assets in order to make a down payment on their first house purchase, then draw down those assets when they buy the home. Soon thereafter, they begin to accumulate liquid assets again. At the same time they are building up home equity by paying off their mortgage and accumulating capital gains on their home. If the wealth in their home is a good substitute for other savings, then one would expect homeowners to have less savings in other assets, holding everything else constant. However, just the opposite is true. Comparing those households in the panel who owned a house continuously from 1970 to 1979 to those who never bought a house, homeowners' non-house savings were $16,000 higher, ceteris paribus. In addition, they had $29,000 in home equity. (For a similar result, see Manchester and Poterba, 1989.)

Another way of looking at the fungibility question is to estimate the MPC from housing wealth. Skinner (1989) took this approach. He first ran a simple regression of the change in real consumption from 1976 to 1981 on the change in housing wealth for those people in his sample who owned a house and did not move. The estimated coefficient was not significantly different from zero. In more complex models, one set of regressions obtained a small but significant effect, while another set that corrected for individual differences across families suggested that shifts in house value had no effect on consumption.

others do not. The Government Accounting Office (GAO/PEMD-88-20FS) reports that participation rates and deferral rates are, if anything, higher in the plans that do *not* permit any withdrawals.

One possible explanation for these results is based on a type of intergenerational transfers argument. If house prices go up, then people want to save more to give their kids money to buy a house. To check this, Skinner investigated whether family size has any effect on savings, and found that it did not.[12] Also, if intergenerational transfers are important then everyone (on average) would respond to an increase in house prices by saving more for their heirs, not just homeowners.

The low MPC from housing wealth is reflected in another life-cycle anomaly, namely that the elderly do not dissave fast enough. This is an additional aspect of the consumption tracks income issues addressed above. The young and the old consume too little, relative to the life-cycle prediction. While the behavior of the young could plausibly be explained by capital market imperfections, the behavior of the elderly is more puzzling, especially for homeowners. Homeowners over 65 rarely have any mortgage debt, and so have considerable home equity they could draw down. The reluctance to spend home equity appears to be voluntary, as shown by Venti and Wise (1989) in a paper entitled "But They Don't Want to Reduce Housing Equity."

Venti and Wise studied this question using the six Retirement History Surveys, from 1969 and 1979. They make use of the fact that those members of the sample who sell one house and buy another can adjust the level of their home equity at low cost, so the desired level of housing equity can be inferred from their behavior. Their behavior suggests that the mean difference between desired and actual house equity was very small, only $1010. To put this in perspective, the desired proportion of wealth in housing equity was .53. The difference between the current and desired proportions was .0107. There was essentially no effect of age on desired housing equity. Also, whether the family had children or not had no effect on desired home equity, rendering a bequest explanation suspect. Venti and Wise concluded (p. 23):

[12]A similar point came up at a seminar I gave once at the University of Chicago. I was discussing the result that the savings *rate* increases sharply with permanent income, though the life-cycle theory says it should be a constant. A seminar participant argued that this result was observed because the poor were actually saving via their children's human capital (by sending their kids through college) which is not captured in normal savings data. I asked whether he would then predict that the childless poor would have middle-class savings rates. "Not necessarily," he said. "A childless family might still have nieces and nephews." I should add that this remark did *not* elicit any laughter from the audience.

"Most elderly are not liquidity constrained. And contrary to standard formulations of the life-cycle hypothesis, the typical elderly family has no desire to reduce housing equity."

LIQUIDITY CONSTRAINTS OR DEBT AVERSION?

In the face of much of the evidence on household consumption, many economists have developed models in which a portion of the population is assumed to be liquidity constrained, in that it cannot borrow to smooth consumption (Hayashi, 1985; Zeldes, 1989). In a model for underdeveloped countries which has much in common with the view presented here, Deaton (1989) assumed that the representative household is impatient and cannot borrow. Such models are important and illuminating. However, I believe that another important source of liquidity constraints are *self-imposed* rules used by households who simply do not like to be in debt.

The evidence presented by Venti and Wise is consistent with this view. The elderly who move do not want to take on a new mortgage if possible. Reverse mortgages (in which a bank buys a house from an elderly family, lets them live in it, and pays them an annuity) have been extremely unpopular, in part, I think, because they are called mortgages.

As a group, homeowners are certainly not liquidity constrained. Manchester and Poterba estimated that in 1988 there was about $3 trillion in home equity in the U.S., about $2.5 trillion of which could be borrowed against on a tax-deductible basis even under the new (more stringent) law. (To give some sense of how big this number is, the total unsecured debt plus vehicle debt in 1985 was $405 billion.) Manchester and Poterba reported that when people do take out second mortgages, they do so primarily to make investments rather than to increase consumption. Roughly half the second mortgages are used to make home improvements, which keeps the funds in the same mental subaccount.[13]

[13]My colleague Jack Knetsch tells me that in British Columbia, Canada, homeowners over age 65 may, if they wish, postpone real estate taxes until they die or sell their home. At that point, the taxes (plus interest at a below market rate) become due. Though many elderly seem cash constrained and are sitting on significant capital gains, especially in Vancouver where house prices have greatly appreciated, only 1 percent of those eligible have elected this option. Knetsch has suggested to the province that the plan might be more popular if a small change were made in the way the plan is described. Tell the

Another relatively untapped source of liquidity is the cash value of whole life insurance. Most whole life insurance policies have a provision that policy holders can borrow against the proceeds, and in older policies the lending rate was very attractive. For example, in 1979 the average policy loan rate was 5.65 percent, while the short-term rate on Treasury bills averaged 9.5 percent. While policy holders could not get rich by borrowing against their policies, they could certainly borrow at a negative real rate. Warshawsky (1987), using 1979 data, found that less than 10 percent of those eligible to use such loans did so. He also examined the hypothesis that people gradually became aware of the arbitrage opportunity. He concluded that if policy holders were learning, they did it very slowly. According to his estimates, it would take 9 years for policy holders to make half of the appropriate adjustment.

The foregoing remarks should not be taken as a claim that liquidity constraints are unimportant. Instead, I am arguing that there are two important sources of liquidity constraints: those imposed by capital markets, and those imposed by individuals on themselves. The latter source has received no attention in the economics literature, but may well be more important.

COMMENTARY

Economists of prior generations offered much more behavioral treatments of saving behavior. For example, Irving Fisher (1930) stressed the roles of foresight, self-control, and habits. Even Friedman's (1957) permanent income hypothesis was a far cry from rational expectations. He said, "The permanent income component is not to be regarded as expected lifetime earnings. . . . It is to be interpreted as the mean income at any age regarded as permanent by the consumer unit in question, which in turn depends on its horizon and foresightedness."[14] The modern theories of saving have made the representative consumer increasingly sophisticated. Expectations are taken to be the same as those which would be held by a sophisticated econometrician.

homeowners that the tax liability would have to be paid by the person who *buys* the house. I would bet that this framing manipulation would increase utilization of the plan. Any takers?

[14] This point is stressed by Carroll and Summers (1989), who quote this passage.

The problem seems to be that while economists have gotten increasingly sophisticated and clever, consumers have remained decidedly human. This leaves open the question of whose behavior we are trying to model. Along these lines, at an NBER conference a couple years ago I explained the difference between my models and Robert Barro's (a well-known rationalist) by saying that he assumes the agents in his model are as smart as he is, while I portray people as being as dumb as I am. Barro agreed with this assessment.

[*10*]

Pari-mutuel
Betting Markets

Well, after many unsuccessful attempts, you have finally gotten a date with the woman of your dreams, and, after debating between going to the ballet (your choice) or a hockey game (hers), you have agreed on a trip to the racetrack. Naturally, you are intent on showing off your keen knowledge of horses and betting strategies, so you buy the racing form, and start studying it studiously. You announce that you are going to bet $10 to win on a 20-1 longshot named "This Old Cowboy." You figure that if you win you will have an impressive wad of cash to spend on dinner, and if you lose, at least you will look appropriately macho. While you have been studying the racing form, she has been just taking in the sun, so you ask her whether she wants to share in your bet. "No," she says, "I'll decide what I am going to do in a minute." At this point, about five minutes before the first race, she starts staring at the "tote board" in the center of the field, and then whips out a calculator and punches in some numbers. After a couple minutes she hands you some money and says: "Bet $50 on Number 3 to show." Horse Number 3 turns out to be one of the favorites in the race, and you patiently explain to her that such a bet will have a small payoff, even if it finishes "in the money." She looks at you sternly, and you go off to place the bets.

With William Ziemba.

Naturally, "This Old Cowboy" comes in dead last, looking like his name was well picked, while Number 3 finishes second and pays $2.80 for a $2.00 bet. This means her bet pays off $70, a tidy $20 profit. The same scenario repeats itself before every race. She never looks at the racing form, or anything else for that matter until five minutes before the race, then punches numbers into her calculator. More than half of the time she makes no bet at all, other times she bets one of the favorites to place or to show. At the end of the day, she has made four bets, all winners, and she is up $75. You, meanwhile, are making sure that the place you had planned to go for dinner takes credit cards.

Finally, you ask her what she is doing with the calculator. She smiles and removes from her massive purse a copy of a book called *Dr. Z's Beat the Race Track*. She says, "Maybe you should read this before you try to impress another date at the racetrack. By the way, do you like to play the lottery?" . . .

Economists have given great attention to stock markets in their efforts to test the concepts of market efficiency and rationality. The next few chapters are devoted to these markets. Before venturing off to Wall Street, however, we think it is useful to consider another set of markets, those for bets or wagers. Wagering markets are, in one key respect, better suited for testing how well markets work. The advantage of wagering markets is that each asset (bet) has a well-defined termination point at which its value becomes certain. The absence of this property is one of the factors that has made it so difficult to test for rationality in the stock market. Since a stock is infinitely lived, its value today depends both on the present value of future cash flows *and* on the price someone will pay for the security tomorrow. Indeed, one can argue that wagering markets have a better chance of being efficient because the conditions (quick, repeated feedback) are those which usually facilitate learning. However, empirical research has uncovered several interesting anomalies. While there are numerous types of wagering markets, legal and otherwise, this chapter will concentrate on racetrack betting and lotto-type lottery games.

RACETRACK BETTING MARKETS

The "market" at the racetrack convenes for about 20–30 minutes, during which time participants place bets on any number of the 6 to 12 horses in the upcoming race. In a typical race, participants can bet on each horse, either to win, place, or show (as well as "exotic" bets which depend on the combined outcomes of two or more horses). The horses that finish the race first, second, or third are said to finish "in-the-money." All participants who have bet a horse to win make money on that bet only if the horse is first, while a place bet pays off if the horse is first or second, and a show bet pays off if the horse is first, second, or third. There is a separate "pool" of money kept for each type of bet. Payoffs are determined in a "*pari-mutuel*" fashion, which means that the winning bets divide the money wagered on losing bets, less transactions costs.[1] The transactions costs, a fixed percentage t, include the "track take" and "breakage," which is the additional cost incurred because all returns per dollar bet are rounded down to the nearest five, ten, or twenty cents. These transactions costs are substantial, typically in the range of 15–25 percent depending on the type of wager and the locale.

The proportion of the money in the win pool that is bet on any given horse can be interpreted as the *subjective probability* that that horse will win the race. By summing over many races, one can check what proportion of the horses with subjective probabilities between, say, .2 and .25 actually won races. The results of this analysis are impressive. Horses rated by the crowd as most likely to win (the "favorites") do win most often (about one-third of the time), and the correlation between subjective and objective probabilities is very high.[2] Apparently the bettors in these markets have considerable expertise.

Does the high correlation between subjective and objective probabilities imply that the racetrack market is efficient? That depends on the definition of market efficiency. If we assume for

[1] Since payoffs depend only the final odds, bettors do not know potential payoffs when they bet. In Britain and some other places bookies accept bets on a fixed odds system where bettors are promised a certain payoff if their horse wins.

[2] See, for example, the studies by Weitzman (1965), Rosett (1965), Ali (1977), and Snyder (1978).

the moment that all bettors are expected value[3] maximizers with rational expectations, then two definitions of market efficiency seem appropriate.

Market efficiency condition 1 (weak). No bets should have positive expected values.

Market efficiency condition 2 (strong). All bets should have the same expected value: (1-t) times the amount bet.

While the racetrack may be surprisingly efficient, there is substantial evidence that both of these conditions are violated. The most robust anomalous empirical regularity is called the *favorite-longshot bias*. Specifically, the expected returns per dollar bet increase monotonically with the probability of the horse winning. Favorites win more often than the subjective probabilities imply, and longshots less often. This means that favorites are much better bets than longshots. Indeed, extreme favorites, those with odds[4] of less than 3-10 (>70 percent chance to win) actually have positive expected values, in violation of condition 1.

Figure 10–1 (taken from Ziemba and Hausch, 1986) illustrates the favorite-longshot bias using data from most of the previously published studies (including over 50,000 races). Expected returns per dollar bet are plotted for horses at various market odds, using a transactions costs assumption of t = 15.33 percent, which applies in the State of California. The horizontal line indicates the point at which returns are the expected .8467 (1-t). This occurs at odds of about 9-2 (i.e., about a 15 percent probability of winning). For odds above 18-1 there is a steep drop in the expected return, with returns falling to only 13.7 cents per dollar wagered at 100-1. This means that if you bet on a horse with 100-1 odds, rather than winning one race in 100, you will only win one race in 730! For odds below 3-10, expected returns are positive, with returns of about 4–5 percent for the shortest-odds horses. (This is

---

[3]Risk neutrality seems like a sensible initial assumption since most bettors probably wager a small portion of their total wealth. Other assumptions about risk attitudes are discussed in the commentary section.

[4]Probabilities at the racetrack are traditionally quoted as "odds." If a horse has odds of "x to 1," then the implicit probability the horse will in is $1/(x + 1)$.

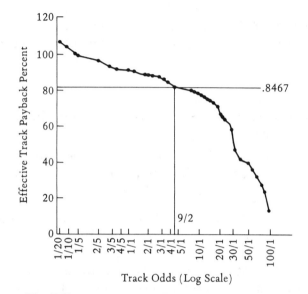

Figure 10–1. The Effective Track Payback Less Breakage for Various Odds Levels in California

Source: Ziemba & Hausch (1986).

partially explained by the existence of a minimum payoff, often $1.05 per dollar bet, at nearly all U.S. tracks.) Although such overwhelming favorites are too rare to get very excited about, other profitable betting strategies will be discussed below.

Another test of market efficiency is to compare the payoffs of equivalent bets. For example, most tracks offer a *daily double* bet, which requires bettors to select the winners of the first two races. Suppose a bettor is considering buying a daily double ticket on horse A in the first race and B in the second race. Then an alternative betting strategy (called a parlay) would be to bet on A in the first race, and, if A wins, bet the proceeds on B to win the second race. Efficiency requires that the daily double payoff on A and B be the same as the parlay on A and B. This proposition has been tested by Ali (1979) and by Asch and Quandt (1987). The conclusion from these tests is that daily double and parlay bets are priced reasonably efficiently relative to each other, though bettors should prefer the daily double because it offers lower transactions costs.

A similar test is possible using *exacta* betting, in which a bettor must correctly pick the first- and second-place horses in the correct order. Just as the relative amounts bet on different horses in the win pool can be used to calculate implicit forecasts of the probability of winning, similar calculations for the exacta can be made using the so-called *Harville* (1973) *formula.* If q_i is the probability that horse i wins, then it is assumed that the probability that horse i is first and horse j is second is $q_i q_j / (1-q_i)$. (Similarly, the probability that i is first, j is second, and k is third is $q_i q_j q_k / [1-q_i]$ $[1-q_i q_j]$).[5] Asch and Quandt (1987) used the Harville formula to compare the subjective probability of winning implied by the betting in the win pool and the exacta pool. They found that the public did not bet in a mathematically consistent fashion. The implicit probabilities of winning for a given horse were often very different in the two pools.

Betting Strategies

Betting strategies at the track, as at the stock market, come in both fundamental and technical varieties. Fundamental strategies commonly are based on publicly available information used to "handicap" races. A bettor using a fundamental or handicapping strategy attempts to determine which horses, if any, have probabilities of winning (or placing, etc.) that exceed the market-determined odds by an amount sufficient to overcome the track take.[6] Technical systems require less information and use only current betting data. Bettors using a technical system attempt to find inefficiencies in the market and bet on such "overlays" when they have positive expected value. Most academic research has concentrated on the latter strategies.[7]

Hausch, Ziemba, and Rubinstein (1981) (HZR) developed and tested a strategy for betting in the place and show markets. They use the amounts bet in the win pool and the Harville formulas to calculate the probabilities of placing and showing for each horse based on the betting in the win pool. Using these methods they are able to identify horses that are underbet to place or show. The

[5]The Harville formulas are quite accurate considering how little data they require. However, they tend to overestimate the probability that a low-odds horse will finish exactly second or third. More accurate estimation formulas are derived in Stern (1987), but these require data on all the horses in the race.

[6]A useful and insightful book on handicapping, based on a multitude of actual data, is Quirin (1979). The current state of the art in handicapping is described in Mitchell (1987) and Quinn (1987).

[7]Asch and Quandt (1986) did investigate whether the advice of professional handicappers ("touts") or computerized handicapping systems can be used to find profitable bets. They concluded that neither was very useful. See also Mitchell (1987).

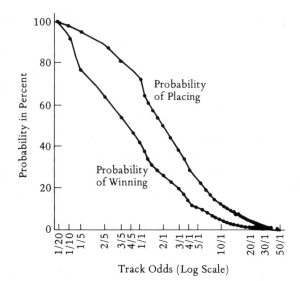

Figure 10–2. The Probability of Winning and Placing at Various Odds Levels in California

Source: Ziemba and Hausch (1986).

basic idea is to compare the proportion of the win pool bet on horse i with the amount of the place or show pool bet on horse i. If, for example, 40 percent of the bets in the win pool are on horse i, but only 15 percent of the bets in the place pool are bet on horse i, then it is profitable to bet on horse i to place. Such profitable betting opportunities typically occur two to four times per racing day. Empirical studies on two seasons of racing data indicate that significant returns on the order of 11 percent per bet are possible in the place and show markets.[8] This violates weak market efficiency. Moreover, publication of the system does not appear to have eliminated the profitable betting opportunities.

Ziemba and Hausch (1986) also developed similar techniques to identify and exploit inefficiencies in the exacta markets. The most frequent profitable bets have the favorite in second position. Plots of the probability of winning and coming in second versus odds in Ziemba and Hausch (1986), as shown in Figure 10–2, show that short-odds horses have a substantial probability of coming in ex-

[8]For details on the system, see Ziemba and Hausch (1987). Hausch and Ziemba (1985) extend the HZR results to analyze the effects of differences in transactions costs, two-horse "entries," and multiple wagers, and provide accurate regression models for varying wealth levels and track "handles" (the size of the betting pool). They also investigate how many bettors have to follow the system for the market to become efficient.

actly second. The betting public might easily underestimate this chance. The other common profitable wagers are derived from the extreme favorite-longshot bias. Betting extreme favorites in the first position can thus yield profitable bets. The public wagers a considerable amount on these super horses, but not as much as they should. Combinations of longshots are almost never a good exacta wager; such bets typically return 10–30 cents on the dollar.

Asch, Malkiel, and Quandt (1984, 1986) and Asch and Quandt (1986) investigated whether a drop in the odds late in the betting period might reflect inside information and thereby point to wagers that may have positive expected returns. Common racetrack folklore suggests that the smart money is bet late. This is borne out by Asch, Malkiel, and Quandt (1982) using data at various points in the betting cycle from 729 races at the Atlantic City Race Course. They found that for winning horses the final odds tend to be lower than the "morning line odds" (predicted odds by the track handicapper), whereas for horses finishing out of the money the final odds are much higher than the morning line odds. The later in the betting period, the more pronounced is the effect for the winners. The final odds for winners are 96 percent of the morning line odds, but for the money bet during the last eight minutes, the marginal odds are 82 percent of the morning line, and in the last five minutes they drop further to 79 percent. The final odds for losers are about 1.5 times the morning line odds. Asch and Quandt (1986) developed a logit model of the probability of winning, using the change in the odds during the last few minutes as one of the independent variables. The logit model was then used to search for profitable investment strategies. They could not find any profitable bets in the win pool, but they did find some in the place and show pools. Apparently, place and show betting on favorites whose odds have fallen in the last few minutes yields small profits. This is consistent with the Ziemba and Hausch (1987) results suggesting inefficiencies in the place and show pools.

Cross Track Betting

A recent development in racetrack betting is the opportunity for bettors to wager at their home track on major thoroughbred races being run at another track. Cross track betting raises new and interesting questions about market efficiency. While arbitrage is made difficult by the high transactions costs and the absence of public telephones inside most racetracks, rational expectations would seem to imply that the odds at every track would be approximately the same. In fact, they frequently vary dramatically. For example, in the 1986 Kentucky Derby, the winner, Ferdinand, paid $16.80 for $2 at Hollywood Park in California where he had run often and was well known. He paid $37.40 at Aqueduct in New York, $79.60 at Woodbine in Toronto, $63.20 at Hialeah in Florida, and $90.00 at Evangeline in Louisiana.

While pure arbitrage may be difficult, profitable betting strategies are possible. Hausch and Ziemba (1987) have developed an optimal betting model for cross track betting under the assumption that final odds at all tracks are known in time to compute and place bets at each track. The essence of the system is to assume that the home track odds are accurate (after correcting for the favorite-longshot bias) and then to select a combination of bets at other tracks to exploit the inefficiencies. If the discrepancies in the odds at the various tracks are large enough (as they have been for some races), it is even possible to create a genuine arbitrage opportunity by betting on every horse at the track where the odds are best. Unfortunately, in the absence of a sophisticated communications system, these strategies are impractical (and probably illegal). However, a Chicago commodities trader has developed and profitably used a workable one-track system using a portable television at the cross track. The bettor views the home odds when they are flashed on television, and then searches for overlays at the cross track.

LOTTO GAMES

Lottery games date at least to biblical days. Israel was divided among the seven tribes by lot. Christ's robe was given to a lottery winner so it would not have to be cut. The Sistine chapel and its paintings were supported by lotteries. The Italian lottery has been running continuously since 1530. Lotteries are played in over 100 countries. Lotteries arrived in North America with the pilgrims. They were used to partially fund the new schools such as Harvard, Princeton, and Yale. Later they were used to raise money and to pay off debts of notables such as Thomas Jefferson. Extreme corruption led to their demise in the late nineteenth century, and they were banned in the U.S. and Canada. They resurfaced in 1964 in New Hampshire. In Canada they arrived to repay the debts from Expo 1967 in Montreal. Since then, there has been explosive growth in popularity and sales. However, with an expected return of between 40 and 60 cents on the dollar, they are usually a poor investment for the rational investor.

Even with such low payout rates, it is possible to obtain positive expected value bets in lotto games. This occurs because not all numbers are equally popular with the public. The possibility of exploiting this pattern was first formalized by Chernoff (1980) (and tested by some of his students) in the context of the Massachusetts numbers game. In this game the object is to pick a number from 0000 to 9999. If your number is drawn then you share a portion of the total pool. A subsidiary prize is awarded if three numbers match. Chernoff found that certain numbers were unpopular: those with 0's, 9's, and to a lesser extent 8's. His theoretical analysis suggested that there were combinations with positive expected values, inducing some of his students to bet systematically on the "good" numbers. However, the students did not fare very well. First, over time the unpopular numbers became less advantageous, due to a combination of learning and simple regression toward the mean. Second, they fell victim to the dreaded "gambler's ruin." The students' bankroll was not sufficient to wait out the time needed to have enough hits to generate substantial profits. Finally, they were unlucky: the unpopular numbers came up less often than would be expected.

The game that has attracted the most attention in North America is Lotto 6/49 or some similar variant. In this game one chooses six of 49 numbers, and if they all match then one wins the jackpot. Lesser prizes are awarded for three to five matches. The probability of selecting the winning combination in this game is one in 13,983,816: if you play twice a week you can expect to win in 134,360 years, a long time horizon even for a rational economist!

Two features make the game interesting for the rational investor. First, as in the numbers game, some numbers are more popular than others. Second, if the grand prize is not won in a given drawing, it is carried over to the next week. Thus prizes can be enormous.[9] Ziemba and his co-workers (1986) have been studying

---

[9]In the U.S. lottery prizes are often announced using the accounting methods favored by University fund raisers and professional athlete agents, namely undiscounted nominal dollars. The after-tax present value of the prize is typically about one-third of the an-

whether these factors can produce favorable investment opportunities. Several estimation methods have been used to calculate the best numbers: simple counts of the frequency with which the numbers are picked, a regression of the log of payoffs on the winning numbers, and a sophisticated constrained maximum likelihood model. All lead to the same conclusion, namely that 15 to 20 of the numbers are quite unpopular. Moreover, the precise numbers are virtually the same from year to year. While there has been some learning over the years, so that these numbers are not quite as unpopular as they used to be, the unpopular numbers tend to remain unpopular. In fact, thousands of combinations of numbers have expected returns over $1 *even when there is no carryover.* The expected value of betting the best numbers increases with the carryover and converges to about $2.25 per $1 for very large pools. The best numbers tend to be high numbers (non-birthdays) and those ending in 0's, 9's, and 8's. According to the regression model, the twelve most unpopular numbers are 32, 29, 10, 30, 40, 39, 48, 12, 42, 41, 38, and 18 which tend to be 15–30 percent less popular than average. Using the marginal approach (those numbers chosen two standard deviations less than average), one finds the nineteen most unpopular numbers to be 40, 39, 20, 30, 41, 38, 42, 46, 29, 49, 48, 32, 10, 47, 1, 37, 28, 34, and 45. These numbers have edges from 26.7 percent down to 3.2 percent. The most popular number is 7, which is selected nearly 50 percent more often than the average number.

The question remains—can you make money in the lotto games playing the unpopular numbers? The answer is a very qualified yes. While you can achieve an expected value of $2 per dollar bet, your chances of winning are very small. Consider a hypothetical carnival game with one million spokes. You pay $1 for a number between 1 and 1 million, and you get $2 million if your choice comes up. While you have an edge, the chance of winning is so small that you probably will go bankrupt before winning the jackpot. To analyze this problem one needs a model of growth of wealth versus security of wealth. MacLean, Ziemba, and Blazenko (1987) develop such a model to investigate questions such as: Can a dynasty enhance its long-term wealth playing lotto games? The answer is that it can. With sufficiently small wagers it can increase its initial stake of, say, $10 million by tenfold before

nounced value. In Canada, however, prizes are paid in cash and incur no Canadian tax liability.

losing $5 million with probability arbitrarily close to one, but this process takes thousands of years even if they play all over the world. For one lotto game it will take them millions of years. A more interesting question for most of us is: Can a group or single investor use the unpopular numbers to become rich? This is even more difficult, especially if one wants low risk. It is easy to bank-roll, as the optimal wager can be as low as 10 cents per week for one of ten syndicate members, but these aspiring millionaires are most likely to be residing in a cemetery when their distant heirs finally reach the goal. It is still best to play unpopular numbers—they have an edge and you will win three to seven times the usual prizes should you hit—but you will expect to play a very long time before winning.

One of the most attractive aspects of lotto games is that the portion of the pool designated for the jackpot is carried over to the next draw when no one wins the jackpot. Indeed it is the prospect of winning a huge jackpot that is the main driving force behind the tremendous interest and sales of lotto tickets. Does it ever pay to buy all the numbers and hence "steal the pot"? Two conditions are necessary for this to be profitable. Roughly speaking these are (1) a large carryover (in 6/49, $7.7 million); and (2) "not very many" tickets sold. While these conditions are unlikely to occur, there are cases that can and have arisen in minor lotto games in Canada and elsewhere where it actually would have been a reasonable idea to buy the pot. It is important to stress, however, that even if the right conditions arose, buying the pot would entail enormous transactions costs since the tickets must be bought and redeemed one by one, and, you would have to hope that no one else tried to buy the pot at the same time (see Ziemba et al., 1986, for details). Similar situations sometimes arise in exotic racetrack betting such as the "pick six" (pick the winners of six consecutive races) and related exotic bets. Substantial carry-overs can exist in these pools, and buying the pot can be profitable. In fact, there are at least two major syndicates that have successfully entered this business.

COMMENTARY

Racetrack Betting

The racetrack betting market is surprisingly efficient. Market odds are remarkably good estimates of winning probabilities. This implies that racetrack bettors have considerable expertise, and that the markets should be taken seriously. Nevertheless, two robust anomalies are present: the favorite-longshot bias, and the inefficiencies of the place and show markets. How can these anomalies be explained?

Quandt (1986) has offered the following argument regarding the favorite-longshot bias (see also Rosett, 1965). The fact that bettors make wagers that are known to have negative expected value implies that they must be "locally" risk seeking.[10] This implies that the usual risk-return relationship will be reversed. In equilibrium, investments (bets) with high variance will have lower average returns than investments with low variance. While this argument is logically consistent, we feel that it is not a satisfactory explanation of the observed behavior. The crucial issue is whether the inference that bettors are risk seeking is a reasonable one to draw from the fact that they are at the track betting.

What does it mean to be "locally risk seeking"? Recognizing that most racetrack fans, including themselves, purchase insurance, Asch and Quandt (1986) suggest that the utility of wealth function may have the shape proposed by Friedman and Savage (1948), namely concave below the current wealth level and convex above it. While this assumption can explain why racetrack bettors also purchase insurance, it is surely not an adequate explanation for bettors' other behavior such as investing. We would venture a guess that when it comes to retirement saving, Professors Asch and Quandt would not be willing to accept a lower mean return in order to obtain a higher level of risk. Indeed, having read their coauthor's book on the stock market (Malkiel, 1985), We surmise that when it comes to investing, many racetrack bettors are normally risk averse. Thus the term *locally risk seeking* may apply to racetrack bettors, but only if the term "locally" refers to physical location rather than wealth level![11]

---

[10]Locally risk seeking means that at the given wealth level of the bettor, he or she would be willing to accept unfair gambles. At other wealth levels, the same individual might be risk averse.

[11]The more basic question is whether individuals display a consistent "trait" that can be captured in an index of risk aversion or risk seeking. Psychologists have found that most such traits are highly context specific, and risk taking is no exception. As Paul Slovic (1972, p. 795) has commented: "Although knowledge of the dynamics of risk taking is still limited, there is one important aspect that has been fairly well researched—that dealing with the stability of a person's characteristic risk-taking preferences as he moves from situation to situation. Typically, a subject is tested in a variety of risk-taking tasks involving problem solving, athletic, social, vocational, and pure gambling situations. The results of

It is true that racetrack fans go to the track to bet—watching a horse race is just not that much fun if you do not have a rooting interest. The real question is to what extent we can explain racetrack betting with the assumptions of rational expectations, expected utility maximization, and a preference for risk. Consider the following stylized facts about racetrack bettors:

1. Most bring a stake that represents a small portion of their wealth. (The average amount bet per person in 1985 was about $150 *for the day*. The median is surely lower).

2. They allocate that stake over the course of the betting day, intending to bet on nearly every race (unless they run out of money before the day ends).

3. Groups of friends who attend the track together rarely bet among themselves, although they could thereby guarantee a zero sum game for the group and increase variance as much as they wanted.

Are these facts consistent with the assumptions stated above?

Another fact that is difficult to explain within this framework is the tendency (first pointed out by McGlothlin, 1956) for the favorite-longshot bias to become more pronounced for the last couple of races of the day. Most observers (e.g., McGlothlin, 1956; Kahneman and Tversky, 1979; Asch and Quandt, 1986) seem to agree about what causes this. Bettors on average are losing toward the end of the day. They would like to go home a winner, but do not want to risk losing much more money. Therefore, they bet on longshots in an attempt to break even for the day. Notice that this behavior is hard to explain within a Friedman-Savage framework. Why should a reduction in wealth increase the tendency for risk seeking?

We feel that a more promising way of modeling racetrack betting (and other gambling behavior) is to introduce the concept of *mental accounting* discussed in Chapter 9. To get the feel of how mental accounting applies here, consider the following thought experiment. A set of identical twins Art and Bart (with identical wealth levels) is at the racetrack, contemplating their bets for the last race of the day.

---

close to a dozen such studies indicate little correlation, from one setting to another, in a person's preferred level of risk taking.''

Art has lost $100 betting so far, though he has another $100 in cash with him.

Bart is even in the betting so far, but between races he read the financial page in the newspaper and discovered that a stock in which he holds 100 shares went down one point the previous day.

Notice that both twins have lost $100, and thus any wealth-based explanation of their betting behavior must predict that they will make similar bets. However, in a mental accounting formulation, Art is behind in the racetrack account while Bart is even; thus, they might well bet differently. (See Thaler and Johnson, 1990, for evidence consistent with this view.) Once the concept of mental accounting is introduced, then it becomes much easier to understand how an individual can be risk neutral or risk seeking at the racetrack but risk averse with respect to retirement savings.

As for the favorite-longshot bias, many behavioral factors are probably at work:

1. Bettors might overestimate the chances that the longshots will win.

2. Bettors might overweight the small probability of winning in calculating the utility of the bet (see Kahneman and Tversky, 1979).

3. Bettors may derive utility simply from holding a ticket on a longshot. After all, $2 is a cheap thrill.

4. It is more fun to pick a longshot to win than a favorite. It is hard to claim much credit for predicting that a 1-5 favorite will win (much less place or show), but if a 20-1 longshot comes through, considerable bragging rights will have been earned.

5. Some bettors may choose horses for essentially irrational reasons (e.g., the horse's name). Since there is no possibility of short sales, such bettors can drive the odds down on the worst horses, with the "smart money" simply taking the better bets on the favorites.

The fact that the place and show pools seem to be less efficient than the win pool is also an interesting observation. One important factor may simply be that these bets are more complicated. For example, the payoff to a bet to show depends not only on the chance the horse will be in the money, but also on which other horses are in the money, and how much has been bet on each. (The greater the share of the money that has been bet on the horses finishing in the top three positions, the smaller the pay-off.) Bettors might prefer simple bets to complicated ones,[12] or they might simply have difficulty determining when an attractive bet occurs in place and show pools.

One important conclusion to draw from this analysis is that modeling gambling behavior is complicated. Bettors' behavior depends on numerous factors such as how they have done in earlier races, and which bets will yield the best stories after the fact. It should be emphasized that these complications apply with equal force to investment behavior. As Merton Miller has said (1986, S467), ''. . . [to many individual investors] stocks are usually more than just the abstract 'bundle of returns' of our economic model. Behind each holding may be a story of family business, family quarrels, legacies received, divorce settlements, and a host of other considerations almost totally irrelevant to our theories of portfolio selection. That we abstract from these stories in building our models is not because the stories are uninteresting but because they may be too interesting and thereby distract us from the pervasive market forces that should be our principal concern.'' While we sympathize with Miller's self-control problem—we also find the stories irresistibly interesting—we feel that to understand the market forces one must enrich the models to incorporate more than ''the bundle of returns.'' Indeed, even professional portfolio managers seem more concerned with beating the S&P index than with maximizing returns. In fact, we suspect that portfolio managers trailing the market in the fourth quarter may behave much like the racetrack bettors who bet on longshots when behind at the end of the day.

Lotteries

What can economic theory say about lotteries? Given the dreadful payout rates, one prediction might be that no one will purchase lottery tickets. However, it is easy to rationalize the purchase of a lottery ticket by saying that for a dollar purchase, the customer is paying 50 cents for a fantasy. That's a pretty good deal. The existence of popular and unpopular numbers is more difficult to

---

[12]For a similar example in the finance literature, see Elton, Gruber, and Rentzler (1982).

rationalize. It seems that economic theory yields the following paradoxical prediction: No one will choose the most popular numbers.[13]

To understand this phenomenon it is useful to point out that lotteries in North America did not become popular until New Jersey introduced a game which allowed players to choose their own numbers. The popularity of this feature seems to be explained by what psychologist Ellen Langer (1975) has called "the illusion of control." Even in purely chance games, players feel they have a better chance to win if they can control their own fate, rather than have it determined by purely "chance" factors. For example, Langer found that subjects in her experiments were more reluctant (charged a higher price) to give up a lottery ticket they had selected themselves, than one selected at random for them.

A news story provides a vivid example of the illusion of control (and the confusion of skill and chance). One year, the winner of the Christmas drawing for the Spanish National Lottery, the El Gordo, was interviewed on television. He was asked: "How did you do it? How did you know which ticket to buy?" Our winner replied that he had searched for a vendor who could sell him a ticket ending in 48. "Why 48?" he was asked. "Well, I dreamed of the number seven for seven nights in a row, and since seven times seven is 48 . . ."[14]

---

[13]This is reminiscent of one of baseball player Yogi Berra's famous quotes: "No one ever goes there anymore because it is too crowded."
[14]This example is cited by Russo and Schoemaker (1989).

[11]

Calendar Effects
in the Stock Market

Your brother-in-law is a stockbroker, and your sister is always after you to listen to him. It's not that you distrust him, as much as you just don't believe him. Anyway, this time he calls with something wild. He tells you that there is a publication called the *Broker's Almanac*, produced by the same people who publish the *Farmer's Almanac*. It seems that this publication, which comes out in December, makes forecasts about which specific days will be good on Wall Street for the upcoming year. Every trading day of the year is given from one to five dollar signs. The publication got some notoriety because October 19, 1987, was given only one dollar sign, and the market fell 500 points. Some people in the firm had actually started paying attention to the publication, much to the amusement of the more sophisticated research types. On a bet, one of the rocket scientists got a few years of past issues together and looked at the Almanac's track record. He was shocked to discover that there was actually a significant correlation between the number of dollar signs given to a day and its actual return! He spent most of the next weekend trying to figure out how they could be doing this. What he found was quite interesting. There were distinct patterns to the Almanac's predictions. Generally, Fridays were predicted to be good while Mondays were bad. Days in January tended to be rated high, especially in the early part of the month. In fact,

averaging over all months, the first few days and the
last day had better-than-average forecasts. Finally, the
days before legal holidays had the highest forecasts of
all. They used this same pattern every year.
Furthermore, all the explanatory power of their forecasts
came from these "special days." Their forecasts on
other days were uncorrelated with the actual outcomes.
Well, this cleared up what these Almanac guys were
doing, but not how it could possibly work. Unless, of
course, these patterns were true . . .

For many reasons, security markets are a good place to look for
anomalies. First of all, there are plenty of data: monthly price data
for individual stocks listed on the New York Stock Exchange are
available back to the 1920s. Second, security markets are thought
to be the most efficient of all markets. If anomalies occur there, it
is difficult to blame them on transactions costs or other market
failures. Third, there are well-developed theories of security
prices, such as the Capital Asset Pricing Model (CAPM),[1] which
add some structure to potential tests. Nevertheless, until the last
ten years or so, anomalies were anomalous in finance. Recent
years, however, have been different. Researchers have reported
that firms with low price-earnings ratios, small firms, firms that
do not pay dividends, and firms that have lost much of their value
in the past all earn returns in excess of what would be predicted
by the CAPM. However, another class of anomalies has surfaced
that is even more puzzling, viz., seasonal patterns.

THE JANUARY EFFECT

The efficient market hypothesis predicts that security prices follow a random walk. It should be impossible to predict returns
from past events. The first attempts to test this hypothesis exam-

---

[1]The CAPM is the cornerstone of the modern theory of financial markets. Its essential
contribution is to incorporate the concept of diversification into asset pricing. Obviously,
holding a portfolio of many stocks is less risky than holding all of your money in just one
stock, as long as the price changes of the individual stocks are not perfectly correlated. In
the CAPM, risky stocks must pay higher returns, where risk is measured by the correlation
with returns on other stocks. This risk measure is commonly called "beta."

ined short-term serial correlations in stock prices. The absence of significant correlations was judged to be evidence consistent with a random walk. Recently, however, researchers have conducted a different type of test. In what proved to be a seminal paper, Rozeff and Kinney (1976) found that there were seasonal patterns in an equal-weighted index of New York Stock Exchange (NYSE) prices over the period 1904–1974. Specifically, the returns in January were much higher than in other months. The average monthly return in January was about 3.5 percent, while other months averaged about 0.5 percent. Almost one-third of the annual returns occurred in January. Interestingly, the high returns in January are not observed in an index that is composed of only large firms, e.g., the Dow Jones Industrial Average. Since an equal-weighted index is a simple average of all firms listed on the NYSE, it gives small firms greater weight than their share of market value. This suggests that the January effect is primarily a small firm effect. Indeed, it is.

In an investigation of the small firm effect (see Banz, 1981), Donald Keim (1983) found that the excess returns to small firms were temporally concentrated. Half of the excess returns to small firms came in January, and half of the January returns came in the first five trading days. Thus the high returns in January for the equal-weighted NYSE index are driven by high returns to small firms in January. Marc Reinganum (1983) clarified the situation further by pointing out that the January returns were higher for small firms that had lost in value during the previous year, and the excess returns in the first five days were not observed for small "winners."

Reinganum's research was motivated by a possible explanation of the January effect based on tax-loss selling. The argument is that the prices of firms which have previously declined in price will decline further in the latter months of the year as owners sell off the shares to realize capital losses. Then, after the new year, prices bounce up in the absence of selling pressure. Whatever the merits of this argument, it must be stressed that it is not based on rational behavior by all market participants. In fact, Richard Roll called the argument "patently absurd" (1983, p. 20). He pointed out that even if the trading of some investors were driven by tax avoidance, other investors could buy in anticipation of the excess returns in January. While Roll described the hypothesis with obvious scorn, he, like Reinganum, found some evidence consistent with it. He reported that stocks with negative returns over the previous year have higher returns in January.

To investigate the tax-loss-selling hypothesis, and also to see whether the January returns might just be a statistical artifact, several researchers have examined the seasonal patterns in other countries. Gultekin and Gultekin (1983) looked at the seasonal pattern in 16 countries and found that January returns were exceptionally large in 15 of them. In fact, the effect in the U.S. is smaller than in many other countries. In Belgium, the Netherlands, and Italy, the January return is bigger than the average return for the whole year! The international evidence also suggests that while taxes seem relevant to the January effect, they are not the entire explanation. First of all, the January effect is observed in Japan where there is no capital gains tax or loss offset (Kato and Schallheim, 1985).[2] Second, in Canada, there was no capital gains tax before 1972, yet there was a January effect before 1972 (Berges, McConnell, and Schlarbaum, 1984). Third, there are January effects in Great Britain and Australia which have April 1 and July 1 beginnings to their tax years, respectively.[3] (Still, returns are high in April in Great Britain, and in July in Australia, so taxes do seem to be part of the story.)

January appears to be special in some other ways. As discussed in the next chapter, the firms which have been the biggest losers over a five-year period subsequently outperform the market. However, they do most of their outperforming in January.

Tinic and West (1984) have re-evaluated the Capital Asset Pricing Model (CAPM) to see whether there are any seasonal patterns to risk premia. They made the startling discovery that the observed return to riskier (higher β) stocks occurs exclusively in January. In all other months, and for the other months together, riskier stocks do not earn higher returns. The CAPM is just a January phenomenon!

A third surprising January effect comes in the most recent contribution to a series of articles investigating whether stocks that

[2] It is also intriguing to note that the good months in Japan are December–January and June–July. These periods coincide with the large semi-annual bonuses most workers receive.

[3] Some authors have pointed out that the January effects in countries with no capital gains tax or other tax years could be explained by trading by non-citizens subject to January-based taxes, but there is little evidence to support this claim. In the case of Japan, studies have found little correlation between stock prices in Japan and the U.S. which seems to weaken the argument considerably.

pay high dividends earn higher returns (to compensate stock-holders for having to pay taxes on the dividends). A recent paper by Keim (1986a) found two anomalous results. Among those firms that pay positive dividends, returns do seem to increase with the dividend yield. However, the highest returns are associated with the firms that pay no dividends. Also, the excess returns in both the high-dividend and zero-dividend groups are concentrated in January.

THE WEEKEND EFFECT

Define the daily return (i.e., price change plus dividends) for a particular day of the week as the return from the close of the previous trading day to the close of trading on that day. Using this definition, how would we expect Monday returns to compare to the returns for other weekdays? The most logical hypothesis (dubbed the "calendar time hypothesis" by French, 1980) is that prices should rise somewhat more on Mondays than on other days because the time between the close of trading on Friday and the close of trading on Monday is three days, rather than the normal one day between other trading days. Accordingly, Monday returns should be three times higher than other weekday returns. French offered an alternative, the "trading time hypothesis," which entails that returns are generated only during active trading and implies that returns should be the same for every trading day. This hypothesis strikes me as unreasonable. Suppose, for example, trading were restricted to one day per week during the summer. Wouldn't we expect the return on those days to be equal to the normal *weekly* return? In any case, neither hypothesis is consistent with the data.

The first study of weekend effects in security markets appeared in the *Journal of Business* in 1931, written by a graduate student at Harvard named M. J. Fields. He was investigating the conventional Wall Street wisdom at the time that "the unwillingness of traders to carry their holdings over the uncertainties of a weekend leads to a liquidation of long accounts and a consequent decline of security prices on Saturday" (Fields, 1931, p. 415). Fields examined the pattern of the Dow Jones Industrial Average (DJIA) for the period 1915–1930 to see if the conventional wisdom was true. He compared the closing price of the DJIA for Saturday with the mean of the closing prices on the adjacent Friday and Monday. He found, in fact, that prices tended to rise on Saturdays. For the 717 weekends he studied, the Saturday price was more than .10 higher than the Friday–Monday mean 52 percent of the time, while it was lower only 36 percent of the time.

The next study of daily return patterns did not appear in the academic literature for four decades. Frank Cross (1973) studied the returns on the Standard and Poor's index of 500 stocks (the S&P 500) over the period 1953 to 1970. He found that the index rose on 62.0 percent of the Fridays, but on only 39.5 percent of the Mondays. The mean return on Fridays was 0.12 percent, while the mean return on Mondays was −0.18 percent. As Cross says, "the probability that such a large difference would occur by chance is less than one in a million."

Kenneth French (1980) also used the S&P 500 index to study daily returns and obtained similar results. He studied the period 1953–1977 and found that the mean Monday return was negative for the full period (mean $= -0.168$ percent, $t = -6.8$) and also for every five-year sub-period. The mean return was positive (as would be expected) for all other days of the week, with Wednesdays and Fridays having the highest returns. French then asked whether the negative returns on Mondays might be due to some unidentified "closed-market effect." If so, the expected return should be lower following holidays, as well as weekends. He found instead that average returns were higher than normal for Mondays, Wednesdays, Thursdays, and Fridays after holidays. On Tuesdays following Monday holidays, returns were negative, perhaps a belated showing of the usual negative weekend returns. He interpreted these results as suggesting that there is something special about weekends, as opposed to general market closings.

The Cross and French studies both measured Monday returns as the differences between the closing price on Friday and the closing price on Monday. This leaves open whether prices fall during the day on Mondays, or between Friday's close and Monday's opening. This issue was investigated by Richard Rogalski (1984). Rogalski obtained opening and closing prices for the DJIA for the period October 1, 1974–April 30, 1984, and for the S&P 500 for the period January 2, 1979–April 30, 1984. He found that prices rose on Mondays from the opening to the close. The negative returns were all between the close of trading on Friday and the opening on Monday. Thus the Monday effect became the weekend effect.[4] He also found that weekends in January are different from other months. During January, weekend and Monday returns are positive. Not surprisingly, in light of the results reported in the previous section, the January returns are also related to firm size. The smallest firms have the highest Monday returns (and the highest returns on all other days for that matter).

If weekends are bad for stocks, what about other securities? Gibbons and Hess (1981) looked at the daily pattern of returns for Treasury bills and found that Monday's return is significantly lower than that of other days. They also investigated several possible explanations of the weekend effect for stocks, the most plausible of which involves "settlement periods." Stocks purchased on one day need not be paid for until several business days later. The length of the settlement period has gradually increased over time. Apparently, the more computerized the process becomes, the longer it takes! From March 4, 1962 to February 10, 1968, the settlement period was four business days; since that time it has been five business days. For the former period, investors who sold stocks on Monday would receive payment in four days, while those who sold on other days would not receive payment for six days. Since the negative Monday returns persist after 1968, the settlement effect cannot be a complete explanation, and Gibbons and Hess showed that even before 1968 the differing settlement periods could not explain the weekend effect.

Odd empirical results such as the weekend effect generate legitimate worries about "data mining." After all, there are many ways to look at the data; and if enough people spin the same tapes long enough, some significant results are bound to be found. Researchers have used two methods to see whether these anomalies may in fact be artifacts. One method is to study different time periods. In the case of the weekend effect, all the recent research can be thought of as replications of Fields' original study which covered 1915–1930. Cross and French used data starting in 1953 (a date chosen because that is when the New York Stock Exchange stopped trading on Saturdays). Since then, Keim and

---

[4]Smirlock and Starks (1986) studied weekend effects for the DJIA over the period 1963–1983. They found that the negative returns have shifted backward in time. In the 1963–1968 period the negative returns occurred during Monday's trading. From 1968 to 1974 the negative returns were concentrated in the opening hours of Monday trading. Since 1974 the losses have occurred between Friday close and Monday opening.

Stambaugh (1984) have confirmed that the weekend effect held for the S&P Composite Index for the period 1928–1982, and Lakonishok and Smidt (1987) studied the seasonal movements of the DJIA for the period 1897–1986 and again found consistent negative Monday returns, even for the previously unstudied 1897–1910 period.

Coursey and Dyl (1986) used a completely different approach to investigate the weekend effect. Using the methods of laboratory market experiments, they introduced trading interruptions and observed the resulting pattern of prices. In their experiments, subjects traded assets with uncertain values. For the first two trading days of each three-day "week", the assets had a lifetime of one day. For the third day, which was followed by a one-period non-trading "weekend," assets had two-day lifetimes. The results were consistent with the evidence in actual security markets. The prices on the days before trading interruptions were significantly higher (per unit of return) than on other days.

HOLIDAYS

In French's investigation of weekend effects he looked at the price behavior after holidays and found nothing special happening. However, in another early study, Fields (1934) found that the DJIA showed a high proportion of advances the day *before* holidays. In this case it took over 50 years for Fields to be resurrected from obscurity by Robert Ariel (1985). Ariel looked at the returns on the 160 days that preceded holidays during the period 1963–1982. For an equal-weighted index of stocks he found that the mean return on the preholidays was .529 percent compared to .056 percent on other days, a ratio of greater than 9 to 1. For a value-weighted index the preholiday returns average .365 percent compared to .026 percent on other days, a ratio of greater than 14 to 1. The differences are both statistically and economically significant. Again, these results were replicated for the 90-year DJIA series by Lakonishok and Smidt (1987). They obtained an average preholiday return of .219 percent compared to the normal daily rate of return of .0094 percent, a ratio of greater than 23 to 1. The size of these numbers is highlighted by the following amazing fact: over the last 90 years, 51 percent of the capital gains in the

DJIA have occurred on the approximately ten preholidays per year.

TURN-OF-THE-MONTH EFFECTS

Ariel (1987) has also examined the pattern of returns within months. For the period 1963–1981 he divided months into two halves, the first half starting with the last day of the prior month. He then compared the cumulative returns for the two periods using both equal-weighted and value-weighted indexes. Again the results are quite startling. The return for the latter half of the month is *negative*. All the returns for the period occur in the first part of the months! This result has been replicated and sharpened by Lakonishok and Smidt. Using their 90-year series for the Dow, they find that the return for the four days around the turn of the month, starting with the last day of the prior month, is .473%. (The average return for a four-day period is .0612 percent.) Also, this four-day return is greater than the average total monthly return which is .35 percent. In other words, aside from the four days around the turn of every month, the DJIA falls!

INTRADAY EFFECTS

The most recent contribution to the analysis of seasonal price movements was made possible by the existence of a new tape that provides a time-ordered record of every common stock transaction (all 15 million!) made on the NYSE for the fourteen months between Dec 1, 1981, and January 31, 1983. Lawrence Harris (1986a) used this tape to investigate intraday price movements. He computed rates of return for every 15-minute period the market was open. He found that the weekend effect spills over into the first 45 minutes of trading on Monday, with prices falling during this period. On all other days, prices rise sharply during the first 45 minutes. Also, returns are high near the very end of the day, particularly on the last trade of the day. Furthermore, the day-end price changes are greatest when the final transaction is within the last five minutes of trading. Harris (1986b) investigated the possibility that this odd result can be attributed to errors in the data or price manipulations by specialists but rejected these possibilities. One fact which argues against these hypotheses is that opening price changes tend to be positive, whereas if the price increases at the end of the day were artifacts, one would expect the subsequent opening changes to be negative. One of the most intriguing aspects of the end-of-the-day results is that similar patterns have been observed in experimental markets. For example, Forsythe, Palfrey, and Plott (1982, 1984) and Plott and Sunder (1982) found positive price blips just before trading closed in their experimental asset markets. This was originally thought to be an experimental markets anomaly, but it appears to be present on the NYSE as well.

COMMENTARY

There is a striking pattern to the price movements described in this chapter. Abnormal price returns occur around the turn of the year, the turn of the month, the turn of the week, the turn of the day, and before holidays. Why? Most of the reasonable, or even not so reasonable, explanations have been tested and rejected. Certainly it is safe to say that no one would have predicted any of these results in 1975, when the efficient market hypothesis was thought by most financial economists to be a well-established fact. While the effects are not large enough for traders with any significant transactions costs to exploit, they remain a genuine puzzle. Investors who plan to trade anyway could alter the timing of their trading to take advantage of the predictable price changes. What new explanations are promising? It is hard to imagine any single factor that can explain all of these effects. However, several kinds of factors seem worth investigating.

1. Price movements may be related to customs that influence the flow of funds in and out of the market. For example, pension funds and mutual funds may receive payments (and make corresponding changes in their portfolios) at dates that coincide with calendar changes because firms and individuals customarily make such payments at regular intervals. At the individual level, Ritter (1987) found that the price movements of small firms near the turn of the year seem to be related to buying and selling by private individuals (who, compared to institutions, own a greater share of small firms than large firms). Specifically, the ratio of buy orders to sell orders for the non-institutional customers of Merrill

Lynch are high in early January and low in late December. In other words, individuals as a group are selling in December and buying in January. Also, the variation in the buy-sell ratio explains 46 percent of the annual variation in the abnormal small-firm January returns (defined as the returns to the smallest decile of NYSE stocks minus the returns on the largest decile). Similar studies of the customs of institutional investors would be very worthwhile.

2. Another reason why institutional investors may make seasonally related changes in their portfolios is the practice that is quaintly referred to as "window dressing." The claim on Wall Street is that investment managers clean up their portfolios before reporting dates, to get rid of embarrassing holdings. Since the reporting dates presumably coincide with natural calendar dates, such actions may be related to some of the seasonal price movements, particularly the year-end and month-end effects.

3. A different type of explanation of calendar effects is that they are related to the systematic timing of the arrival of good and bad news. This hypothesis seems most plausible for the weekend effect, if the announcement of bad news is systematically postponed until after the close of trading on Friday. Several of the authors cited above mention this hypothesis, though it has not been seriously investigated.

These hypotheses all can explain why there might be patterns of buying and selling that coincide with calendar time. Of course, they are not consistent with the efficient market hypothesis since that hypothesis assumes that there is an infinitely elastic supply of arbitrageurs and traders ready to buy or sell whenever prices vary from their intrinsic values. However, there is reason to believe that the supply and demand elasticities of arbitrageurs is finite. For example, articles published nearly simultaneously by Shleifer (1986) and by Harris and Gurel (1986) found that in recent years when stocks are added to the S&P 500 index their prices rise immediately by a little under 3 percent. The authors argue convincingly that there is no information about quality embedded in the announcement that a stock has been added to the index. Rather, they attribute the price appreciation to the increased demand for the stocks by index funds, mutual funds that attempt to mimic the S&P index. Consistent with this explanation, the effect is more pronounced in the last few years as index funds have become an important segment of the institutional investment community. Also, Harris and Gurel found that the price increase is temporary: the price increases are dissipated within three weeks. Once the possibility of downward-sloping demand curves for stocks is conceded, then many possible explanations of anomalous price behavior can no longer be dismissed out of hand.

The three explanations described above are based on institutional considerations. One argument against these hypotheses is that some of the effects have been observed in experimental markets in which the relevant institutional features are missing. There are no cash inflows, no portfolios to be window dressed, and no news announcement in the experimental markets studied. Thus, Coursey and Dyl suggest that the weekend effect might be explained by psychological factors, such as a preference for compound gambles over simple gambles. Other behavioral explanations might incorporate variations in the mood of the market participants (good moods on Fridays and before holidays, bad moods on Mondays, etc.) It is well known, for example, that suicides occur more frequently on Mondays than on any other day.

What conclusions can be drawn from the seasonal anomaly literature at this time? Marc Reinganum (1984), one of the participants in this field, interprets the results as a challenge to theorists: ''What then do the anomalies mean? They mean that the theories of capital asset pricing (at least as they pertain to equity markets) have been toppled. They mean that the most interesting insights into the pricing behavior of stocks are being discovered by tedious and painstakingly thorough examination of data. They mean that, in the constant ebb and flow between theory and empirics, empirics currently holds the upper hand'' (p. 839). I don't agree. The ball is still in the empiricists' court. The clues that will allow us to understand these puzzles must come from additional econometric and experimental investigations. Only then can the formal modelers try to put the pieces together conceptually. The challenge, then, is really to all economists to try to understand why the seasonal price movements occur, and how they can persist for at least 90 years, and for at least 50 years after their existence has been published.

[12]

A Mean Reverting Walk Down Wall Street

It is your brother-in-law the stockbroker on the phone again. This time, he has been reading up on his statistics, an admirable thing to do. He excitedly tells you about his current "discovery"—regression toward the mean (or mean reversion). Mean reversion refers to the fact that in a chance process, very extreme observations are likely to be followed by less extreme observations. Children of very tall parents are likely to be tall, but shorter than their parents. A company that doubles its sales in one year is likely to grow less quickly in the next year. And so forth. Mean reversion is a fact of nature. Your brother-in-law's idea is that this concept could be applied to the stock market. He figures that stocks that have done very poorly over some period should do better in the next period, and, conversely, last period's big winners should be next period's losers. He asks you what you think.

Patiently, you explain to him that his idea must be wrong. You remind him of Burton Malkiel's famous book *A Random Walk Down Wall Street* which summarizes the massive evidence that stock prices follow a "random walk." That is, future stock prices cannot be predicted from past price movements. If stock prices were mean reverting, then they would be predictable, and all economists know that can't be true. "Hah!" he says. "I

With Werner F. M. De Bondt.

> thought you might mention that. It is obvious that you
> have not been keeping up with the recent literature in
> finance. Randomness is passé—mean reversion is in!"
> He hangs up, and you scurry off to the library.

Few propositions in economics are held with more fervor than the view that financial markets are "efficient" and that the prices of securities in such markets are equal to their intrinsic values. For stocks, prices should reflect a rational forecast of the present value of future dividend payments. The efficient market hypothesis has also been traditionally associated with the assertion that future price changes are unpredictable[1] or, in the language of finance texts, efficient capital markets "have no memory" (Brealey and Myers, 1988, p. 289). The logic of this assertion is simple and compelling. If stock prices were predictable, knowledgeable investors would buy cheap and sell dear. Soon, the forces of competition and rational arbitrage would guarantee that prices adjust, only to move again, randomly, in response to unanticipated events.

Many early observers of financial markets, however, believed that security prices could diverge from their fundamental values. For example, in *The General Theory*, Keynes (1936, pp. 153–54) argued that "day-to-day fluctuations in the profits of existing investments, which are obviously of an ephemeral and non-significant character, tend to have an altogether excessive, and even an absurd, influence on the market." Williams (1938; 1956, p. 19) notes in his *Theory of Investment Value* that "prices have been based too much on current earning power, too little on long-run dividend paying power."

More recently, the idea that fashions and fads in investor attitudes (or other types of systematic "irrationality") may affect stock prices has gained new respectability with work by, among others, Shiller (1984), De Long, Shleifer, Summers, and Waldmann (1987), and Shefrin and Statman (1988). These papers investigate economies with both rational "information" traders and

---

[1]Price changes would be expected to be totally unpredictable if expected returns were zero. Actually, since stock prices drift up, there is a predictable positive return. However, over short time intervals, expected returns are so small that they are swamped by the return volatility. Some adherents of the efficient market hypothesis no longer believe that predictability implies market inefficiency. The new view is explained below.

irrational "noise" traders. Even though specifics differ, *rational information trading* is usually thought to be based upon the objectivity correct probability distribution of returns, conditional on what is known at the time. In contrast, *noise trading* is based upon incorrect conditional probability assessments. In a world populated by noise traders, there is no theoretical certainty that rational traders dominate the market or that noise traders become extinct, even in the long run. In fact, under plausible conditions, noise traders can even outperform "rational arbitrageurs." Also, prices do not necessarily equal intrinsic value. However, so long as prices have any tendency to gravitate back to fundamentals, they will be mean reverting over long horizons, i.e. they are somewhat predictable and not a random walk.

Whether stock prices *are* predictable is an old question. Eugene Fama's classic (1965, p. 34) paper on this subject begins as follows: "For many years the following question has been a source of continuing controversy in both academic and business circles: To what extent can the past history of a common stock's price be used to make meaningful predictions concerning the future price of the stock?" He concludes some sixty pages later (p. 98): "It seems safe to say that this paper has presented strong and voluminous evidence in favor of the random-walk hypothesis." However, a more recent paper by Fama and French (forthcoming, p. 1) has a rather different opening sentence: "There is much evidence that stock returns are predictable."

Indeed, stock prices do appear to be somewhat predictable. In particular, if one takes a long-term perspective (three–seven years) or examines individual securities that have experienced extreme price movements, then stock returns display significant negative serial correlation, in other words, prices are mean reverting. This chapter reviews some of this evidence.[2]

MEAN REVERSION IN STOCK MARKET AVERAGES

The early empirical investigations which led to Fama's 1965 conclusion that stock prices were unpredictable stressed simple

[2]For a more extensive survey of the literature and a more complete bibliography, see De Bondt (forthcoming). One topic that we do not discuss is what (prior to October 1987) used to be called the excess volatility "debate." For a review of this literature, see West (1988). As Campbell and Shiller (1988) stress, excess volatility implies predictability, so the issues are closely related.

short-run correlations using data bases that, at least by modern standards, seem small. Fama's study investigated whether there was any serial correlation in the day-to-day price changes of the 30 stocks composing the Dow Jones Industrial Average for the period 1957–1962. Though Fama found statistically significant positive serial correlation, he concluded that the correlations were too small to be of any economic significance. However, if the time period is lengthened, and the number of stocks are increased, new patterns emerge. For example, French and Roll (1986) repeat Fama's tests for all NYSE and AMEX stocks during the 1963–1982 period. They report small but significant negative serial correlation in daily returns—positive returns are likely to be followed by negative returns, and vice versa.

Much larger and economically more important correlations are found by examining longer time periods. For example, the procedure adopted by Fama and French (1988) is simply to regress the return on a stock market index over some time period of length T, on returns over the prior period of equal length. If prices are a random walk, then the slope in the regression should be zero. If prices are mean reverting, then the slope should be negative. Fama and French used monthly nominal return data from 1926 to 1985 for firms listed on the New York Stock Exchange. They studied both equal-weighted and value-weighted indexes as well as the returns to decile portfolios formed on the basis of the size of the firms.[3]

The results reveal considerable mean reversion. The slopes of the regressions are generally negative for horizons from 18 months to five years. Both the explanatory power (R^2) and the slope increase with the length of the horizon, T, up to 5 years, then decrease. The mean reversion is stronger for portfolios of smaller firms and for the equal-weighted index than for the large-firm portfolios or the value-weighted index. The mean reversion also has declined over time, with the results for the sub-period 1941–1985 weaker than for the earlier period.

The fact that prices are mean reverting implies that prices are

---

[3]An equal-weighted index counts every stock the same, whereas a value-weighted index counts bigger firms more heavily. The procedure for creating size-based decile portfolios is to rank all the NYSE firms that appear on the Center for Research in Security Prices (CRSP) computer tape based on their market value (price of the stock times number of shares outstanding). Then decile portfolios are formed with the smallest 10 percent of the firms in the first portfolio, etc.

predictable. Regressing a three- to five-year future return on past annual returns yields substantial forecasting power. For the equal-weighted index and the smallest quintile the R^2 is about .4. The R^2 is about .3 for the middle quintiles, and above .2 for the largest quintile and the value-weighted index. Thus about 25–40 percent of the three- to five-year returns are predictable from past returns. Even better forecasts are possible using the current market dividend yield, that is, the price divided by the dividend (Fama and French, forthcoming).

Fama and French's results have been replicated and extended by Poterba and Summers (forthcoming) using a variance ratio test. This test exploits the fact that if the log of stock prices follows a random walk, then the return variance should be proportional to the return horizon. That is, the variance of monthly returns should be one-twelfth of the variance of annual returns, which in turn should be one-fifth of the variance of five-year returns. The variance ratios are scaled so that if returns are uncorrelated the ratios equal 1.0. A variance ratio of less than one implies negative serial correlation; a ratio greater than one implies positive serial correlation. While Poterba and Summers conclude that the variance ratio test is best, they show that even it has limited power to test the random walk model against plausible alternatives. They argue that it may be appropriate to reject the null hypothesis (of a random walk) at confidence levels higher than the conventional .05. The point is that while the tests may not always reject the random walk, they clearly do not reject mean reversion either.

Poterba and Summers first confirmed Fama and French's results for both real returns and returns in excess of a treasury bill yield. They found that the variance of eight-year returns is about four (rather than eight) times the variance of annual returns. For horizons of less than one year, however, returns display some positive serial correlation (see also Lo and MacKinlay, 1988). They also examine various sub-periods. The evidence for mean reversion over long horizons is weaker if the depression years before World War II are excluded. However, there appears to be substantial mean reversion in nominal and excess returns over the period 1871–1925.[4]

Poterba and Summers also investigated whether mean rever-

[4]The mean reversion for real returns is weaker. Poterba and Summers argue that this may be produced by the ''jagged character of the Consumer Price Index series in the years before 1900.''

sion can be found on the stock exchanges of other countries. They used data for Canada since 1919, Britain since 1939, and fifteen other countries for shorter post-war periods. The Canadian and British markets display patterns similar to those found in the U.S., namely strong mean reversion over long time horizons, and some positive serial correlation over short horizons. The eight-year variance ratios are .585 for Canada and .794 for Britain. Most of the other countries also display negative serial correlation at long horizons, the only exceptions being Finland, South Africa, and Spain. The average eight-year variance ratio for all non-U.S. counties is .754 (or .653 if Spain, a distinct outlier, is excluded.) From the international evidence, Poterba and Summers concluded that mean reversion is more pronounced in less broad-based and less sophisticated (foreign) equity markets.

In the face of this evidence, adherents of efficient markets must search for rational explanations of why equilibrium expected returns vary over time. Following a line of argument suggested by Shiller (1981), one might ask how much expected returns in the stock market would have to vary to account for the observed changes in stock prices. Poterba and Summers (forthcoming) calculated that the annual standard deviation of expected returns would have to be between 4.4 percent and 15.8 percent. Given the fact that investors will only put money into stocks if there is a positive expected return—if the expected return in stocks is not positive, they can always keep their money in a bank account—the variances calculated by Poterba and Summers would imply that expected returns must exceed 20 percent fairly regularly. They judged 20 percent to be too high an expected return to be plausible in a world with only rational investors. (We agree. Wouldn't you buy stocks if you thought the expected return were 20 percent?). Since the power of the statistical tests is low and the tests do not permit us to reject either hypothesis, judgments of this sort are a necessary part of evaluating the evidence.

MEAN REVERSION IN THE CROSS SECTION

One type of mean reversion in cross-sectional stock prices has been discussed in the literature at least since the time of Benjamin Graham (1949), one of the pioneers of security analysis. He advocated the purchase of stocks whose prices seemed low relative to their fundamental value. This *contrarian* advice is based on the premise that such prices are temporarily low, and can be expected to bounce back after one or two years.

Modern empirical work suggests that simple contrarian strategies do yield excess returns. For example, Basu (1977) showed that the strategy of buying stocks with low price to earnings per share ratios (P/E-ratios) yields "abnormal" returns over and above the "normal" required returns that represent compensation for risk. (Similarly, firms with high P/Es earn below-normal returns.) Basu offers the "price-ratio hypothesis" to explain the results. Companies with low P/Es are temporarily undervalued because the market gets inappropriately pessimistic about current or future earnings. Eventually, however, actual earnings growth differs predictably from the growth rate impounded in the price. Price corrections and the P/E anomaly inexorably follow. Also consistent with the hypothesis, earning yields affect the association between annual income numbers and share prices (Basu, 1978). During the 12 months that lead up to the announcement date, unanticipated increases in earnings cause larger positive residual returns to securities with low P/Es than to securities with high P/Es.

Similar results apply to other contrarian indicators such as the dividend yield (high dividend yields may suggest that a firm's stock price is too low) or the ratio of the price of the stock to the book value per share, an accounting measure of the value of the firm's assets. Stocks with very high dividend yields or very low price to book value ratios also earn abnormal returns after normal risk adjustments (Keim, 1985; Rosenberg, Reid, and Lanstein, 1985).

Our own research on this topic (De Bondt and Thaler, 1985, 1987) was motivated by the hypothesis that the contrarian strategies are successful because of systematic investor overreaction. There is substantial evidence in the psychology literature that individuals tend to overweight recent data in making forecasts and judgments (Kahneman and Tversky, 1973; Grether, 1980). If this behavior is manifest in financial markets, then we expected to observe mean reverting returns to the stocks that had experienced extremely good or bad returns over the past few years.

To test for this possibility, our 1985 paper studied the investment performance of (35 stock, 50 stock, or decile) portfolios of

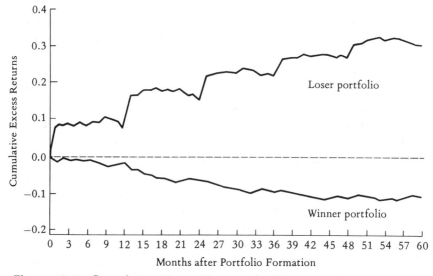

Figure 12–1. Cumulative Excess Returns for Winner and Loser Portfolios

Source: De Bondt and Thaler (1985).

long-term winners and losers, i.e. exceptional performers over prior "formation periods" ranging between one to five years. We used monthly return data for the 1926–1982 period and considered all stocks listed on the NYSE for possible inclusion. In one such experiment, portfolios of the 35 most extreme winners and losers over the five years between January 1928 and December 1932 were formed and then followed for the next five years (the "test period"). The same experiment was conducted 46 times by advancing the starting data one year each time. Finally, average test period performance in excess of the mean return on a NYSE index (giving equal weight to each company on the exchange) was computed.

The test period findings are displayed in Figure 12–1. Three aspects of the results stand out. First, the returns for both winners and losers are mean reverting. Prior losers outperform the market average, while prior winners underperform.) Second, the price reversals for losers[5] are more pronounced than for winners (about

---

[5]The excess returns to the losers are not caused by a "survivorship bias." To enter the sample a firm must only be listed as of the start of the test period. If a firm goes bankrupt, or is otherwise delisted during the test period, we "sell" the stock at the next price at which the stock is traded; if necessary at zero. In fact, however, few NYSE firms actually go bankrupt, even within our loser sample.

+30 percent versus about −10 percent excess return). Third, most of the excess returns for losers occur in January, as shown by the five sharp jumps in the return line. These three qualitative results are observed in all the versions of the study we conducted. In addition, and consistent with overreaction, it appears that the more extreme are the initial price movements, the greater are the subsequent reversals. For formation periods of three to five years, an "arbitrage" strategy that buys losers by selling winners short earns average annual returns ranging between 5 and 8 percent, with most of the returns occurring in Januaries.[6]

Two sorts of explanations have been offered for the apparent excess returns earned by the losers. 1. The losers tend to be smaller than average firms. It has been established that small firms earn abnormally high returns (though mostly in January; see Banz, 1981, Keim, 1983), so perhaps the "losing firm effect" is simply a reincarnation of the small firm effect. 2. Since the losers have obviously been having a rough time financially, perhaps they have become substantially riskier, and the apparent excess return is simply a normal return to their high level of risk. We find neither explanation completely satisfactory.

There is, certainly, a relationship between the size effect and the losing firm effect. The firms in our loser portfolios have lost a substantial portion of their value. Since firm size is usually measured by the market value of equity (share price times number of shares outstanding), the losing firms became much "smaller" during the formation period. Nevertheless, the losers are not the same very small firms normally associated with the small firm effect. In our 1987 paper we replicated our original results with NYSE and AMEX firms from a COMPUSTAT sample covering the period 1966–1983. We found that even quintile portfolios of losing firms (less extreme performers than the stocks studied in our earlier paper) earn about 25 percent above the market over a four-year period after portfolio formation. These firms had an average market value of $304 million. In contrast, the mean market value of the smallest quintile of firms is only $9 million. Also, these very small firms have, on average, fallen in price over the past few years. That is, they are losers. So, while losing firms tend to be smaller than average, and small firms tend to be prior losers, it seems that there are two anomalies here, not one.

---

[6]The excess returns in January do not depend on when the investment strategy starts. There are still excess returns in January for portfolios formed, say, in July.

Nevertheless, Fama and French (1986) and Zarowin (1988) both argue that the losing firm effect is subsumed by the size effect. Fama and French first formed decile portfolios ranked by size. Then within each size portfolio they examined the returns for three-year winner and loser *quartiles*. They found that the losers outperform the winners, but insignificantly except in January. In contrast to our results, they found stronger reversals for the winners than for the losers. Using a similar approach Zarowin found that the three-year return on an arbitrage (loser minus winner) portfolio ranges from 7 to 19 percent for the smallest four quintiles, but is virtually zero for the largest quintile. However, none of the returns are significantly different from zero.

Since both winners and losers tend to be relatively small, it follows mechanically that computing excess returns relative to a size-matched portfolio will decrease the returns to losers and increase the returns to winners. However, without any theory explaining how the market value of a company may proxy for its investment risk, it is difficult to interpret size-adjusted returns. Why should a portfolio of many small firms represent a more risky investment than just one conglomerate firm of equivalent size?

More generally, the argument that the apparent excess return to losers or small firms is compensation for risk, however understood, cannot be falsified in the absence of operational risk measures suggested by economic theory. The most common risk measure used in finance remains the capital asset pricing model (CAPM) beta. The CAPM beta is the coefficient of the return on the security regressed on the return on the market index. Beta measures the degree to which a security's price variability cannot be smoothed out and diversified away, even by an investor who chooses to hold the market portfolio. Only this "systematic" risk should be priced in equilibrium.

If the CAPM beta is an adequate risk measure, then the difference between the winner and the loser returns cannot be attributed to differences in risk. If beta is measured over the formation period, in fact, the losers have lower betas than the winners. However, Chan (1988) argues that one should look at the test period betas, since risk may have changed as the losers were losing and the winners were winning. Still, the test period betas are only slightly higher for losers than for winners (1.263 versus 1.043) and this estimated risk difference is not capable of explaining the gap in returns. Actually, it may well be argued, at least intuitively, that the beta difference is misleading because both winners and losers have very peculiar time patterns of returns. In De Bondt and Thaler (1987) we estimated for both portfolios two types of betas: one for periods when the market portfolio is rising in value, and one for periods when the market is falling. (An implicit assumption of the CAPM is that these two betas are equal.) In the test period, the loser portfolio has a bull market beta of 1.39 and a bear market beta of .88. This implies that the losers go up 13.9 percent when the market goes up to 10 percent, but the losers only fall 8.8 percent when the market falls 10 percent. This doesn't seem too risky to us! In contrast, the loser portfolio's bull and bear betas are .99 and 1.20, respectively. Combining them we find that the arbitrage portfolio has a bull beta of .40 and a bear beta of − .32. This means that, on average, the arbitrage portfolio goes up when the market goes up, and goes up when the market falls.

SHORT-TERM MEAN REVERSION

One way of testing the size and risk explanations of the loser price reversals is to examine shorter time horizons. If a stock falls or rises 10 percent in a day, it is unlikely that the objective risk of the stock has changed significantly, and obviously its size has changed only by 10 percent. Thus if mean reversion is observed over very brief time periods, factors other than size or objective risk can be assumed to be at work.

Several studies have used a design similar to the one we used to examine short-term price movements. We will describe one of these studies in detail, and present the key results of the other studies in Table 12–1. The study we will concentrate on is by Bremer and Sweeney (1991). For the period July 1962 to December 1986 they considered all the cases where a Fortune 500 company had a one-day price change of 10 percent or greater. (They also reported the results for cutoffs of 7.5 percent or 15 percent.) By considering only large firms, Bremer and Sweeney eliminated several possible objections to their results. For example, for very

Table 12–1 Short-Term Price Reversals: An Overview of the Literature

	Sample	Methods	Summary of selected findings
Dyl and Maxfield (1987)	daily returns 1974–1984 NYSE and AMEX companies	buy/sell 3 stocks with largest price one-day loss/gain on 200 trading days selected at random	next 10 trading days winners: −1.8 percent losers: +3.6 percent
Bremer and Sweeney (1991)	daily returns 1962–1986 Fortune 500 companies	all one-day (absolute) returns in excess of 7 1/2, 10, or 15 percent	next 5 trading days winners: −.004 percent losers: + 3.95 percent
Brown, Harlow and Tinic (1988)	daily returns 1963–1985 200 largest companies in the S&P 500	all one-day (market model) residual returns in excess of (absolute) 2 1/2 percent	next 10 trading days winners: +.003 percent losers: +.37 percent
Howe (1986)	weekly returns 1963–1981 NYSE and AMEX companies	all returns that rise or fall more than 50 percent within one week	next 10 weeks winners: −13.0 percent losers: +13.8 percent
Lehmann (1988)	weekly returns 1962–1986 NYSE and AMEX companies	buy all stocks that lagged the market during the previous week ("losers") and sell short the equivalent "winners"	for $1 long in zero-investment arbitrage portfolio, earn 39 cents every 6 months; 2/3 of profits generated by prior "losers"
Rosenberg, Reid, and Lanstein (1985)	monthly returns 1981–1984 NYSE companies	buy stocks with negative residuals (relative to multi-factor model) and sell short stocks	arbitrage portfolio earns 1.36 percent per month; profits mostly gener-

	Sample	Methods	Summary of selected findings
		with positive residuals over the previous month	ated by prior "losers"
Jegadeesh (1987)	monthly returns 1945–1980 NYSE companies	regressions relating Sharpe-Lintner residual returns to raw returns of previous month and returns in earlier years	extreme decile portfolios: difference in residual returns is 2.5 percent per month
Brown and Van Harlow (1988)	1- to 6-month returns; 1946–1983 NYSE companies	study stocks with residual returns that gain/lose (between absolute) 20 and 65 percent between one to six months	large rebounds for losers; no decline for winners except in first month

low-priced stocks large percentage price changes could reflect (in part) the bid-ask spread. However, since large firms' stock prices tend to be traded for more than $10 a share, this problem should not be of great importance.[7] Also, it is clear that the small firm effect cannot be invoked to explain any anomalous results.

For Bremer and Sweeney's sample there are 1,305 price declines and 3,218 increases. Stock prices are then tracked for 20 days after the jump. For losers, after five days the stocks have earned a 3.95 percent return. (The average initial drop was about 13 percent.) For the cutoff values of 7.5 percent and 15 percent, the five-day excess returns are 2.84 percent and 6.18 percent. Winners, on the other hand, show virtually no excess returns in the period immediately following the event.

Notice that the pattern of returns following these large one-day jumps is remarkably similar to that observed for long-term winners and losers. That is, there is a significant correction for losers but not for winners, and the correction increases with the size of

[7]Indeed, Bremer and Sweeney tested for this problem by deleting all firms with share prices less than $10 and found that the first post-event day returns were virtually unaffected.

the initial price jump. As shown in Table 12–1, this pattern is repeated in most of the other studies of large, short-run price changes.

There is one more study of short-term price reversals that deserves mention but differs from the other papers summarized in Table 12–1. This is the paper by Lehmann (1988). Using weekly returns, Lehmann studied the profitability of a return reversal strategy which finances its purchases of short-term losers (the stocks that underperformed the market over the previous week) by selling short winners (the stocks that outperformed the market). Unlike the other papers summarized in Table 12–1, Lehmann's research was not limited to extreme performers. Almost all securities listed on the NYSE and AMEX over the period 1962–1986 are included in his strategy. However, the dollar amount invested in each security is proportional to its (absolute) weekly excess return, i.e., extreme performers carry more weight in the arbitrage portfolio. Typically, there are more than 2,000 round trip transactions per week.

Because of the large number of transactions, the profitability of this strategy depends critically on the level of transactions costs. For floor traders, however, the strategy is extraordinarily successful. If transactions costs are assumed to be 0.1 percent each way, then portfolios which are long $100 million of losers and short $100 million of winners earn average six-month profits of $38.77 million, with about two-thirds of the profit generated by the losers. Consistent with the other studies, the winners and losers that gained or lost the most experience the largest reversals.

COMMENTARY

Risk and Perceived Risk. Many fields of inquiry have idiosyncratic disclaimers. In finance, a popular disclaimer in papers reporting anomalies is this: "Of course, it is not possible to test for market efficiency directly. It is only possible to conduct *joint* tests of market efficiency and some model of equilibrium prices." In light of this problem, Fama and French (1986, p. 23) conclude:

> The tendency toward reversal . . . may reflect time-varying expected returns generated by rational investor behavior and the

dynamics of common macro-economic driving variables. On the other hand, reversals generated by a stationary component of prices may reflect market-wide waves of over-reaction of the kind assumed in models of an inefficient market. . . . Whether predictability reflects market inefficiency or time-varying expected returns generated by rational investor behavior is, and will remain, an open issue.

This is an open-minded but pessimistic conclusion. Are market rationality and irrationality indistinguishable? We think it is premature to give up.

Consider the problem of discriminating between overreaction and risk as explanations for mean reversion. If the excess return to losers or the mean reversion in market indexes is to be satisfactorily explained by some as yet poorly understood risk measure, then it will also be necessary to show that the (time-varying) risk is "real." There is substantial evidence in other domains that perceived risk and actual risks can diverge. For example, people judge the risk of death by homicide to be greater than the risk of death by diabetes or stomach cancer, though the actual numbers of deaths are about 18,000, 39,000, and 95,000 per annum, respectively (Slovic, Fischhoff, and Lichtenstein, 1982).

To get a sense of how a model with faulty risk perceptions might work, suppose that (marginal) investors judge the risk of both extreme winners and losers to be greater than the objective risk. Losers might be considered very risky because bankruptcy risk is overestimated. Winners might be considered risky because they appear to have so much "down-side potential." Such firms will bear an excess risk premium, forcing prices lower. Suppose further that investors have a tendency to overreact to recent trends, failing to make proper Bayesian forecasts. This combination of misperceived risks and faulty judgments could explain the observed asymmetry in returns to winners and losers. That is, losers show price reversals because the overreaction effect and the excess risk premium both work in the same direction (lowering prices). When information comes in and investors discover that their fears and predictions were biased, prices increase. For winners, however, the overreaction effect drives prices too high while the excess risk premium forces prices down. Since the two effects go in the opposite direction, the reversals to winners should be smaller or non-existent, as observed.

Event Studies. The assumption of efficient capital markets is incorporated in the *event study* methods now popular in accounting, industrial organization, and finance. Event studies attempt to measure the financial impact of a change in the company's environment by focusing on the change in the firm's stock market value around the time that news about it first became known to the public. Typical events include takeover bids, new equity issues, changes in accounting rules, or a change in the tax law. Many event studies, e.g., those which draw policy conclusions, take it as an article of faith that the change in market value is an unbiased estimate of the change in "fundamentals." It is an article of faith because, as far as we know, there is no evidence to support this claim. Suppose one firm buys another and increases in value by 10 percent. This represents the market's estimate of the net present value of the acquisition. To test whether this estimate is unbiased, one would want to look at a long enough period of time for the actual results of the merger to be realized. Do the managers get along? Does the synergy that was hoped for actually occur? Is top management overextended? Were the buyers subject to the winner's curse? Perhaps after five years or so it would be possible to answer most of these questions. So, one measure of whether the event day price is unbiased is whether it is an accurate forecast of the price five years later. Unfortunately, stock prices are so variable that we have no real way to test this hypothesis.

In this context, the Bremer and Sweeney paper may be thought of as an "event study of event studies." Since such studies focus on large price changes, what Bremer and Sweeney have done in essence is to collect a series of events without specifying what they are. For positive events, the market yields unbiased estimates (as judged two weeks or so later) while, for negative events, the immediate price reaction appears biased. Our own results for long-term losers suggest a similar conclusion. For companies that experience a series of "bad events," the price correction may take several years.

Concluding Remarks. Financial markets are fertile territory for anomaly mining. However, we do not think that anomalies are so abundant in finance because the theories are worse than in other areas of economics. Rather, anomalies are common because the theories are unusually well specified (so they can be tested) and the data are unusually rich. This combination of well-specified models, good data, and many anomalies makes finance an extremely exciting research area. The real challenge facing the field is to develop new theories of asset pricing that are consistent with known empirical facts *and* offer new testable predictions. We are pessimistic about the chances of success for traditional models in which all agents are assumed to be fully rational. Models in which some agents have non-rational expectations of future cash flows, or have faulty risk perceptions, seem to us to offer greater promise. However, the current state of these models does not permit them to be carefully tested. When such tests become possible, it may well turn out that these models are in as much conflict with the data as is the traditional framework.

[13]

Closed-End Mutual Funds

Y our brother-in-law the stockbroker is on the phone
again. This time he starts out badly: "Have I got a deal
for you! I have found a way for you to buy stocks at a
discount!" You ask him (hopefully) whether he means
that you should switch to a discount broker (which he
isn't). "No," he says. "That's peanuts. Even my fees
are less than 1 percent of the price of the stock. I am
talking here about buying stocks at 10–20 percent off the
'retail' price, sometimes even more." You, of course, are
suspicious of this concept, so you press him on how he
can do this. "Closed-end funds," he says. He asks if
you know what they are and you mumble so he tells
you. "Closed-end funds are mutual funds whose shares
are traded on the major exchanges. If you own shares in
these funds and want to sell them, you sell the shares
on the market, rather than redeem them from the fund.
It turns out that some of these funds sell at prices which
are substantially less than the value of the stocks that
they own. A fund with assets worth $20 a share might
sell for only $17 a share—a healthy 15 percent discount.
Pretty good deal, huh!" You tell him that there must be
a catch, but you will look into these things . . .

Testing the efficient markets hypothesis is often difficult. For example, one implication of the hypothesis is that there are no free
lunches, no easy ways to make money. However, apparent viola-

With Charles M. C. Lee and Andrei Shleifer.

tions of this implication, such as mean reversion in asset prices, are said by many to be evidence of variation in risk, which is consistent with the efficient markets hypothesis. Another implication of the efficient markets hypothesis is that asset prices should be equal to their intrinsic or fundamental values, that is, the expected present values of future cash flows. One finance professor we know used to refer to this version of the efficient markets hypothesis as *The Price is Right!* Testing whether the price is right is hard, of course, because intrinsic values are not easily observable. How are we to know, now, what the present value of IBM's future dividends will be?

There does turn out to be one class of securities whose intrinsic values are relatively easy to measure, the so-called *closed-end mutual funds* (now officially known as *publicly traded funds*). Most mutual funds are open-end funds in the sense that the fund stands ready to accept more money at any time and will redeem shares for current stockholders at the "net asset value" of fund, that is, the market value (per share) of the securities the fund holds. In the case of a closed-end fund, the management raises a certain amount of capital, say $100 million, buys a portfolio of securities which it will manage according to its charter, and then issues a fixed number of shares, say 10 million. The shares are traded on organized stock markets, including the New York Stock Exchange. Any stockholder who wants to liquidate must sell the shares at the market price. The share price, of course, is set by supply and demand, and therefore can diverge from the net asset value. Indeed, the stock prices of closed-end funds often do diverge from net asset values. Funds selling for less than their net asset value are said to trade at a discount, while those selling for more than net asset value are said to sell at a premium. During 1989, for example, it was possible to find some funds selling at substantial discounts (greater than 30 percent) and others selling for enormous premia (in one case over 100 percent). In the case of closed-end funds, therefore, it is common to find that the price is wrong!

A FOUR-PART ANOMALY

The pricing of closed-end funds presents several puzzles. The following are the four sets of facts that any theory of closed-end fund pricing must address.

1. New funds appear on the market with some regularity. New funds tend to get started when the existing funds are selling at premia or small discounts (Lee, Shleifer, and Thaler, 1991a). When the new funds are released, they are sold with a commission of roughly 7 percent. This means that investors have to pay $107 to obtain $100 worth of assets. When they first start to trade, the funds usually trade at a small premium. Weiss (1989), Peavy (1988), and Laing (1987) all document striking evidence of underperformance by new closed-end funds. Weiss (1989), for example, found that from 1985 to 1987, 20 days after the initial offering, U.S. stock funds traded at an average premium of almost 5 percent. However, 120 days after the initial offering, these funds sold for an average discount of over 10 percent. This means that the returns to holding these stocks over this period were −25.1 percent. So: Why does anyone buy these funds when they are first issued?

2. Closed-end funds usually trade at substantial discounts relative to their net asset values. Over the period 1965–1985 the (value-weighted) average discount on a portfolio of major closed-end stock funds in the U.S. was 10.1 percent. Though discounts are the norm, some funds (and in some unusual periods, most funds) sell at premia. In recent years, premia have been most common for funds specializing in investment in foreign countries. So, puzzle two: Why aren't prices equal to net asset values, and why are discounts the norm?

3. Discounts (and premia) are subject to wide variation, both over time and across funds. The largest stock fund traded in the U.S. is the Tricontinental Fund (Tricon) which holds a diversified portfolio of common stocks. The year-end price for Tricon has varied over the last 30 years from a 2.5 percent premium to a 25 percent discount. In 1988, the price at each week's end ranged from a 6.7 percent premium to a 17.9 percent discount.

Though fund discounts vary greatly over time, their movements are positively correlated. Lee, Shleifer, and Thaler (1991a) studied nine of the largest and oldest funds over the period 1965–1985 and found that discounts were highly correlated. Monthly levels of discounts for individual firms typically had correlation coefficients of greater than .5. Monthly changes were also positively correlated, with coefficients typically between .2 and .4. Average discounts also display a seasonal pattern which will not be a surprise in light of the evidence in Chapters 11 and 12. Yes, discounts tend to shrink in the month of January. This result is quite striking because Brauer and Chang (1989) found that the assets the funds own did not display a January effect.

Discounts also vary widely across funds. It is common to see some funds selling for large discounts while others sell at substantial premia. Even within specific categories of funds, such as diversified domestic funds, or single country foreign funds, there is wide variation in the discounts at a point in time. So, why do discounts move together and why do they vary so much, over time and across funds?

4. When closed-end funds are terminated, either through merger, liquidation, or being converted to an open-end fund, prices converge to reported net asset value (Brauer, 1984; Brickley and Schallheim, 1985). This fact may not seem to be a puzzle. If a fund is converted to an open-end fund, or liquidated, its assets will be redeemed at net asset value, so of course the price should be equal to net asset value at the time of termination. However, some theories of closed-end fund pricing argue that reported net asset values are mismeasured. If this were the case, then net asset value would fall to the market price when a fund is liquidated, rather than the price rising to the net asset value. So, when funds are open-ended, why does the price rise to eliminate the discount?

These four puzzles raise basic questions about the operation of financial markets. How can prices diverge from fundamental values? Why don't the forces of arbitrage drive prices back in line? These are the questions addressed in this chapter.

STANDARD EXCUSES

To what extent can these facts be explained within the standard paradigm of rational expectations and efficient markets? Two types of explanations have been offered. The first is based on misbehavior by the fund's managers. The second is based on miscalculation of net asset value.

Agency Costs

Might the mere existence of fund managers explain the closed-end fund puzzles? There are two possibilities worth considering.

First, the funds charge a management fee, typically between .5 and 2.0 percent of the asset value, annually. One argument is that the existence of these fees implies that funds will sell at a discount in equilibrium. Consider a fund with a 1 percent annual fee. At a discount rate of 10 percent, the present value of these fees accumulated forever corresponds to a discount of roughly 10 percent. Upon scrutiny, however, this argument does not hold up. Large closed-end funds, such as Tricon, charge fees that are comparable to those of large no-load mutual funds. Since both are providing similar services, it would seem that both should sell at the same price. But if closed-end funds sell at a discount, investors are getting a higher yield from them than from open-end funds (since they are buying more assets for their money). The existence of fees, then, does not imply that funds should sell at discounts.[1] There is also no evidence that discounts are correlated with management fees (Malkiel, 1977; Lee, Shleifer, and Thaler, 1991b).

The second aspect to consider is managerial performance. Boudreaux (1973) pointed out that the net asset value represents expected returns of the present portfolio, but since fund managers buy and sell securities, discounts might reflect their differential ability to perform this task. But unless some managers have figured out a way to systematically underperform the market (itself an anomaly, of course), this explanation does not explain why funds usually trade at discounts. For relative performance to explain the variation in discounts, large discounts should forecast poor future performance, and premia should forecast extraordinary future returns. So, for example, the premia observed when funds start should forecast superior returns. In contrast, discounts observed a few months later suggest that investors quickly become disenchanted, and are predicting below-normal performance. Logic suggests that it is impossible for both predictions to be rational, and the empirical evidence suggests that neither prediction is fulfilled. Malkiel (1977) investigated the relationship between the *past* performance of the fund's assets and discounts, and Roenfeldt and Tuttle (1973) investigated contemporaneous performance. The former found no relationship and the latter a weak one. However, Lee, Shleifer, and Thaler (1991b) found that *future* net asset value performance is weakly related to present

---

[1] This argument was suggested by Ken French. Timothy Taylor has pointed out to us that one could alternatively view the fact that people are willing to invest in open-end funds without a discount as the anomaly.

discounts and the relationship has the "wrong" sign. That is, funds with bigger discounts tend to have higher future performance than those with smaller discounts. We conclude that agency costs cannot even explain the primary fact they are alleged to address, the existence of discounts. Agency costs do even less well on the other parts of the puzzle. For example, if agency costs are positive, then funds should never get started (at a premium) as long as no-load open-end funds exist. Indeed, a premium for any fund implies negative agency costs in this framework. Agency costs also cannot explain the wide variations of discounts over time. Neither management fees (which are extremely stable) nor expectations of performance can possibly vary enough to explain the observed time-series movement of individual fund discounts, nor the variation in the average discount across funds. The only fact consistent with agency costs is the disappearance of discounts when funds are terminated.

Restricted Stocks

A divergence between price and net asset value is not an anomaly if net asset value does not reflect the true value of the fund to the shareholders. One way in which the portfolio might be misvalued is if the fund held large quantities of stocks which cannot be freely sold in the open market. It makes sense for closed-end funds to hold illiquid stocks, since unlike open-end funds, they cannot be forced to liquidate their shares because of a sudden rash of redemptions of fundholders. Such stocks, some have argued, are valued too highly in the calculation of net asset value. In fact, both Malkiel (1977) and Lee, Shleifer, and Thaler (1991b) find that restricted stock holdings can explain some portion of the cross-sectional variation in discounts. Nevertheless, restricted stock holdings cannot explain much of the closed-end fund puzzle. Most closed-end funds, including Tricon, hold little or no restricted stocks and yet still sell at discounts. Also, the amount of restricted stock any given fund holds does not vary much over time, so this variable cannot explain much of the time-series variability of discounts. Finally, and most fundamentally, when funds are open-ended, the price rises to net asset value. If restricted holdings were overvalued, the net asset value should instead drop down to the price.

Taxes

Another reason why the true value of the fund's portfolio might be misvalued by net asset value is capital gains taxation. When a fund realizes a capital gain it must report this to the Internal Revenue Service. The tax liability is borne by the existing shareholders at the time the gain is realized by the fund. So if you buy a fund today and it realizes a large capital gain tomorrow, you must pay a tax even if you haven't made any money. This implies that a fund with large unrealized capital appreciation is worth less than net asset value to both existing and potential shareholders, and should thus sell at a discount. This explanation, like the others, has some apparent merit but fails to explain all the facts. Malkiel (1977) calculated that under fairly generous assumptions, taxes could not explain a discount of more than 6 percent. Obviously, the larger discounts that are often observed remain a mystery. Also, according to the tax story, discounts should increase when the market rises, since unrealized capital gains will be accumulating. Lee, Shleifer, and Thaler (1991a) present evidence counter to this implication. And, once again, the fact that prices rise to net asset values upon liquidation suggests that the tax liabilities are not major.

In summary, a number of reasons have been put forth to explain closed-end fund discounts in the context of the efficient markets hypothesis and rational agents. Several of these factors do have some merit, but, taken together, these factors explain only a small portion of the total variations in discounts.

Closed-End Fund Premia

Although most of the work on closed-end funds has focused on the fact that typically they sell at discounts, some of the most puzzling evidence concerns closed-end fund premia. We have already mentioned that in the mid-1980s, closed-end funds went from an average 7 percent premium at the time of initial offer to an average 10 percent discount within 100 trading days. These large and rapid negative returns to initial investors raise substantial doubts about these investors' rationality. None of the standard explanations even begin to deal with the question of why anyone ever buys new issues at a premium.

Initial public offerings (IPOs) are not the only case of funds selling at premia. Historically, there have been periods when even diversified funds sold at premia, such as the late 1960s and particularly the late 1920s right before the crash. Even when the median fund sells at a discount, some funds sell at premia. These premia pose a serious challenge to agency costs, taxes, and other explanations of why funds should sell at a discount.

Consider the case of the 1929 stock market boom. De Long and Shleifer (1990) found that the median fund in their sample sold at a premium of 47 percent in the third quarter of 1929, right before the crash. They also found that $1.9 billion in closed-end funds were issued in that quarter. Adjusted for the change in the price level and the size of the U.S. economy, this amounts to roughly $55 billion today—at least five times more than the current total outstanding value of closed-end funds. The closed-end fund boom that summer was extraordinary, never to be repeated. The boom ended with the Great Crash, as closed-end funds moved to discounts which have remained a rule since then. Not surprisingly, observers of closed-end funds before the Great Crash did not consider the possibility of discounts on closed-end funds. Unschooled in efficient markets, they reasoned that a fund's value consists of the value of its assets plus the skills of its management, and so premia should be a rule. Some observers thought premia of 50 to 100 percent were reasonable. During this wave of enthusiasm, theories explaining why closed-end funds should sell at discounts were not advanced.

Such investor optimism about funds has not been common in recent years, with the possible exception of country funds. Some country funds (e.g. Korea, Spain, Taiwan, Brazil, and Germany) were introduced in the mid-1980s. The new, but not the old, country funds have sold at large premia. Some of these funds such as Korea and Brazil invest in countries that prevent unrestricted foreign direct investment, while others such as Germany and Spain invest in completely open markets. Both types of funds sold at large premia in the 1980s, sometimes above 100 percent. What drove these country funds to a premium, especially the funds in countries with open capital markets? Those investors who drove the price of the Spain fund to a premium over 100 percent, when they could have put their money in the Spanish market directly, must either have been overoptimistic about the management of the Spain fund or just ignorant of other ways to invest in Spain. The premia on many country funds have been gradually reduced by the entry of new country funds. In the space of a few months, three competitors each emerged for the Spain and Germany funds which had been selling at large premia. Two interesting things happened when the new funds appeared. First, the premia on the existing funds fell. Second, the premia on the new funds were lower than on the old funds. The fact that an increase in supply reduces price would not be considered anomalous in most economic markets, but in financial markets, where price is allegedly equal to value and value is independent of the supply of substitutes, this evidence is anomalous.

In sum, premia on closed-end funds seem to occur at the times of great investor enthusiasm about stocks in general such as the late 1920s or late 1980s, or the times of investor enthusiasm about particular securities such as country stocks. These premia are very hard to fathom when investors are supposed to be cool-headed and when arbitrage should keep prices equal to values. This raises the next question: How can mispricing of closed-end funds survive arbitrage by smart investors?

MONEY FOR NOTHING

If closed-end funds are so clearly mispriced, can't a smart investor make money? Consider funds selling at premia. Why can't a smart investor sell them short, and buy their portfolio, or something close to their portfolio, as a hedge? One argument usually given is that for funds investing in countries with restricted markets, one cannot buy stocks directly so the hedge is not possible. However, this is not very persuasive. Why can't a family with some members in Korea and some in the U.S. have its American branch short the fund and have the Korean branch buy its portfolio? Besides, a lot of funds from unrestricted countries, such as Spain and Germany, have sold at large premia. What prevents arbitrage in these cases?

The problems with arbitrage turn out to lie right here in the United States. First, borrowing shares is often very difficult, so one can't sell the funds short. This has been the case with many country funds recently, whether from restricted or from unrestricted markets, as well as with closed-end fund IPOs. Even if an investor could sell them short, the proceeds are not received immediately,[2] raising the cost of this trade. Second, even if an investor manages to sell a fund short and buy its portfolio, the premium can get larger before it gets smaller, leading to a capital loss on the position and the demand by the broker for more funds. If you shorted the Spain fund at a 20 percent premium, you might be broke as the premium rose to 100 percent. Unless the investor is very patient and has deep pockets, this arbitrage trade would not pay.

What about the more typical case of funds selling at discounts? In this case, the first obvious way to make money is to take the fund over and liquidate or convert it to an open-ended fund. While this is a good idea in theory, in practice there are multiple obstacles to taking over a closed-end fund. Fund managers fiercely resist takeovers, raising the bidder's costs. Herzfeld (1980) reported that by 1980 Lehman and Tricontinental—the two largest diversified funds—had each defeated four attempts to reorganize them. In the past decade, many new funds have explicitly enacted anti-takeover provisions. If the anti-takeover provisions do not work, the managers can count on the help of the Securities and Exchanges Commission, which regulates investment companies and has frequently contributed to raising bidders' costs.

Even if bidders can circumvent this resistance, there is another problem raised by Grossman and Hart (1980). Once a buyer's holdings in a company, including a closed-end fund, exceed 5 percent, the buyer must announce her intentions regarding the company. If the buyer announces that she intends to liquidate the fund, the other shareholders of the fund have an incentive not to tender, to wait for the liquidation, and then to realize the full net asset value. But if the bid is for full net asset value, there is nothing left for the bidder, except the profit on the original 5 percent investment. Not surprisingly, the bids that succeed are typically for 95 to 98 percent of net asset value. What this all means is that taking over closed-end funds is not as good a deal as it looks, which explains why so many of them selling at large discounts are still around.

A more passive strategy for a discounted fund is to buy the fund and to sell short its portfolio, which is to some extent possi-

[2]An investor's proceeds on short sales are only paid, net of costs, when the position is closed. The credit position created by the short sale typically earns no interest for the investor.

ble (Herzfeld, 1980). But here again one runs into the costs of only partial proceeds from short sale, as well as the risk that the discount will widen, bringing a loss to a smart investor with a short horizon.

Clearly, the more obvious "easy money" strategies are not without costs and risks. Nevertheless, there is some evidence that excess risk-adjusted returns can be had by trading in closed-end funds. These strategies are based on the observation that discounts are mean reverting. This suggests buying the funds with the largest discounts, hoping they will shrink over time. Thompson (1978) investigated the profitability of buying a portfolio of funds at discount where the amount of each fund purchased was proportional to the discount. He found that over his 32-year sample period, the strategy earned an annual excess return of more than 4 percent.[3] Brauer (1988) improved on this strategy somewhat by incorporating variables which are related to the probability that a fund will be open ended. His strategy earns an abnormal return of 5 percent a year. Anderson (1986), studying the 1965–1984 period, also found significant excess returns to closed-end fund investment. Thus, a long-run bet on funds with high discounts appears to offer some opportunities for excess returns.

INVESTOR SENTIMENT—
A POSSIBLE SOLUTION TO THE PUZZLES

De Long, Shleifer, Summers, and Waldmann (1990) and Lee, Shleifer, and Thaler (1991a) have explored one possible explanation of the closed-end fund puzzle based on a model of noise traders. Here we can only give a skeleton of the argument.

De Long, Shleifer, Summers, and Waldmann (1990) presented a model with two kinds of investors: rational traders, who invest based on fundamentals, and noise traders, who base their investment decisions partly on irrational factors. The rational investors have unbiased expectations, whereas the noise traders make systematic forecasting errors. Put differently, noise trader sentiment shifts over time—sometimes it is excessively optimistic

---

[3]As we indicated at the beginning, one problem with findings such as Thompson's (1978) is that they are conditional on the pricing model being able to properly measure risk. In his conclusion, Thompson cautions that his findings are only inconsistent with the joint hypothesis of market efficiency and a well-specified pricing model.

about the future, at other times it is excessively pessimistic. This variability in noise trader sentiment creates a new source of risk in the markets where they trade. A final assumption is that the rational traders are risk averse, and have finite horizons, two characteristics that seem to describe most investors, even (or maybe especially) those who manage other people's money. As a result, the risk from shifting noise trader sentiment deters rational investors from attempting aggressive arbitrage strategies.

Closed-end funds are a good illustration of how the model works. Suppose there is a higher concentration of noise traders in the ownership of closed-end funds than in the ownership of the funds' assets. When noise traders become pessimistic about the future, they drive down the price of closed-end funds below net asset value. Why don't rational traders buy the funds up at the bargain prices? The answer is that buying a closed-end fund, even at a discount, a rational trader must bear two kinds of risk. The first is that the net asset value of the fund will underperform the market. The second risk is that when the rational trader wishes to sell the fund, the discount may have widened, because noise traders have become even more pessimistic. This analysis implies that rational investors will only be willing to buy closed-end funds if they are compensated for the noise trader risk, that is, if they can buy the funds at a discount! This is the noise trader explanation for the most salient fact about closed-end funds, that, on average, the funds sell at discounts from net asset value. It should be stressed that this explanation does not rely on the average pessimism of noise traders; it stems completely from the risk aversion of the rational investors. Interestingly, Martin Zweig (1973) also stressed the role of investor sentiment in closed-end fund pricing, and has since started two closed-end funds that bear his name. What about the other parts of the closed-end fund puzzle? To explain why investors buy funds initially at a premium one needs to have noise traders, or "suckers," who are sufficiently optimistic to buy overpriced assets. It helps to have a gimmick. Some recent start-ups, such as the Zweig funds, are run by famous portfolio managers; other new funds, such as the country funds, feature specialized investment strategies. Start-ups of generic diversified closed-end funds are rare, except during bubble periods such as 1929. The people who buy the new funds when issued are those most optimistic about the fund's future returns. When they subsequently try to sell their shares to other, possibly rational investors, the price falls. The fact that new funds start when existing funds are selling at premia or small discounts is also consistent with the theory. These are times when investor sentiment is high.

The fact that discounts vary over time and move together is necessary to this theory. Discounts must vary, else there would not be any risk associated with their changes. That they move together reinforces the view that discounts are a measure of investor sentiment. The fact that discounts disappear when funds are liquidated or open ended also fits, since when either of these events happen, noise trader risk is eliminated.

The noise trader model makes several additional predictions which are tested in Lee, Shleifer, and Thaler (1991a). Specifically, closed-end funds are taken to be a measure of a particular type of noise trader sentiment, namely, the sentiment of individual investors. Closed-end funds are held almost entirely by individuals, rather than institutions, in part because institutions have a hard time explaining to their clients why they are sub-contracting some of the money and thus imposing two management fees. The model implies that for a type of noise trader risk to be priced, it must affect other types of assets, otherwise it would be diversifiable. In this case, the logical place to look is other markets in which individuals are the predominant investors. One such market is small capitalization stocks. The investor sentiment theory predicts that when individual investors are pessimistic about closed-end funds, widening the discount, they will also be pessimistic about small firms, driving down their returns. This prediction is borne out by the data. For the period 1965–1985 we studied monthly returns for each of ten portfolios of New York Stock Exchange firms, where the portfolios were formed by ranking the firms by market value of equity. The smallest 10 percent of the firms were in the first decile portfolio, and so forth. Each of these decile returns was regressed on the return on the value-weighted NYSE index, and the change in a value-weighted index of closed-end fund discounts. We found that the returns are significantly related to the change in the value-weighted discount for every decile. The nine smaller deciles are negatively related—when discounts fall stock prices go up, however, the relationship declines in magnitude and significance as size increases. For the largest decile, the relationship is reversed. Discounts do seem to reflect the sentiment of individual investors.

COMMENTARY

Benjamin Graham (1949, p. 242), in his seminal book on security analysis, *The Intelligent Investor,* called the discounts on closed-end funds "an expensive monument erected to the inertia and stupidity of stockholders." Burton Malkiel, another well-known observer of financial markets (1977, p. 857) concluded his analysis of closed-end funds with the observation that "market psychology has an important bearing on the level and structure of discounts." How can stockholder stupidity or market psychology matter? In an efficient market, arbitrageurs buy and sell securities to assure that prices cannot diverge from their intrinsic values. If some investors prefer ounces of gold purchased in London to those purchased in Chicago, their preferences will not drive up the price of gold in London since other investors will be happy to buy in Chicago and sell in London. This analysis does not apply to closed-end funds. As discussed above, mispricing can occur because no riskless arbitrage opportunity exists,[4] and the supply of rational investors willing to make long-term bets against the prevailing investor sentiment is limited.

The major lesson we take from this analysis is that the demand for securities can influence price, even if that demand is based on irrational beliefs. In situations when this analysis applies—which includes many of the most interesting financial markets—it is important to remember that the statement "price is equal to intrinsic value" is a testable proposition, not an axiom.

[4]See Russell and Thaler (1985) and Shleifer and Summers (1990) for more details on the limits of arbitrage.

[*14*]

Foreign Exchange

 T he one person in your family who ever listens to your advice about economics is your uncle, who is in the import-export business. A while back he called you about a foreign exchange issue. "Let's suppose I owe a million German marks, payable in one month," he said. "We have the money to pay the bill in dollars, so the issue is whether to put the money into marks now or later. I figure we should put the money wherever it would earn the highest interest rate, but my treasurer, one of those MBA hotshots, tells me that this is irrelevant because if the interest rate is high in Germany that means that the mark is expected to go down. When I ask her what we *should* do, she says that it doesn't matter. 'Flip a coin,' she says! Is this what I am paying her so much money for? To flip coins?" You tried to calm your uncle down, and explain the idea of efficient markets to him, but he was unconvinced. "OK," you told him, "if you think you can do better, why don't you run an experiment? You invest some of your money your way, while your treasurer flips coins, and then see who does better." He thought this was a great idea, and promised to let you know what happened.

Much to your surprise, your uncle calls back a few months later. He claims to have a strategy that beats his coin-flipping treasurer. "Here's what I do," he crows. "When interest rates rise in other countries I put my money there, and take my chances on the currency falling. On the other hand, if rates in the foreign

With Kenneth A. Froot.

country fall relative to U.S. rates, I keep my money
here. It's simple, I admit, but it seems to be working.
Of course, my treasurer claimed it was just luck, and
said she would do some testing with historical data to
prove her point. Well, she just came sheepishly into my
office with piles of computer output and has agreed my
theory beats her coin flipping. What do you think of
this, wise guy?''

Baffled, you decide to look into the literature on
foreign exchange rates.

The foreign exchange market is among the most active of all financial markets. As of mid-1989, the average volume of trading
activity (adjusted for double counting) was about $430 billion per
day. To get a sense for just how big this number is, consider that
daily U.S. GNP is about $22 billion, and daily world trade in
goods and services is about $11 billion. Since foreign exchange
trading is so much greater in volume than is trade in real goods
and services, foreign exchange markets would seem to be highly
liquid and efficient.

Partly as a result of the sheer volume of trading, many researchers have focused on the foreign exchange market to examine
questions of speculative efficiency. One view—argued initially by
Milton Friedman (1953)—is that because speculators buy low and
sell high their activity ensures that exchange rates reflect the fundamental or long-run determinants of currency values. A second
strand of literature, often attributed to Ragnar Nurske (1944),
holds that speculation in foreign exchange can be destabilizing,
and that excess volatility imposes large costs on producers and
consumers who as a consequence make less efficient allocative
decisions.

Recently this debate has escalated, as both sides try to come to
grips with the dramatic, *temporary* 65 percent appreciation in the
value of the dollar during the mid-1980s. Some hold that these
swings in the dollar's value were attributable to changes in fundamentals, and that given those fundamentals the appreciation was
both predictable and optimal. Others, however, point to the experience as evidence of a capricious delinking of the dollar from its
usual determinants, and argue that at least some of the dollar's
appreciation could have been prevented beneficially. The debate

about whether exchange rates are "correctly priced" is particularly important (in comparison to similar debates about the pricing of other assets), since the exchange rate simultaneously affects the prices of *all* foreign assets, goods, and factors of production. If Nurske's followers are right that speculation drives prices away from fundamentals, then the argument for intervention might be considered strongest in the market for foreign exchange.

In this chapter we concentrate on the efficiency of foreign exchange markets. Readers interested in more complete treatments should refer to Mussa (1979), Levich (1985), Boothe and Longworth (1986), Hodrick (1987), and Froot (1990). To keep things as simple as possible (which, unfortunately, won't be all that simple), the question of efficiency is viewed below from the perspective of a single type of test: the test for what is called the *forward discount bias*. This test is easy to understand, and since the empirical tests strongly reject the null hypothesis, statistical power is not an issue. Along the way we will also mention a variety of other empirical work designed to shed light on alternative explanations of the results.

TESTS OF FORWARD DISCOUNT BIAS

If investors are risk neutral and have rational expectations, then the market's forecast of the future exchange rate is implicit in international differences in interest rates. To see this, suppose that the one-year dollar interest rate is 10 percent, and that the comparable German mark interest rate is 7 percent. The dollar *interest differential* is then said to be 3 percent. Risk neutral, rational investors then must expect the dollar to depreciate against the mark by 3 percent over the next year. This amount of depreciation would just equalize the expected returns on dollar and mark denominated deposits. If instead these investors expected a different rate of dollar depreciation, say 4 percent, they would all wish to borrow in dollars and lend in marks. Consequently, dollar interest rates would tend to rise and mark interest rates would tend to fall until the interest differential also became 4 percent. This simple relationship between interest differentials and expected currency depreciation is called *uncovered interest parity* (uncovered because forward markets are not used as a hedge). Thus, uncovered inter-

est parity implies that the interest differential is implicitly an estimate of future exchange rate changes. If expectations are rational,
then this estimate of future exchange rate changes provided by
the interest differential should be unbiased.

Unbiasedness is usually tested by regressing the change in the
exchange rate on the interest differential.

(1) $$\Delta s_{t+k} = \alpha + \beta(i_t - i_t^*) + \eta_{t+k},$$

where Δs_{t+k} is the percentage depreciation of the currency (the
change in the log of the spot dollar price of foreign exchange)
over k periods and $(i_t - {}_t^*)$ is the current k-period dollar interest
rate less the k-period foreign interest rate. The null hypothesis is
that $\beta = 1$. Some authors include $\alpha = 0$ in the null hypothesis as
well. In other words, the realized depreciation of the spot rate is
equal to the interest differential plus a purely random error term,
η_{t+k}.

A second specification of equation (1) replaces the interest differential by the forward discount, i.e., the percentage difference
between the current forward and spot exchange rates. (The forward rate is today's dollar price of foreign exchange to be deliv-
ered on a specific date in the future.) By arbitrage, the forward
discount must equal the interest differential. If it did not, then a
strategy of borrowing in the foreign currency, changing the proceeds into dollars, investing those dollars and then selling them
forward would yield a riskless profit. Most observers agree that
the market respects this arbitrage condition, as banks allow forward rates to be set by interest differentials. Under risk neutrality
and rational expectations, the forward discount should also be
an unbiased estimate of the subsequent exchange rate change.
Indeed, the failure of regressions such as (1) to yield estimates of
$\beta = 1$ is often referred to as the forward discount bias.

A very large literature has tested the unbiasedness hypothesis
and found that the coefficient β is reliably less than one. In fact,
β is frequently estimated to be less than zero. The average coefficient, across some 75 published estimates, is -0.88 (see Froot,
1990). A few are positive, but, *not one is equal to or greater than the
null hypothesis of $\beta = 1$.*

A coefficient of approximately minus one is difficult to explain.
It implies that, for example, when U.S. interest rates exceed foreign rates by one percentage point, the dollar subsequently tends
to *appreciate* at an annual rate of 1 percent. This is in stark contrast

to the 1 percent *depreciation* dictated by the unbiasedness hypothesis.

Two interpretations of these results are common in the literature. Some authors argue that $\beta < 1$ is evidence of a time-varying risk premium on foreign exchange: when the dollar interest rate rises, investments in dollar assets become relatively more risky.[1] Alternatively, others assume that exchange-rate risk is purely diversifiable or that investors are risk neutral. They therefore interpret any bias as evidence of expectational errors. In the next two sections, we evaluate the merit of these two types of explanations.

EXCHANGE RISK PREMIA

If the marginal investors in foreign exchange markets are risk averse, and if foreign exchange risk is not fully diversifiable, then the interest differential or forward discount can no longer be interpreted as a pure estimate of the expected change in future exchange rates. Rather, the interest differential is the sum of the expected change in the exchange rate plus a risk premium. Thus, if the dollar is viewed as riskier than the foreign currency, dollar interest rates would have to be higher, even if the exchange rate is not expected to change. If the assumption of rational expectations is maintained, then a finding of β not equal to one implies that interest rate movements are related to changes in the risk premium. A finding of β less than one implies that a 1 percent increase in the dollar interest differential is associated with a less than 1 percent expected drop in the value of the dollar. Since the risk premium is just equal to the interest differential less the expected change in exchange rates, this implies that the risk premium on dollar assets must rise with the interest differential, or equivalently, the required return on foreign exchange must fall.[2]

---

[1]Similarly, the results would then also imply that when the foreign interest rate rises (relative to the dollar interest rate), investments in foreign assets become relatively more risky.

[2]Readers may find it difficult to understand how assets denominated in one currency can be riskier than assets denominated in the other currency when there is only a single exchange rate to connect them. The following example may help. Suppose that there are two equally sized countries with perfectly integrated trade in goods and assets. Each produces it own good, but consumes both goods in equal amounts. Each country also has an asset which pays off in future consumption of that country's good. Now suppose that country A's asset represents claims to a greater fraction of country A's goods than B's asset represents to country B's good. In other words, the outstanding supply of country A's asset is larger than country B's. Since investors will consume the same amount of each good, all else equal, they will want to invest half of their portfolio in the assets of each

Naturally, a finding of a negative β is more extreme: an increase in the interest differential is then associated with a *decline* in expected depreciation (since the dollar subsequently appreciates on average) and therefore with an even larger rise in the risk premium. As Fama (1984) pointed out, this implies that: (1) the variance of the risk premium is greater than the variance of both expected depreciation and the interest differential; and (2) the covariance of expected depreciation and the risk premium is negative.

By itself, a negative correlation between expected depreciation and the risk premium might be considered plausible: higher expected inflation in the U.S. might sensibly be associated with both greater expected dollar depreciation and increased riskiness of dollar-denominated assets (see Hodrick and Srivastava, 1986). This would be the case if, for example, higher expected inflation reflects greater uncertainty about the future course of monetary policy. The real problem for explanations based on risk premia is whether they can explain why a change in interest rates should produce an even larger change in risk premia. Three approaches have been advanced to evaluate the merit of the risk-premium interpretation—none of which offers the hypothesis much support.

The first approach specifies and tests what one might call "statistical" models of risk. Rather than exploring whether underlying economic determinants of risk can help explain excess returns on foreign exchange, this approach tests for certain patterns in or across excess currency returns. While this class of tests has provided rich information about the predictable components of exchange rate changes, it has not provided much evidence that these components are actually attributable to risk. Another statistical test asks whether predictable returns can be explained by the expected variance in future returns. This kind of test may, in principle, be more able to distinguish between risk and expectational errors. In practice, however, there is no evidence that measures of expected variance are related to the forward discount bias.

---

country. Investors will agree to hold a greater fraction of their portfolio in the assets of country A—as they must in equilibrium—only if they get paid a premium on the return of A's asset relative to B's. In such a case, we would say that assets denominated in A's goods are "riskier" than those denominated in B's.

A second strand of tests for the exchange risk premium looks beyond relative asset returns themselves and examines various specifications of the fundamental determinants of required returns. One approach, taken initially by Frankel (1982), notes that the capital asset pricing model (CAPM) requires an asset's risk premium to be systematically related to that asset's value share in investors' portfolios. His tests provide no evidence that required returns are positively related to systematic risk in exchange rates. Indeed, using these models it is not possible to reject the hypothesis that the systematic risk is zero, i.e., that the exchange risk premium is zero. There is no evidence here that risk premia vary in a way that can explain predictable excess returns in foreign exchange (see Frankel and Engel, 1984, and Hodrick, 1987). Later work has examined more complex models of time-varying risk, but with similar results (see Engel and Rodrigues, 1989; Giovannini and Jorion, 1989; Mark, 1985; and Obstfeld, 1990).

The third approach for assessing the risk-premium interpretation attempts to measure expected depreciation directly, thereby avoiding reliance on inferences from realized depreciation. If one could actually observe expectations it would be possible to decompose the interest differential's bias into separate components attributable to risk premia and to expectational errors. This would not tell us how the risk premium is formed, but it could tell us the importance of risk and market efficiency in explaining the bias.

The problem, of course, is that market expectations are not observable. However, by gathering independent measures of expectations, one might nevertheless hope to gain insights. Froot and Frankel (1989) used survey data on the expectations of foreign exchange traders as their independent measure of expected depreciation. If the survey expectations are accepted as a measure of expected depreciation, then the bias in the interest differential can be decomposed into a risk premium and a bias in expectations. When this decomposition is performed, the component attributable to risk turns out to be small and insignificantly different from zero. This is not to say that the surveys don't contain a risk premium, as would be true if the surveys were always equal to the interest rate differential. In fact, the risk premia implied by the surveys are substantially different from zero and move over time. However, the survey risk premia are uncorrelated with the forward discount.

Risk and the 1980–1985 Dollar

Finally, we might put the alternative hypothesis of a time-varying risk premium to a more informal sensibility check, asking how it would explain the unprecedented behavior of the dollar in the 1980s. From late 1980 until early 1985, dollar interest rates were above foreign rates so the dollar sold at a forward discount, implying that the value of the dollar should fall. However, the dollar *appreciated* (more or less steadily) at a rate of about 13 percent per year. Under the risk-premium scenario, these facts would suggest that investors' (rational) expectation of dollar appreciation was strongly positive (perhaps even the full 13 percent), but that the risk premium was also positive. Therefore, according to this view, dollar-denominated assets were perceived to be much riskier than assets denominated in other currencies, exactly the opposite of the "safe-haven" hypothesis which was frequently offered at that time as an explanation for the dollar's strength.

The subsequent rapid fall in the value of the dollar would conversely imply a reversal in the risk premium's sign, as investors in 1985 switched to thinking of the dollar as relatively safe. Something very dramatic must have happened to the underlying determinants of currency risk to yield such enormous swings in the dollar's value: during the appreciation investors must have been willing to give up around *16 percent per year* (13 percent from dollar appreciation plus 3 percent from an interest differential in favor of the dollar) in order to hold the "safer" foreign currency, whereas during the later depreciation phase they must have been willing to forgo about 6 percent in additional annual returns (8 percent average annual depreciation minus the 2 percent average interest differential) in order to hold dollars. These premia are very large. It is hard to see how one could rely on the risk-premium interpretation alone to explain the dollar of the 1980s.[3]

EXPECTATIONAL ERRORS

The other main alternative hypothesis is that expectational errors explain the bias in the forward discount and the interest differen-

[3]These conclusions can be softened by arguing that investors were repeatedly surprised at the strength (and subsequent weakness) of fundamentals over this period. Rationally expected appreciation (and depreciation) and estimates of the risk premium would then

tial. Under this alternative the risk premium is constant (or at least uncorrelated with the forward discount). It follows that an increase in the interest differential is associated with an equivalent increase in expected depreciation. If this increase in expected depreciation is rational, a 1 percent increase in the interest differential tends to be followed by a 1 percent drop in the value of the dollar. The coefficient estimates above, however, suggest that when the interest differential implies a depreciation of 1 percent, the spot rate on average *appreciates* by almost 1 percent. How could these expectational errors arise, and how could they persist?

Even if such expectational errors appear ex post to be economically significant for the period studied, they may not imply market inefficiency or unexploited profit opportunities ex ante. Perhaps the period studied was unrepresentative, in which case the usual methods of statistical inference may lead to incorrect conclusions. If investors are in the process of learning about floating exchange rates, or other regime changes, this may be a possible source of "unrepresentative" exchange rate changes. Lewis (1989) explored whether an explanation of this sort could explain the persistence of the 1980–1985 dollar appreciation. She presented evidence that investors' slow learning about an unobservable shift in the U.S. money supply process could explain about half of the error implicit in the forward rate. However, as Lewis noted, the errors do not seem to have died out over time, which is evidence against models of learning about once-and-for-all shifts in regime.

Another example which would generate misleading inferences from regressions is that of *peso problems*. This term derives from the 1955–1975 Mexican peso, which was fixed by the Mexican government at a constant rate against the U.S. dollar, yet all the while sold at a forward discount. Of course, the large depreciation apparently expected by investors did eventually occur, validating the prediction from interest rates and the forward market— but one could not have guessed this from the 1955–1975 sample alone (see Rogoff, 1979). In these as well as less extreme circumstances, peso problems will invalidate standard statistical inference procedures.

be closer to zero than calculated above. We address such explanations directly in the next section.

Michael Mussa (1979) has suggested why peso problems might indeed be expected to plague regressions of the type we have been discussing. He argued that the distribution of inflation rates is skewed: most of the time inflation hovers in a restricted range, but occasionally hyperinflation breaks out. For periods in which no hyperinflation actually occurs, increases in expected inflation overpredict the subsequent realized inflation rate. Since such increases in expected inflation are likely to be associated with increases in nominal interest rates and expected depreciation, the β coefficients will be less than one in more than half of the regression samples.

We can evaluate whether the peso problem is a reasonable explanation for the dollar of the early 1980s by using a skewness argument similar to that proposed by Mussa. During the 1980–1985 period, the dollar was above its 1980 level by an average of about 33 percent, and appreciated at an average annual rate of 13 percent. Suppose that the market did indeed expect the dollar to appreciate at 13 percent per year *if* it appreciated at all, but that the alternative was an expected collapse back to its 1980 level. Expected depreciation would then be equal to the probability of collapse, π, times the average size of the expected collapse, 33 percent, minus the probability of appreciation, $1-\pi$, times the amount of appreciation, 13 percent. If we assume that expected depreciation was the 3 percent given by the interest differential, then the probability of collapse in any one year is: $\pi = \$(13+3)/(13+33) = 35$ percent. This would imply that the probability that the exchange rate went five years without collapsing was $.65^5 = .12$. If we take this computation seriously, the result suggests that the peso problem hypothesis is unlikely to be true, although it cannot be rejected at standard levels of statistical significance.

Interest Differentials and Secular Exchange Rate Changes

The bias in the interest differential seems less severe for certain types of fluctuations in interest rates. Tests of the bias during the buildup to hyperinflations, in which nominal interest rates move from being small to very large, show βs that are positive and nearer one. In addition, casual inspection of cross-sectional evidence suggests that interest differentials lead to reasonable predictions: high-inflation countries, such as Italy, typically have had higher nominal interest rates than the U.S., and their currencies indeed did tend to depreciate secularly. Just the reverse has been true for the currencies of low-inflation countries such as West Germany which has had relatively low interest rates. In other words, the average level of the interest differentials points the right way in forecasting long-run currency changes, even though the short-run correlations usually point the wrong way in forecasting near-term exchange rate changes.

This evidence might be taken as supporting the slow learning or peso explanations of the bias, since both explanations predict that interest differentials on average correctly forecast long-run currency changes (even if there might appear to be bias in short-run predictions). However, by the same logic, these explanations should also lead us to expect that estimates of β should be equal to one on average. Also, if slow learning were behind the bias, we should see the estimated coefficients get closer to one in later sub-samples, but there is no sign of such an evolution.

The preponderance of evidence that β is less than one across different sub-samples, currencies, forecast horizons, and asset markets, coupled with the near-rejection of the peso explanation of the behavior of the dollar in the early 1980s, casts some doubt on the validity of learning and peso problems. In order to keep these explanations intact, one would need to argue that there is little independence across these many estimates of β. Perhaps there is the possibility of some important event that has not yet occurred—like complete nuclear annihilation—that somehow conditions investors' expectations in such a way as to create the appearance of bias. As the time-series and cross-sectional size of the statistical sample continues to increase, however, such arguments become increasingly strained.

A POSSIBLE EXPLANATION

The primary conclusions reached so far have been negative: a rational efficient markets paradigm provides no satisfactory explanation for the observed results. One thing to try to do is to offer a simple and parsimonious explanation, one that has other testable restrictions but does not require full rationality of all investors. Consider, as an example, the hypothesis that at least some investors are slow in responding to changes in the interest differential. It may be that these investors need some time to think about trades before executing them, or that they simply cannot respond quickly to recent information. These investors might also be called "central banks," who seem to "lean against the wind" by trading in such a way as to attenuate the appreciation of a currency as interest rates increase. Other investors in the model are fully rational, albeit risk averse and liquidity constrained, and may even try to exploit the first group's slower movements.[4]

A simple story along these lines has the potential for reconciling the above facts. First, it yields negative coefficient estimates of β, as long as some changes in nominal interest differentials also reflect changes in real interest differentials. While changes in nominal interest rates have different instantaneous effects on the exchange rate across different exchange-rate models, most of these models predict that an increase in the dollar real interest rate (all else equal) should lead to instantaneous dollar appreciation. If only part of this appreciation occurs immediately, and the rest takes some time, then we might expect the exchange rate to appreciate in the period subsequent to an increase in the interest differential. Hence the possibility of a negative relationship between short-run changes in interest rates and exchange rates. Second, this hypothesis can also explain the cross-sectional and hyperinflation results, in which the interest differential correctly forecasts secular exchange rate changes. Short lags in the responsiveness of some investors would not affect the long-term relationship between interest differentials and exchange-rate changes. A test of this hypothesis could be based on the additional implication that past (not just current) levels of the forward discount should help in predicting exchange-rate changes. In fact, this hypothesis suggests that if past levels of the interest differential are added to equation (1), the estimated coefficient should be positive and near one. Froot (1990) presents evidence which is supportive of this latter implication.

If You Are So Smart . . .

Such an explanation (which stresses the lack of "efficiency" in the usual sense) seems to fit the facts well enough, but has an apparently serious flaw: Isn't there money to be made by trading on contemporaneous interest rate changes? The empirical case for

[4]For examples of such models see Cutler, Poterba, and Summers (1990).

foreign exchange market inefficiency was made forcefully by Bilson (1981). He argued that the speculative rule suggested by the finding of B < 1—buy the currency whose interest rate is relatively high—could actually provide expected profits without bearing much risk. Indeed, word has it that he in fact made quite a bit of money using this strategy.[5]

Dooley and Shafer (1983) and Sweeney (1986) also examined several types of "filter rules"—trading strategies that are triggered by the past behavior of spot rates. A typical filter rule might specify that an investor should sell the dollar short if the dollar has appreciated by more than 2 percent in the last 24 hours. Such rules appear profitable, although the profits are not always statistically significant. Also, Schulmeister (1987) and Cumby and Modest (1987) studied a number of trading rules derived from "technical analysis" and found that these rules generate statistically significant profits.

Whether or not there is really money to be made based on the apparent inefficiency of foreign exchange markets, it is worth emphasizing that the risk-return trade-off for a single currency is not very attractive. The annualized standard error of the regression estimates of equation (1) is about 36 percent. This implies that a strategy that generates expected profits $1 comes with a standard deviation of profits of $15. To see this, note that with β equal to minus one, a one-percentage-point increase in the dollar interest rate is associated with an additional two-percent higher annual return on dollar assets than on foreign assets. On a monthly basis, a $500 investment therefore yields about $1 in expected profit, ($500 × .02)/12 ≈ $1—ignoring compounding. The standard error of profits is then ($500 × .36)/12 = $15. With transactions costs, the risk-return trade-off becomes even less favorable. Although much of the "risk" in these strategies may be diversifiable in principle, more complex diversified strategies may be much more costly, unreliable, or difficult to execute.

COMMENTARY

Anomalies in financial markets are often "explained" by economists with the use of some type of risk argument. For example,

[5]Hodrick and Srivastava (1984) reported less favorable risk-return tradeoffs using Bilson's (1981) data.

small firms which earn higher returns than large firms are said to be riskier, though differentials in traditional risk measures such as CAPM betas are not high enough to explain the differentials in returns. Similarly, mean reversion in asset prices is often attributed to alleged time-varying risk premia—the amount of risk investors are willing to bear is said to vary over time in a manner that can explain the pattern of returns. Such explanations are often thought to have a decisive debating advantage: untestability. Since risk premia are unobservable directly, how can the explanation ever be disproven? This type of thinking can lead to a false sense of security, because clever researchers often think of ways of testing such untestable propositions. An analogy is the concept of utility maximization, often considered an untestable tautology. However, as discussed in Chapter 7 on preference reversals, people can be induced to make conflicting choices when faced with two different versions of the same problem, and of course it is impossible for both answers to be consistent with utility maximization.

As we have seen in this chapter, researchers in foreign exchange markets have been inventive in devising methods of testing whether risk can explain the anomalies. Indeed, the conclusion we draw from the tests completed so far is that there is no positive evidence that the forward discount's bias is due to risk (as opposed to expectational errors). Risk premia which are derived from economists' asset-pricing models show no sign of being systematically related to the predictable excess returns derived from econometricians' regressions.

In addition, there *is* positive evidence which suggests the reverse: that the bias is attributable to expectational errors and not to risk. Attempts to separate the forward discount into expected depreciation and a risk premium using survey data on exchange-rate expectations suggest that the bias is entirely due to expectational errors and that none is due to time-varying risk. While such a decomposition cannot itself shed light on whether the expectational errors are generated by learning, peso problems, or market inefficiency, neither learning nor peso problems seem to offer complete explanations of the facts. Taken as a whole, the evidence suggests that explanations which allow for the possibility of market inefficiency should be seriously investigated.

What are the policy implications of the apparent inefficiency in foreign exchange markets? Because the evidence for inefficiency is ambiguous, and because there exists no good general equilibrium model of exchange rates, we can say little about whether exchange rate fluctuations are costly enough to merit government intervention. Although the kind of inefficiency discussed above can lead to very large distortions in the level of the exchange rate, interventions such as transactions taxes or an exchange rate peg also involve costs to welfare. Future research may help to determine how consumers and producers are affected by the use of such blunt policy instruments.

[15]

Epilogue

What are we to make of these anomalies? Do they together call for the demise of economic theory? For several reasons, the answer is no. First, while the standard economics paradigm has limitations and weaknesses, there is no good substitute available. For many domains, economists are the only social scientists doing any research at all. Consider the stock market. My experience has been that Wall Street professionals are very open to the idea that psychological factors have major influences in financial markets. However, there are at most a handful of non-economist social scientists who have seriously studied financial markets, and there is nothing resembling a behavioral alternative to the capital asset pricing model. If one should emerge it is more likely to come from behaviorally oriented economists than from psychologists or sociologists. Change must come from within the profession.

What should the new kind of economic theory be? The most important advance I would like to see is a clear distinction made between normative and descriptive theories. Profit maximization, expected utility maximization, game theory, and so forth, are theories that describe optimal behavior. Setting price so that marginal cost equals marginal revenue is the right answer to the problem of how to maximize profits. Whether firms *do* that is another matter. I try to teach my MBA students that they should avoid the winner's curse and equate opportunity costs to out-of-pocket costs, but I also teach them that most people don't. I also tell them that cooperation is often a good strategy, even if economic theory suggests defection. I think that it helps you to be a good manager if you know both the kinds of mistakes you, and your employees, customers, and competitors are likely to make, and the surprising ways in which they may be cooperative. This can't be controversial. I also think that the same knowledge about human nature is useful to an economist trying to explain and predict behavior. I don't think this should be controversial, but it is. Then, if we get the normative versus descriptive distinction down, we can begin to work on prescriptive theories, such as how to play a game against other human beings. In the absence of such prescriptive theories, economics has little advice to offer someone playing an ultimatum game or bidding in an auction.

The primary lesson here is admittedly a depressing one for economic theorists. The lesson is that their job is much harder than we may have previously thought. Writing down a model of rational behavior and turning the crank may not be enough, and writing down a good model of less than fully rational behavior is difficult for two reasons. First, it is not generally possible to build good descriptive models without collecting data, and many theorists claim to have a strong allergic reaction to data. Second, rational models tend to be simple and elegant with precise predictions, while behavioral models tend to be complicated, and messy, with much vaguer predictions. But, look at it this way. Would you rather be elegant and precisely wrong, or messy and vaguely right?

References

ABRAMS, BURTRAN A., and MARK A. SCHMITZ (1978). "The Crowding Out Effect of Government Transfers on Private Charitable Contributions." *Public Choice*, 33, 29–39.

ABRAMS, BURTRAN A., and MARK A. SCHMITZ (1984). The Crowding Out Effect of Government Transfers on Private Charitable Contributions: Cross Sectional Evidence." *National Tax Journal*, 37, 563–68.

AINSLIE, GEORGE (1975). Specious Reward: A Behavioral Theory of Impulsiveness and Impulse Control." *Psychological Bulletin*, 82, 463–509.

AINSLIE, GEORGE (forthcoming). *Picoeconomics: The Interaction of Successive Motivational States within the Individual*. Cambridge, U.K.: Cambridge University Press.

AKERLOF, GEORGE A. (1982). "Labor Contracts as Partial Gift Exchange." *Quarterly Journal of Economics*, 87, November, 543–69.

AKERLOF, GEORGE A. (1984). "Gift Exchange and Efficiency Wages: Four Views." *American Economic Review*, 73, 79–83.

AKERLOF, GEORGE A., ANDREW ROSE, and JANET YELLEN (forthcoming). "Job Switching and Job Satisfaction in the U.S. Labor Market." *Brookings Papers on Economic Activity*.

AKERLOF, GEORGE A., and JANET YELLEN (1988). "The Fair Wage/Effort Hypothesis and Unemployment." Unpublished, Department of Economics, University of California, Berkeley.

ALI, MUKHTAR M. (1977). "Probability and Utility Estimates for Racetrack Bettors." *Journal of Political Economy*, 85, 803–15.

ALI, MUKHTAR M. (1979). "Some Evidence of the Efficiency of a Speculative Market." *Econometrica*, 47, 387–92.

ANDERSON, S. C. (1986). "Closed-end Funds versus Market Efficiency." *Journal of Portfolio Management*, Fall, 63–65.

ANDREONI, JAMES (1988). "Why Free Ride? Strategies and Learning in Public Goods Experiments." *Journal of Public Economics*, 37, 291–304.

ANDREONI, JAMES (1990). "Impure Altruism and Donations to Public Goods: A Theory of Warm-Glow Giving." *Economic Journal,* June.

ARIEL, ROBERT A. (1985). "High Stock Returns Before Holidays." Unpublished Working Paper, Department of Finance, MIT.

ARIEL, ROBERT A. (1987). A Monthly Effect in Stock Returns." *Journal of Financial Economics,* 18, March, 161–74.

ARROW, KENNETH A. (1986). "Rationality of Self and Others in an Economic System." *Journal of Business,* 59, October, S385–s400.

ASCH, PETER, BURTON G. MALKIEL, and RICHARD E. QUANDT (1982). "Racetrack Betting and Informed Behavior." *Journal of Financial Economics,* 10, 187–94.

ASCH, PETER, BURTON G. MALKIEL, and RICHARD E. QUANDT (1984). "Market Efficiency in Racetrack Betting." *Journal of Business,* 57, 65–75.

ASCH, PETER, BURTON G. MALKIEL, and RICHARD E. QUANDT (1986). "Market Efficiency in Racetrack Betting: Further Evidence and a Correction." *Journal of Business,* 59, 157–60.

ASCH, PETER, and RICHARD E. QUANDT (1986). *Racetrack Betting: The Professors' Guide to Strategies.* Dover, Mass.: Auburn House.

ASCH, PETER, and RICHARD E. QUANDT (1987). "Efficiency and Profitability in Exotic Bets." *Economica,* 59, August, 278–98.

ASQUITH, P. (1983). "Merger Bids, Uncertainty, and Stockholder Returns." *Journal of Financial Economics,* 11, 51–83.

AXELROD, ROBERT (1984). *The Evolution of Cooperation.* New York: Basic Books.

BANZ, ROLf, W. (1981). "The Relationship between Return and Market Value of Common Stocks." *Journal of Financial Economics,* 9, 3–18.

BARRO, ROBERT (1978). *The Impact of Social Security on Private Saving.* Washington, D.C.: American Enterprise Institute.

BARRO, ROBERT (1989). "The Ricardian Approach to Budget Deficits." *Journal of Economic Perspectives,* 3, 37–54.

BASU, SANJOY (1977). "Investment Performance of Common Stocks in Relation to Their Price-Earnings Ratios: A Test of the Efficient Market Hypothesis." *Journal of Finance,* 33, June, 663–82.

BASU, SANJOY (1978). "The Effect of Earnings Yield on Assessments of the Association between Annual Accounting Income Numbers and Security Prices." *Accounting Review,* 53, July, 599–625.

BAZERMAN, MAX H., and WILLIAM F. SAMUELSON (1983). "I Won the Auction But Don't Want the Prize." *Journal of Conflict Resolution,* 27, December, 618–34.

BECKER, GORDON M., MORRIS H. DeGROOT, and JACOB MARSCHAK (1964).

"Measuring Utility by a Single-Response Sequential Method." *Behavioral Science*, 9, July, 226–32.

BELL, DAVID, HOWARD RAIFFA, and AMOS TVERSKY, (1988). "Descriptive, Normative, and Prescriptive Interactions in Decision Making." In David Bell, Howard Raiffa, and Amos Tversky, eds., *Decision Making: Descriptive, Normative, and Prescriptive Interactions*. New York: Cambridge University Press.

BENZION, URI, AMNON RAPOPORT, and JOSEPH YAGIL (1989). "Discount Rates Inferred from Decisions: An Experimental Study." *Management Science*, 35, March, 270–84.

BERGES, A., J. J. MCCONNELL, and G. G. SCHLARBAUM (1984). "An Investigation of the Turn-of-the-Year Effect, the Small Firm Effect and the Tax-Loss-Selling-Pressure Hypothesis in Canadian Stock Returns." *Journal of Finance*, 39, March, 185–92.

BERGSTROM, THEODORE, LAWRENCE E. BLUME, and HAL VARIAN (1986). "On the Private Provision of Public Goods." *Journal of Public Economics*, 29, 25–49.

BILSON, JOHN (1981). "The Speculative Efficiency Hypothesis." *Journal of Business*, 54, 433–451.

BINMORE, KEN, AVNER SHAKED, and JOHN SUTTON (1985). "Testing Noncooperative Bargaining Theory: A Preliminary Study." *American Economic Review*, 75, 1178–80.

BLACKBURN, MCKINLEY, and DAVID NEUMARK (1987). "Efficiency Wages, Inter-Industry Wage Differentials, and the Returns to Ability." Unpublished, Finance and Economics Discussion Series, Federal Reserve Board.

BOOTHE, PAUL, and DAVID LONGWORTH (1986). "Foreign Exchange Market Efficiency Tests: Implications of Recent Findings." *Journal of International Money and Finance*, 5, 135–52.

BOSTIC, RAPHAEL, RICHARD J. HERRNSTEIN, and R. DUNCAN LUCE (1990). "The Effect on the Preference-Reversal Phenomenon of Using Choice Indifferences." *Journal of Economic Behavior and Organization*, 13, 2, March, 193–212.

BOUDREAUX, K. J. (1973). "Discounts and Premiums on Closed-end Mutual Funds: A Study in Valuation." *Journal of Finance*, May.

BRAUER, GREGORY A. (1984). "Open-ending Closed-end Funds." *Journal of Financial Economics*, 13.

BRAUER, GREGORY A. (1988). "Closed-End Fund Shares' Abnormal Returns and the Information Content of Discounts and Premiums." *Journal of Finance*, March.

BRAUER, GREGORY, A., and ERIC CHANG (1989). "Return Seasonality in Stocks and Their Underlying Assets: Tax Loss Selling Versus Information Explanations." Working Paper, University of Washington and University of Maryland.

BREALEY, RICHARD A., and STEWART C. MYERS (1988). *Principles of Corporate Finance*, 3rd edition. New York: McGraw-Hill.

BREMER, M. A., and RICHARD J. SWEENEY (1991). "The Information Content of Extreme Negative Rates of Return." *Journal of Finance*, March.

BRICKLEY, JAMES A., STEVE MANASTER, and JAMES S. SCHALLHEIM (1989). "The Tax Timing Option and the Discounts on Closed-End Investment Companies." Working Paper, Graduate School of Business, University of Utah.

BRICKLEY, JAMES A., and JAMES S. SCHALLHEIM (1985). "Lifting the Lid on Closed-end Investment Companies: A Case of Abnormal Returns." *Journal of Financial and Quantitative Analysis*, 20, 1, March.

BROWN, CHARLES, and JAMES MEDOFF (forthcoming). "The Employer Size Wage Effect." *Journal of Political Economy*.

BROWN, KEITH (1974). "A Note on the Apparent Bias of Net Revenue Estimates for Capital Investment Projects." *Journal of Finance*, 29, 1215–16.

BROWN, KEITH C., and W. VAN HARLOW (1988). "Market Overreaction: Magnitude and Intensity." *Journal of Portfolio Management*, Winter, 6–13.

BROWN, KEITH C., W. VAN HARLOW, and SEHA M. TINIC (1988). "Risk Aversion, Uncertain Information, and Market Efficiency." Working Paper, University of Texas at Austin, January.

CAGAN, PHILIP (1965). *The Effect of Pension Plans on Aggregate Savings*. New York: National Bureau of Economic Research.

CAMPBELL, JOHN, and ANGUS DEATON (1987). "Is Consumption Too Smooth?" Working Paper, Department of Economics, Princeton University.

CAMPBELL, JOHN Y., and N. GREGORY MANKIW (1989). "Consumption, Income, and Interest Rates: Reinterpreting the Time Series Evidence." National Bureau of Economic Research, Working Paper #2924.

CAMPBELL, JOHN Y., and ROBERT J. SHILLER (1988). "Stock Prices, Earnings, and Expected Dividends." *Journal of Finance*, 43, July 661–76.

CAPEN, E. C., R. V. CLAPP, and W. M. CAMPBELL (1971). "Competitive Bidding in High-Risk Situations." *Journal of Petroleum Technology*, 23, June, 641–53.

CARROLL, CHRIS, and LAWRENCE H. SUMMERS (1987). "Why Have Private Savings Rates in the United States and Canada Diverged?" *Journal of Monetary Economics*, 20, 249–79.

CARROLL, CHRIS, and LAWRENCE H. SUMMERS (1989). "Consumption Growth Parallels Income Growth: Some New Evidence." Department of Economics, Harvard University.

CASSING, JAMES, and RICHARD W. DOUGLAS (1980). "Implications of the Auction Mechanism in Baseball's Free Agent Draft." *Southern Economic Journal*, 47, July, 110–21.

CHAN, K. C. (1988). "On the Return of the Contrarian Investment Strategy." *Journal of Business*, 61, 147–63.

CHERNOFF, HERMAN (1980). "An Analysis of the Massachusetts Numbers Game." Department of Mathematics, MIT, Technical Report No. 23, November.

CLOTFELTER, CHARLES T. (1985). *Federal Tax Policy and Charitable Giving.* Chicago: The University of Chicago Press.

COHEN, DAVID, and JACK L. KNETSCH (1990). "Judicial choice and Disparities between Measures of Economic Values." Working Paper, 19 Department of Economics, Simon Fraser University.

CONSTANTINIDES, GEORGE (1988). "Habit Formation: A Resolution of the Equity Premium Puzzle." Unpublished Working Paper, Graduate School of Business, University of Chicago.

COURANT, PAUL, EDWARD GRAMLICH, and JOHN LAITNER (1986). "A Dynamic Micro Estimate of the Life Cycle Model," In Henry G. Aaron and Gary Burtless, eds., *Retirement and Economic Behavior*. Washington D.C.: Brookings Institution.

COURSEY, DONALD L., and EDWARD A. DYL (1986). "Price Effects of Trading Interruptions in an Experimental Market." Unpublished Working Paper, Department of Economics, University of Wyoming, March.

COURSEY, DONALD L., JOHN L. HOVIS, and WILLIAM D. SCHULZE (1987). "The Disparity between Willingness to Accept and Willingness to Pay Measures of Value." *The Quarterly Journal of Economics*, 102, 679–90.

COX, JAMES C. and R. M. ISAAC (1984). "In Search of the Winner's Curse." *Economic Inquiry*, 22, 579–92.

CROSS, FRANK (1973). "The Behavior of Stock Prices on Fridays and Mondays." *Financial Analysts Journal*, November–December, 67–69.

CUMBY, ROBERT, and DAVID MODEST (1987). "Testing for Market Timing Ability: A Framework for Forecast Evaluation." *Journal of Financial Economics*, 169–89.

CUMMINGS, RONALD G., DAVID S. BROOKSHIRE, and WILLIAM D. SCHULZE, eds. (1986). *Valuing Environmental Goods*. Totowa, N.J.: Rowman and Allanheld.

CUTLER, DAVID M., JAMES M. POTERBA, LAWRENCE H. SUMMERS (1990).

"Speculative Dynamics and the Role of Feedback Traders." *American Economic Review*, 80, May, 63–68.

DARK, F. H., and K. KATO (1986). "Stock Market Overreaction in the Japanese Stock Market." Working Paper, Department of Economics, Iowa State University.

DAWES, ROBYN M., JOHN M. ORBELL, RANDY T. SIMMONS, and ALPHONS J. C. VAN DE KRAGT (1986). "Organizing Groups for Collective Action.: *American Political Science Review*, 80, 1171–85.

DAWES, ROBYN M., and RICHARD H. THALER (1988). "Cooperation." *Journal of Economic Perspectives*, 2, Summer, 187–97.

DE BONDT, WERNER F. M. (forthcoming). "Stock Price Reversals and Overreaction to New Events: A Survey of Theory and Evidence." In S. J. Taylor, B. G. Kingsman, and R. M. C. Guimaraes (eds.), *A Reappraisal of the Efficiency of Financial Markets*. Heidelberg: Springer-Verlag.

DE BONDT, WERNER F. M., and RICHARD H. THALER (1985). "Does the Stock Market Overreact?" *Journal of Finance*, 40, July, 793–805.

DE BONDT, WERNER F. M., and RICHARD H. THALER (1987). "Further Evidence on Investor Overreaction and Stock Market Seasonality." *Journal of Finance*, 42, July, 557–81.

DE LONG, J. BRADFORD, ANDREI SHLEIFER, LAWRENCE H. SUMMERS, and ROBERT J. WALDMANN (1990). "Noise Trader Risk in Financial Markets." *Journal of Political Economy*, 98, August, 703–38.

DEATON, ANGUS (1987). "Life-cycle Models of Consumption: Is the Evidence Consistent with the Theory?" In Truman F. Bewley, *Advances in Econometrics: 5th World Congress*, Vol. II. New York: Cambridge University Press, 121–48.

DEATON, ANGUS (1989). "Saving in Developing Countries: Theory and Review." Working Paper, Department of Economics, Princeton University.

DESSAUER, JOHN P. (1981). *Book Publishing*. New York: Bowker.

DICKENS, WILLIAM T. (1986). "Wages, Employment and the Threat of Collective Action by Workers." Unpublished, University of California, Berkeley.

DICKENS, WILLIAM T., and LAWRENCE F. KATZ (1987a). "Inter-Industry Wage Differences and Industry Characteristics." In Kevin Lang and Jonathan S. Leonard, eds., *Unemployment and the Structure of Labor Markets*. Oxford: Basil Blackwell.

DICKENS, WILLIAM T., and LAWRENCE F. KATZ (1987b). "Inter-Industry Wage Differences and Theories of Wage Determination." National Bureau of Economic Research, Working Paper #2271.

DOMOWITZ, IAN, and CRAIG HAKKIO (1985). "Conditional Variance and the Risk Premium in the Foreign Exchange Market." *Journal of International Economics*, 19, 47–66.

DOOLEY, MICHAEL P., and JEFF SHAFER (1983). "Analysis of Short-Run Exchange Rate Behavior: March 1983 to November 1981." In D. Bigman and T. Taya, eds., *Exchange Rate and Trade Instability: Causes, Consequences, and Remedies.* Cambridge, Mass.: Ballinger.

DYER, DOUGLAS, JOHN KAGEL, and DAN LEVIN (1987). "The Winner's Curse in Low Price Auctions." Unpublished manuscript, Department of Economics, University of Houston.

DYL, EDWARD A., and KENNETH MAXFIELD (1987). "Does the Stock Market Overreact? Additional Evidence." Working Paper, Department of Economics, University of Arizona, June.

ELSTER, JON (1979). *Ulysses and the Sirens.* New York, Cambridge University Press.

ELSTER, JON (1986). "The Market and the Forum: Three Varieties of Political Theory." In Jon Elster and Aanund Hylland, eds., *Foundations of Social Choice Theory: Studies in Rationality and Social Change.* Cambridge, U.K.: Cambridge University Press, 103–132.

ELTON, E., M. GRUBER, and J. RENTZLER (1982). "Intra Day Tests of the Efficiency of the Treasury Bills Futures Market." Working Paper No. CSFM-38, Columbia University Business School, October.

ENGEL, CHARLES M., and JAMES HAMILTON (1990). "Long Swings in the Foreign Exchange Market: Are They There, and Do Investors Know It?" National Bureau of Economic Research, Working Paper, *American Economic Review.*

ENGEL, CHARLES M., and ANTHONY P. RODRIGUES (1989). "Tests of International CAPM with Time-Varying Covariances." *Journal of Applied Econometrics,* 4 119–38.

EVANS, GEORGE W. (1986). "A Test for Speculative Bubbles in the Sterling-Dollar Exchange Rate: 1981–84." *American Economic Review,* 76, September, 621–36.

FAMA, EUGENE F. (1965). "The Behavior of Stock Market Prices." *Journal of Business,* 38, January, 34–105.

FAMA, EUGENE F. (1984). "Forward and Spot Exchange Rates." *Journal of Monetary Economics,* 36, 697–703.

FAMA, EUGENE F., and KENNETH R. FRENCH (1986). "Common Factors in the Serial Correlation of Stock Returns." Working Paper, Graduate School of Business, University of Chicago, October.

FAMA, EUGENE F., and KENNETH R. FRENCH (1988). "Permanent and Temporary Components of Stock Prices." *Journal of Political Economy,* 98, April, 246–74.

FAMA, EUGENE F., and KENNETH R. FRENCH (forthcoming). "Dividend Yields and Expected Stock Returns." *Journal of Financial Economics.*

FEENBERG, DANIEL, and JONATHAN SKINNER (1989). "Sources of IRA Saving." In Lawrence Summers, ed., *Tax Policy and the Economy*, Vol. 3. Cambridge: MIT Press, 25–46.

FEINSTEIN, JONATHAN, and DANIEL MCFADDEN (1987). "The Dynamics of Housing Demand by the Elderly: Wealth, Cash Flow, and Demographic Effects." National Bureau of Economic Research, Working Paper #2471.

FIELDS, M. J. (1931). "Stock Prices: A Problem in Verification." *Journal of Business,*

FIELDS, M. J. (1934). "Security Prices and Stock Exchange Holidays in Relation to Short Selling." *Journal of Business*, 328–38.

FISHBURN, PETER C. (1985). "Nontransitive Preference Theory and the Preference Reversal Phenomenon." *Rivista Internazionale di Scienze Economiche e Commerciali*, 32, January, 39–50.

FISHER, IRVING (1930). *The Theory of Interest*. London: Macmillan.

FLAVIN, MARJORIE (1981). "The Adjustment of Consumption to Changing Expectations about Future Income." *Journal of Political Economy*, 89, 974–1009.

FORSYTHE, ROBERT, THOMAS R. PALFREY, and CHARLES R. PLOTT (1982). "Asset Valuation in an Experimental Market." *Econometrica*, 50, May, 537–67.

FORSYTHE, ROBERT, THOMAS R. PALFREY, and CHARLES R. PLOTT (1984). "Futures Markets and Informational Efficiency: A Laboratory Examination." *Journal of Finance*, 39, September, 55–69.

FRANK, ROBERT (1987). "If *Homo Economicus* Could Choose His Own Utility Function, Would He Want One with a Conscience?" *American Economic Review*, 77, September, 593–605.

FRANK, ROBERT, and ROBERT HUTCHENS (1990). "Feeling Better vs. Feeling Good: A Life-Cycle Theory of Wages." Working Paper, Department of Economics, Cornell University.

FRANKEL, JEFFREY A. (1982). "A Test of Perfect Substitutability in the Foreign Exchange Market." *Southern Economic Journal*, 48, 406–16 (a).

FRANKEL, JEFFREY A., and CHARLES M. ENGEL (1984). "Do Asset Demand Functions Optimize over the Mean and Variance of Real Returns? A Six Currency Test." *Journal of International Economics*, 17, 309–23.

FRANKEL, JEFFREY A., and KENNETH A. FROOT (1987). "Using Survey Data to Test Standard Propositions on Exchange Rate Expectations." *American Economic Review*, 77, March, 133–53.

FREEMAN, RICHARD B., and JAMES L. MEDOFF (1984). *What Do Unions Do?* New York: Basic Books.

FRENCH, KENNETH (1980). "Stock Returns and the Weekend Effect." *Journal of Financial Economics*, 8, March, 55–69.

FRENCH, KENNETH R., and RICHARD ROLL (1986). "Stock Return Variances: The Arrival of Information and the Reaction of Traders." *Journal of Financial Economics*, 17, September, 5–26.

FRIEDMAN, MILTON (1953). "The Case for Flexible Exchange Rates." In his *Essays in Positive Economics*. Chicago: University of Chicago Press, 157–203.

FRIEDMAN, MILTON (1957). *A Theory of the Consumption Function.* Princeton: Princeton University Press.

FRIEDMAN, MILTON, and L. J. SAVAGE (1948). "The Utility Analysis of Choices Involving Risk." *Journal of Political Economy*, 56, August, 279–304.

FROOT, KENNETH A. (1990). "Short Rates and Expected Asset Returns." National Bureau of Economic Research Working Paper, #3247, January.

FROOT, KENNETH A., and JEFFREY A. FRANKEL (1989). "Forward Discount Bias: Is it an Exchange Risk Premium?" *Quarterly Journal of Economics*, 416, February, 139–61.

GATELY, DERMOT (1980). "Individual Discount Rates and the Purchase and Utilization of Energy-using Durables: Comment." *Bell Journal of Economics*, 11, 1, 373–74.

GIBBONS, MICHAEL, and PATRICK HESS (1981). "Day of the Week Effects and Asset Returns." *Journal of Business*, 54, October, 579–96.

GIBBONS, ROBERT S., and LAWRENCE F. KATZ (1987). "Learning, Mobility, and Inter-Industry Wage Differences." Unpublished Working Paper, MIT.

GILOVICH, THOMAS, ROBERT VALLONE, and AMOS TVERSKY (1985). "The Hot Hand in Basketball: On the Misperceptions of Random Sequences." *Cognitive Psychology*, 17, 295–314.

GIOVANNINI, ALBERTO, and PHILLIPE JORION (1989). "The Time-Variation of Risk and Return in the Foreign Exchange and Stock Markets." *Journal of Finance*, 44, 2.

GOETZE, DAVID, and JOHN M. ORBELL (forthcoming). "Understanding and Cooperation." *Public Choice.*

GOLDSTEIN, WILLIAM M., and HILLEL J. EINHORN (1987). "Expression Theory and the Preference Reversal Phenomena." *Psychological Review*, 94, April, 236–54.

GRAHAM, BENJAMIN (1949). *The Intelligent Investor: A Book of Practical Counsel.* New York: Harper and Brothers.

GREEN, FRANCIS (1981). "The Effect of Occupational Pension Schemes on Saving in the United Kingdom: A Test of the Life Cycle Hypothesis." *Economic Journal*, 91, March, 136–44.

GRETHER, DAVID M. (1980). "Bayes' Rule as a Descriptive Model: The Representativeness Heuristic." *Quarterly Journal of Economics*, 95, November, 537–57.

GRETHER, DAVID M., and CHARLES PLOTT (1979). "Economic Theory of Choice and the Preference Reversal Phenomenon." *American Economic Review*, 75, 623–38.

GROSHEN, ERICA L. (1988). "Sources of Wage Dispersion: The Contribution of Interemployer Differentials within Industry." Unpublished, Federal Reserve Bank of Cleveland.

GROSSMAN, SANFORD J., and OLIVER D. HART (1980). "Takeover Bids, the Free-rider Problem, and the Theory of the Corporation." *Bell Journal of Economics and Management Science*, Spring, 42–64.

GULTEKIN, MUSTAFA N., and N. BULENT GULTEKIN (1983). "Stock Market Seasonality: International Evidence." *Journal of Financial Economics*, 12, 469–81.

GÜTH, WERNER, ROLF SCHMITTBERGER, and BERND SCHWARZE (1982). "An Experimental Analysis of Ultimatum Bargaining." *Journal of Economic Behavior and Organization*, 3, 367–88.

GÜTH, WERNER, and REINHARD TIETZ (1987). "Ultimatum Bargaining for a Shrinking Cake: An Experimental Analysis." Unpublished, J. W. Goethe-Universität.

HALL, ROBERT (1988). "Intertemporal Substitution in Consumption." *Journal of Political Economy*, 86, 339–57.

HALL, ROBERT, and FREDRICK MISHKIN (1982). "The Sensitivity of Consumption to Transitory Income: Estimates from Panel Data on Households." *Econometrica*, 50, 461–81.

HARRIS, LAWRENCE (1986a). "A Transaction Data Study of Weekly and Intradaily Patterns in Stock Returns." *Journal of Financial Economics*, 16, 99–117.

HARRIS, LAWRENCE (1986b). "A Day-End Transaction Price Anomaly." Unpublished Working Paper, Department of Finance, University of Southern California, March.

HARRIS, LAWRENCE, and EITAN GUREL (1986). "Price and Volume Effects Associated with Changes in the S&P 500 List: New Evidence for the Existence of Price Pressures." *Journal of Finance*, 41, September, 815–29.

HARRISON, J. R., and J. G. MARCH (1984). "Decision Making and Postdecision Surprises." *Administrative Science Quarterly*, March, 26–42.

HARTMAN, RAYMOND, MICHAEL J. DOANE, and CHI-KEUNG WOO (forthcoming). "Consumer Rationality and the Status Quo." *Quarterly Journal of Economics.*

HARVILLE, DAVID A. (1973). "Assigning Probabilities to the Outcomes of Multi-Entry Competitions." *Journal of the American Statistical Association*, 68, 312–16.

HATSOPOULOS, GEORGE N., PAUL R. KRUGMAN, and JAMES M. POTERBA (1989). "Overconsumption: The Challenge to U.S. Economic Policy." American Business Conference.

HAUGEN, ROBERT A., and JOSEF LAKONISHOK (1986). *Only in January. An Investor's Guide to the Unsolved Mystery of the Stock Market. The Incredible January Effect.* Unpublished manuscript, University of Illinois, Urbana-Champaign.

HAUSCH, DONALD B., and WILLIAM T. ZIEMBA (1985). "Transactions Costs, Extent of Inefficiencies, Entries and Multiple Wagers in a Racetrack Betting Model." *Management Science*, 31, 381–94.

HAUSCH, DONALD B., and WILLIAM T. ZIEMBA (1987). "Cross Track Betting on Major Stakes Races." Working Paper No. 975, Faculty of Commerce, University of British Columbia, Vancouver, June.

HAUSCH, DONALD B., WILLIAM T. ZIEMBA, and MARK RUBINSTEIN (1981). "Efficiency of the Market for Racetrack Betting." *Management Science*, 27, 1435–52.

HAUSMAN, JERRY (1979). "Individual Discount Rates and the Purchase and Utilization of Energy-Using Durables." *Bell Journal of Economics*, 10, 33–54.

HAYASHI, FUMIO (1985). "The Effect of Liquidity Constraints on Consumption: A Cross-Sectional Analysis." *Quarterly Journal of Economics*, 100, 183–206.

HENDRICKS, KENNETH, ROBERT H. PORTER, and BRYAN BOUDREAU (1987). "Information, Returns, and Bidding Behavior in OCS Auctions: 1954–1969." *Journal of Industrial Economics*, 35, 517–42.

HERRNSTEIN, RICHARD J. (1961). "Relative and Absolute Strength of Response as a Function of Frequency of Reinforcement." *Journal of Experimental Analysis of Behavior.* 4, 267–72.

HERSHEY, JOHN, ERIC JOHNSON, JACQUELINE MESZAROS, and MATTHEW ROBINSON (1990). "What Is the Right to Sue Worth?" Unpublished paper, Wharton School, University of Pennsylvania, June.

HERSHEY, JOHN C., and PAUL J. H. SCHOEMAKER (1985). "Probability versus Certainty Equivalence Methods in Utility Measurement: Are They Equivalent?" *Management Science*, 31, October, 1213–31.

HERZFELD, THOMAS J. (1980). *The Investor's Guide to Closed-end Funds.* New York: McGraw-Hill.

HIRSHLEIFER, JACK (1985). "The Expanding Domain of Economics." *American Economic Review,* 75, 6, December, 53–70.

HODRICK, ROBERT J. (1987). "The Empirical Evidence on the Efficiency of Forward and Futures Foreign Exchange Markets." In Jacques Lesourne, Hugo Sonnenstein ed., *Fundamentals of Pure and Applied Economics,* #24 Chur, Switzerland: Harwood Academic Publishers.

HODRICK, ROBERT J., and SANJAY SRIVASTAVA (1984). "An Investigation of Risk and Return in Forward Foreign Exchange." *Journal of International Money and Finance,* 3, April 5–30.

HODRICK, ROBERT J., and SANJAY SRIVASTAVA (1986). "The Covariation of Risk Premiums and Expected Future Spot Rates." *Journal of International Money and Finance,* 5, S5–S22.

HOFFMAN, ELIZABETH, and MATTHEW L. SPITZER (1982). "The Coase Theorem: Some Experimental Tests." *Journal of Law and Economics,* 25, 73–98.

HOFFMAN, ELIZABETH, and MATTHEW L. SPITZER (1985). "Entitlements, Rights and Fairness: An Experimental Examination of Subjects' Concepts of Distributive Justice." *Journal of Legal Studies,* 14, 259–97.

HOFSTEADTER, DOUGLAS (1983). "Metamagical Themas." *Scientific American,* 248, 14–28.

HOLCOMB, JOHN H., and PAUL S. NELSON (1989). "An Experimental Investigation of Individual Time Preference." Unpublished Working Paper, Department of Economics, University of Texas at El Paso.

HOLMES, OLIVER WENDELL (1897). "The Path of the Law." *Harvard Law Review.* 10, 457–78.

HOLT, CHARLES A. (1986). "Preference Reversals and the Independence Axiom." *The American Economic Review,* 76, June, 508–15.

HOROWITZ, JOHN K. (1988). "Discounting Money Payoffs: An Experimental Analysis." Working Paper, Department of Agricultural and Resource Economics, University of Maryland.

HOWE, JOHN S. (1986). "Evidence on Stock Market Overreaction." *Financial Analysts Journal,* July/August, 74–77.

ISAAC, R. MARK, KENNETH F. MCCUE, and CHARLES PLOTT (1985). "Public Goods Provision in an Experimental Environment." *Journal of Public Economics,* 26, 51–74.

ISAAC, R. MARK, and JAMES M. WALKER (forthcoming). "Group Size Effects in Public Goods Provision: The Voluntary Contributions Mechanism." *Quarterly Journal of Economics.*

ISAAC, R. MARK, JAMES M. WALKER, and SUSAN H. THOMAS (1984). "Divergent Evidence on Free Riding: An Experimental Examination of Possible Explanations." *Public Choice,* 43, 113–49.

ISHIKAWA, TSUNEO, and KAZUO UEDA (1984). "The Bonus Payment System and Japanese Personal Savings." In Masahiko Aoki, ed., *The Economic Analysis of the Japanese Firm*. Amsterdam: North-Holland.

JEGADEESH, NARASIMHAN (1987). "Evidence of Predictable Behavior of Security Returns." Working Paper, Columbia University, May.

KAGEL, JOHN H., and DAN LEVIN (1986). "The Winner's Curse and Public Information in Common Value Auctions." *The American Economic Review*, 76, December, 894–920.

KAGEL, JOHN H., DAN LEVIN, and RONALD M. HARSTAD (1987). "Judgment, Evaluation and Information Procession in Second-Price Common Value Auctions." Unpublished manuscript, Department of Economics, University of Houston.

KAHNEMAN, DANIEL, JACK KNETSCH, and RICHARD H. THALER (1986a). "Fairness as a Constraint on Profit Seeking: Entitlements in the Market." *American Economic Review*, 76, September, 728–41.

KAHNEMAN, DANIEL, JACK L. KNETSCH, and RICHARD H. THALER (1986b). "Fairness and the Assumptions of Economics." *Journal of Business*, 59, S285–S300.

KAHNEMAN, DANIEL, JACK L. KNETSCH, and RICHARD THALER (1990). "Experimental Tests of the Endowment Effect and the Coase Theorem." *Journal of Political Economy*, 98, December, 1325–48.

KAHNEMAN, DANIEL, and AMOS TVERSKY (1973). "On the Psychology of Prediction." *Psychological Review*, 80, 237–51.

KAHNEMAN, DANIEL, and AMOS TVERSKY (1979). "Prospect Theory: An Analysis of Decision under Risk." *Econometrica*, 47, 2 363–91.

KAHNEMAN, DANIEL, and AMOS TVERSKY (1984). "Choices, Values and Frames." *American Psychologist*, 39, April, 341–50.

KARNI, EDI, and ZVI SAFRA (1987). "'Preference Reversal' and the Observability of Preferences by Experimental Methods." *Econometrica*, 55, May, 675–85.

KATO, KIYOSHI, and JAMES S. SCHALLHEIM (1985). "Seasonal and Size Anomalies in the Japanese Stock Market." *Journal of Financial and Quantitative Analysis*, 20, June, 107–18.

KATONA, GEORGE (1965). *Private Pensions and Individual Saving*. Ann Arbor: University of Michigan.

KATZ, LAWRENCE F. (1986). "Efficiency Wage Theories: A Partial Evaluation." *National Bureau of Economics Research Macroeconomics Annual*, 1, 235–76.

KATZ, LAWRENCE F., and LAWRENCE H. SUMMERS (forthcoming). "Industry Rents and Industrial Policy." *Brookings Papers on Economic Activity*.

KEIM, DONALD B. (1983). "Size-Related Anomalies and Stock Return Seasonality: Further Empirical Evidence." *Journal of Financial Economics*, June, 13–32.

KEIM, DONALD B. (1985). "Dividend Yields and Stock Returns: Implications of Abnormal January Returns." *Journal of Financial Economics*, 14, 473–89.

KEIM, DONALD B. (1986a). "Dividend Yield and the January Effect." *The Journal of Portfolio Management*, Winter, 54–60.

KEIM, DONALD B. (1986b). "The CAPM and Equity Return Regularities." *Financial Analysts Journal*, May–June, 19–34.

KEIM, DONALD B., and ROBERT F. STAMBAUGH (1984). "A Further Investigation of the Weekend Effect in Stock Returns." *Journal of Finance*, 39, 3 July, 819–40.

KEYNES, JOHN M. (1936). *The General Theory of Employment, Interest and Money*. London: Harcourt Bruce Jovanovich.

KIM, OLIVER, and MARK WALKER (1984). "The Free Rider Problem: Experimental Evidence." *Public Choice*, 43, 3–24.

KLEIDON, ALLAN W. (1986). "Anomalies in Financial Economics." *Journal of Business*, 59, Supplement, December.

KNETSCH, JACK L. (1989). "The Endowment Effect and Evidence of Nonreversible Indifference Curves." *The American Economic Review*, 79, 1277–84.

KNETSCH, JACK L. (1990). "Derived Indifference Curves." Working Paper, Department of Economics, Simon Fraser University.

KNETSCH, JACK L., and J. A. SINDEN (1984). "Willingness to Pay and Compensation Demanded: Experimental Evidence of an Unexpected Disparity in Measures of Value." *Quarterly Journal of Economics*, 99, 507–21.

KNETSCH, JACK L., and J. A. SINDEN (1987). "The Persistence of Evaluation Disparities." *Quarterly Journal of Economics*, 99, 691–95.

KNEZ, PETER, VERNON SMITH, and ARLINGTON W. WILLIAMS (1985). "Individual Rationality, Market Rationality, and Value Estimation." *American Economic Review*, 75, May, 397–402.

KOTLIKOFF, LAWRENCE J., and LAWRENCE H. SUMMERS (1981). "The Role of Intergenerational Transfers in Aggregate Capital Formation." *Journal of Political Economy*, 89, 706–32.

KRAMER, R. M., and MARILYN BREWER (1986). "Social Group Identity and the Emergence of Cooperation in Resource Conservation Dilemmas." In H. Wilke, D. Messick, and C. Rutte, eds, *Psychology of Decision and Conflict* Vol. 3, *Experimental Social Dilemmas*. Frankfurt am Main: Verlag Peter Lang, 205–30.

KREPS, DAVID, PAUL MILGROM, JOHN ROBERTS, and ROBERT WILSON (1982). "Rational Cooperation in Finitely Repeated Prisoner's Dilemmas." *Journal of Economic Theory, 27*, 245–52.

KRUEGER, ALAN B., and LAWRENCE H. SUMMERS (1987). "Reflections on the Inter-Industry Wage Structure." In Kevin Lang and Jonathan S. Leonard, eds., *Unemployment and the Structure of Labor Markets*. Oxford: Basil Blackwell.

KRUEGER, ALAN B., and LAWRENCE H. SUMMERS (1988). "Efficiency Wages and the Inter-Industry Wage Structure." *Econometrica, 56*, March, 259–93.

KRUGMAN, PAUL R. (1989). *Exchange Rate Instability*. Cambridge, Mass.: MIT Press.

KRUMM, RONALD, and NANCY MILLER (1986). "Household Savings, Homeownership, and Tenure Duration." Office of Real Estate, Research Paper #38.

KUNREUTHER, HOWARD, DOUGLAS EASTERLING, WILLIAM DESVOUSGES, and PAUL SLOVIC (forthcoming). "Public Attitudes toward Citing a High Level Nuclear Waste Depository in Nevada." *Risk Analysis*.

LAING, JOHNATHAN R. (1987). "Burnt Offerings: Closed-end Funds Bring No Blessings to Shareholders." *Barron's*, 10, August, 6–7, 32–36.

LAKONISHOK, JOSEF, and MAURICE LEVI (1982). "Weekend Effects on Stock Returns." *Journal of Finance, 37*, 883–89.

LAKONISHOK, JOSEF, and SEYMOUR SMIDT (1984). "Volume and Turn of the Year Behavior." *Journal of Financial Economics*, September, 435–55.

LAKONISHOK, JOSEF, and SEYMOUR SMIDT (1987). "Are Seasonal Anomalies Real? A Ninety-Year Perspective." Unpublished Working Paper, Department of Finance, Cornell University.

LANDSBERGER, MICHAEL (1966). "Windfall Income and Consumption: Comment." *American Economic Review, 56*, June, 534–39.

LANGER, ELLEN J. (1975). "The Illusion of Control." *Journal of Personality and Social Psychology, 32*, 311–28.

LAWRENCE, COLIN, and ROBERT Z. LAWRENCE (1985). "Manufacturing Wage Dispersion: An End Game Interpretation." *Brookings Papers on Economic Activity*, 47–106.

LAZEAR, EDWARD (1981). "Agency, Earnings Profiles, Productivity, and Hours Restrictions." *American Economic Review, 61*, 606–20.

LEE, CHARLES, ANDREI SHLEIFER, and RICHARD THALER (1991a). "Investor Sentiment and the Closed-end Fund Puzzle." *Journal of Finance, 46*, 75–110.

LEE, CHARLES, ANDREI SHLEIFER, and RICHARD THALER (1991b). "Explaining Closed-end Fund Discounts: A Cross-Examination of the Evidence." Unpublished manuscript, Johnson School of Management, Cornell University, June.

LEHMANN, BRUCE N. (1988). "Fads, Martingales, and Market Efficiency." Working Paper, Hoover Institution, Stanford University, January.

LEVICH, RICHARD (1985). "Empirical Studies of Exchange Rates: Price Behavior, Rate Determination and Market Efficiency." In R. W. Jones and P. B. Kenen, eds., *Handbook of International Economics*, Vol. 2. Amsterdam: North-Holland.

LEWIS, KAREN K. (1989). "Changing Beliefs and Systematic Rational Forecast Errors with Evidence from Foreign Exchange." *American Economic Review*, 79, September, 621–36.

LICHTENSTEIN, SARAH, and PAUL SLOVIC (1971). "Reversals of Preference between Bids and Choices in Gambling Decisions." *Journal of Experimental Psychology*, 89, January, 46–55.

LICHTENSTEIN, SARAH, and PAUL SLOVIC (1973). "Response-induced Reversals of Preference in Gambling: An Extended Replication in Las Vegas." *Journal of Experimental Psychology*, 101, November, 16–20.

LIND, ROBERT (forthcoming). "Reassessing the Government's Discount Rate Policy in Light of New Theory and Data in a World Economy with a High Degree of Capital Mobility," *Journal of Environmental Economics and Management*.

LINDBECK, ASSAR, and DENNIS SNOWER (1988). "Cooperation, Harassment, and Involuntary Unemployment: An Insider-Outsider Approach." *American Economic Review*, 78, March, 167–88.

LO, ANDREW W., and A. CRAIG MACKINLAY (1988). "Stock Prices Do Not Follow Random Walks: Evidence from a Simple Specification Test." *Review of Financial Studies*, 1, 1, 41–66.

LOEWENSTEIN, GEORGE (1987). "Anticipation and the Valuation of Delayed Consumption." *Economic Journal*, 97, 666–84.

LOEWENSTEIN, GEORGE (1988). "Frames of Mind in Intertemporal Choice." *Management Science*, 34, 200–214.

LOEWENSTEIN, GEORGE, and DANIEL KAHNEMAN (1991). "Explaining the Endowment Effect." Working Paper, Department of Social and Decision Sciences, Carnegie-Mellon University.

LOEWENSTEIN, GEORGE, and DRAZEN PRELEC (1989a). "Anomalies in Intertemporal Choice: Evidence and Interpretation." Working Paper, Russell Sage Foundation.

LOEWENSTEIN, GEORGE, and DRAZEN PRELEC (1989b). "Decision Making over Time and under Uncertainty: A Common Approach." Working Paper, Center for Decision Research, University of Chicago.

LOEWENSTEIN, GEORGE, and NACHUM SICHERMAN (1989). "Do Workers Prefer Increasing Wage Profiles?" Unpublished Working Paper, Graduate School of Business, University of Chicago.

LOOMES, GRAHAM, and ROBERT SUGDEN (1983). "A Rationale for Preference Reversal." *American Economic Review,* 73, June, 428–32.

MACLEAN, LEONARD, WILLIAM T. ZIEMBA, and GEORGE BLAZENKO (1987). "Growth versus Security in Dynamic Investment Analysis." Mimeo, Faculty of Commerce and Business Administration, University of British Columbia, 1987.

MALKIEL, BURTON G. (1977). "The Valuation of Closed-end Investment Company Shares." *Journal of Finance,* June.

MALKIEL, BURTON G. (1985). *A Random Walk Down Wall Street.* New York: Norton.

MANCHESTER, JOYCE M., and JAMES M. PORTERBA (1989). "Second Mortgages and Household Saving." *Regional Science and Urban Economics,* 19, 2, May, 325–46.

MARK, NELSON C. (1985). "On Time Varying Risk Premia in the Foreign Exchange Market: An Econometric Analysis." *Journal of Monetary Economics,* 16, 3–18.

MARKOWITZ, HARRY (1952). "The Utility of Wealth." *Journal of Political Economy,* 60, 151–58.

MARSH, T. A., and R. C. MERTON (1986). "Dividend Variability and Variance Bounds Tests for the Rationality of Stock Market Prices." *American Economic Review,* 76, June, 483–98.

MARSHALL, ALFRED (1891). *Principles of Economics,* 2nd ed. London: Macmillian.

MARWELL, GERALD, and RUTH AMES (1981). "Economists Free Ride, Does Anyone Else?" *Journal of Public Economics,* 15, 295–310.

MCAFEE, R. PRESTON, and JOHN MCMILLAN (1987). "Auctions and Bidding." *Journal of Economic Literature,* 25, June, 699–738.

MCGLOTHLIN, WILLIAM H. (1956). "Stability of Choices among Uncertain Alternatives." *American Journal of Psychology,* 69, 604–15.

MEAD, WALTER J., ASBJORN MOSEIDJORD, and PHILIP E. SORENSEN (1983). "The Rate of Return Earned by Lessees under Cash Bonus Bidding of OCS Oil and Gas Leases." *The Energy Journal,* 4, 37–52.

MEDOFF, JOHN, and KATHRINE ABRAHAM (1980). "Experience, Performance, and Earnings." *Quarterly Journal of Economics,* 94, 703–36.

MILGROM, PAUL R., and R. J. WEBER (1982). "A Theory of Auctions and Competitive Bidding." *Econometrica,* 50, 1089–1122.

MILLER, E. M. (1977). "Risk, Uncertainty, and Divergence of Opinion." *Journal of Finance,* 32, September, 1151–68.

MILLER, MERTON H. (1986). "Behavioral Rationality in Finance: The Case of Dividends." *Journal of Business,* 59, October, S451–S468.

MITCHELL, DICK (1987). *A Winning Thoroughbred Strategy.* Los Angeles: Cynthia Publishing.

MODIGLIANI, FRANCO (1988). "The Role of Intergenerational Transfers and Life Cycle Saving in the Accumulation of Wealth." *Journal of Economic Perspectives,* 2, Spring, 15–40.

MURPHY, KEVIN M., and ROBERT H. TOPEL (1987). "Unemployment, Risk, and Earnings: Testing for Equalizing Wage Differences in the Labor Market." In Kevin Lang and Jonathan S. Leonard, eds., *Unemployment and the Structure of Labor Markets.* Oxford: Basil Blackwell.

MUSSA, MICHAEL (1979). "Empirical Regularities in the Behavior of Exchange Rates and Theories of the Foreign Exchange Market." In K. Brunner and A. H. Meltzer, eds., *Policies for Employment Prices and Exchange Rates,* Vol. 11. Carnegie-Rochester Conference Series on Public Policy, supplement to the *Journal of Monetary Economics,* 9–57.

NEELIN, JANET, HUGO SONNENSCHEIN, and MATTHEW SPIEGEL (1987). "A Further Test of Bargaining Theory." Unpublished manuscript, Department of Economics, Princeton University.

NURKSE, RAGNAR (1944). *International Currency Experience.* Geneva: League of Nations.

OBSTFELD, MAURICE (1990). "The Effectiveness of Foreign-Exchange Intervention: Recent Experience 1985–1988." In W. Branson, J. Frenkel, and M. Goldstein, eds., *International Policy Coordination and Exchange Rate Determination.* Chicago: University of Chicago Press.

OCHS, JACK, and ALVIN E. ROTH (1988). "An Experimental Study of Sequential Bargaining." Unpublished, Department of Economics, University of Pittsburgh.

ORBELL, JOHN M., ROBYN M. DAWES, and ALPHONS J. C. VAN DE KRAGT (forthcoming). "Explaining Discussion Induced Cooperation." *Journal of Personality and Social Psychology.*

PEAVY, JOHN W. (1988). "Closed-end Fund New Issues: Pricing and Aftermarket Trading Considerations." Working Paper 88-8, CSFIM, Southern Methodist University.

PLOTT, CHARLES R., and SHYAM SUNDER (1982). "Efficiency of Experimental Security Markets with Insider Information: An Application of Rational Expectation Models." *Journal of Political Economy,* 90, August, 663–98.

POTERBA, JAMES M., and LAWRENCE H. SUMMERS (forthcoming). "Mean Reversion in Stock Prices: Evidence and Implications." *Journal of Financial Economics.*

PRATT, JOHN W., DAVID WISE, and RICHARD ZECKHAUSER (1979). "Price

Differences in Almost Competitive Markets." *Quarterly Journal of Economics*, 93, 189–211.

QUANDT, RICHARD E. (1986). "Betting and Equilibrium." *Quarterly Journal of Economics*, 101, 201–7.

QUINN, JAMES (1987). *The Best of Thoroughbred Handicapping: 1965–1986.* New York: Morrow.

QUIRIN, WILLIAM L. (1979). *Winning at the Races: Computer Discoveries in Thoroughbred Handicapping.* New York: Morrow.

RAFF, DANIEL M. G., and LAWRENCE H. SUMMERS (1987). "Did Henry Ford Pay Efficiency Wages?" *Journal of Labor Economics*, 5, S57–S86.

RAPOPORT, ANATOL, and A. M. CHAMMAH (1965). *Prisoner's Dilemma.* Ann Arbor: University of Michigan Press.

REINGANUM, MARC R. (1983). "The Anomalous Stock Market Behavior of Small Firms in January: Empirical Tests for Tax-loss Selling Effects." *Journal of Financial Economics*, June, 89–104.

REINGANUM, MARC R. (1984). "Discussion." *Journal of Finance*, 39, July, 837–40.

RITOV, RITA, and JONATHAN BARON (forthcoming). "Status-quo and Omission Biases." *Journal of Risk and Uncertainty.*

RITTER, JAY R. (1987). "An Explanation of the Turn of the Year Effect." Working Paper, Graduate School of Business Administration, University of Michigan.

ROENFELDT, RODNEY L., and DONALD L. TUTTLE (1973). "An Examination of the Discounts and Premiums of Closed-end Investment Companies." *Journal of Business Research*, Fall.

ROGALSKI, RICHARD (1984). "New Findings Regarding Day-of-the-Week Returns over Trading and Non-Trading Periods: A Note." *Journal of Finance*, 34, 5, December, 1603–14.

ROGOFF, KENNETH (1979). "Essays on Expectations and Exchange Rate Volatility." Ph.D. dissertation, Massachusetts Institute of Technology.

ROLL, RICHARD (1983). "Vas ist Das? The Turn-of-the-Year Effect and the Return Premia of Small Firms." *Journal of Portfolio Management*, Winter, 18–28.

ROLL, RICHARD (1986). "The Hubris Hypothesis of Corporate Takeovers." *Journal of Business*, 59, April, 197–216.

ROSEN, SHERWIN (1986). "The Theory of Equalizing Differences." In Orley Ashefelter and Richard Layard, eds., *Handbook of Labor Economics*, Vol. 1. New York: Elsevier Science Publishers BV.

ROSENBERG, BARR, KENNETH REID, and RONALD LANSTEIN (1985). "Persuasive Evidence of Market Inefficiency." *Journal of Portfolio Management*, 11, Spring, 9–16.

ROSETT, RICHARD N. (1965). "Gambling and Rationality." *Journal of Political Economy,* 73, 595–607.

ROTH, ALVIN E. (1987). "Bargaining Phenomena and Bargaining Theory." In A. E. Roth, ed., *Laboratory Experimentation in Economics: Six Points of View.* New York: Cambridge University Press.

ROZEFF, MICHAEL S., and WILLIAM R. KINNEY, JR. (1976). "Capital Market Seasonality: The Case of Stock Returns." *Journal of Financial Economics,* 3, 379–402.

RUBINSTEIN, ARIEL (1982). "Perfect Equilibrium in a Bargaining Model." *Econometrica,* 50, 97–109.

RUDERMAN, HENRY, MARK LEVINE, and JAMES MCMAHON (1986). "Energy-Efficiency Choice in the Purchase of Residential Appliances." In Willett Kempton and Max Neiman, eds., *Energy Efficiency: Perspectives on Individual Behavior.* Washington, D.C.: American Council for an Energy Efficient Economy.

RUSSELL, THOMAS, and RICHARD H. THALER (1985). "The Relevance of Quasi Rationality in Competitive Markets." *American Economic Review,* 75, December, 1071–82.

RUSSO, J. EDWARD, and PAUL J. H. SCHOEMAKER (1979). *Decision Traps.* New York: Doubleday.

SALOP, STEVEN C. (1979). "A Model of the Natural Rate of Unemployment." *American Economic Review,* 69, March, 117–25.

SAMUELSON, WILLIAM F., and MAX H. BAZERMAN (1985). "The Winner's Curse in Bilateral Negotiations." *Research in Experimental Economics,* 3, 105–37.

SAMUELSON, WILLIAM, and RICHARD ZECKHAUSER (1988). "Status Quo Bias in Decision Making." *Journal of Risk and Uncertainty,* 1, 7–59.

SCHELLING, THOMAS (1984). "Self-command in Practice, in Policy, and in a Theory of Rational Choice." *American Economic Review,* 74, 2, 1–11.

SCHKADE, DAVID A., and ERIC J. JOHNSON (1989). "Cognitive Processes in Preference Reversals." *Organization Behavior and Human Performance,* 44, June, 203–31.

SCHULMEISTER, STEPHAN (1987). "An Essay on Exchange Rate Dynamics." WZB, Berlin Discussion Paper No. 87-8, July.

SEGAL, UZI (1988). "Does the Preference Reversal Phenomenon Necessarily Contradict the Independence Axiom?" *The American Economic Review,* 78, March, 233–36.

SEN, AMARTYA K. (1977). "Rational Fools: A Critique of the Behavioral Foundations of Economics Theory." *Journal of Philosophy and Public Affairs,* 6, 317–44.

SHAPIRO, CARL, and JOSEPH E. STIGLITZ (1984). "Equilibrium Unemployment as a Worker Discipline Device." *American Economic Review*, 74, 433–44.

SHEFRIN, HERSH, and MEIR STATMAN (1988). "Noise Trading and Efficiency in Behavioral Finance." Working Paper, Leavey School of Business, Santa Clara University, August.

SHEFRIN, HERSH, and RICHARD H. THALER (1988). "The Behavioral Life-Cycle Hypothesis." *Economic Inquiry*, 26, October, 609–43.

SHILLER, ROBERT J. (1981). "Do Stock Prices Move Too Much to be Justified by Subsequent Changes in Dividends?" *American Economic Review*, 71, June, 421–36.

SHILLER, ROBERT J. (1984). "Stock Prices and Social Dynamics," *Brookings Papers on Economic Activity*, 457–510.

SHLEIFER, ANDREI (1986). "Do Demand Curves for Stocks Slope Down?" *Journal of Finance*, 41, July, 579–89.

SHLEIFER, ANDREI, and LAWRENCE SUMMERS (1990). "The Noise Trader Approach." *Journal of Economic Perspectives*, 4, 19–34.

SKINNER, JONATHAN (1989). "Housing Wealth and Aggregate Saving." *Regional Science and Urban Economics*, 19, 2, May, 305–24.

SLICHTER, SUMMER (1950). "Notes on the Structure of Wages." *Review of Economics and Statistics*, 32, 80–91.

SLOVIC, PAUL (1972). "Psychological Study of Human Judgment: Implications for Investment Decision Making." *Journal of Finance*, 27, 779–99.

SLOVIC, PAUL, BARUCH FISCHHOFF, and SARAH LICHTENSTEIN (1982). "Facts versus Fears: Understanding Perceived Risk." In Daniel Kahneman, Paul Slovic, and Amos Tversky, eds., *Judgment under Uncertainty: Heuristics and Biases*. Cambridge, U.K.: Cambridge University Press.

SLOVIC, PAUL, DALE GRIFFIN, and AMOS TVERSKY (1990). "Compatibility Effects in Judgment and Choice." In Robin M. Hogarth, ed., *Insights in Decision Making: Theory and Applications*. Chicago: The University of Chicago Press.

SLOVIC, PAUL, and SARAH LICHTENSTEIN (1968). "The Relative Importance of Probabilities and Payoffs in Risk-Taking." *Journal of Experimental Psychology Monograph Supplement*, 78, November, Part 2, 1–18.

SLOVIC, PAUL and SARAH LICHTENSTEIN (1983). "Preference Reversals: A Broader Perspective." *American Economic Review*, 73, September, 596–605.

SMIRLOCK, MICHAEL, and LAURA STARKS (1986). "Day of the Week and Intraday Effects in Stock Returns." *Journal of Financial Economics*, 17, 197–210.

SMITH, ADAM (1976). *The Theory of Moral Sentiments*. Oxford: Clarendon Press. (Originally published in 1759.)

SNYDER, WAYNE W. (1978). "Horse Racing: Testing the Efficient Markets Model." *Journal of Finance*, 33, 1109–18.

SOLOW, ROBERT M. (1979). "Another Possible Source of Wage Stickiness." *Journal of Macroeconomics*, 1, 79–82.

STAHL, INGOLF (1972). *Bargaining Theory*. Economic Research Institute, Stockholm.

STERN, HAL (1987). "Gamma Processes, Paired Comparisons and Ranking." Ph.D. dissertation, Department of Statistics, Stanford University, August.

STIGLITZ, JOSEPH E. (1974). "Alternative Theories of Wage Determination and Unemployment in L.C.D.'s: The Labor Turnover Model." *Quarterly Journal of Economics*, 88, May, 194–227.

STIGLITZ, JOSEPH E. (1976). "Prices and Queues as Screening Devices in Competitive Markets." IMSSS Technical Report No. 212, Stanford University, August.

STIGLITZ, JOSEPH E. (1987). "The Causes and Consequences of the Dependence of Quality on Price." *Journal of Economic Literature*, 25, March, 1–48.

STROTZ, ROBERT H. (1955). "Myopia and Inconsistency in Dynamic Utility Maximization." *Review of Economic Studies*, 23, 165–80.

STULZ, RENE (1986). "An Equilibrium Model of Exchange Rate Determination and Asset Pricing with Non-Traded Goods and Imperfect Information." Mimeo, Ohio State University.

SUMMERS, LAWRENCE (1986a). "Reply to Galper and Byce." *Tax Notes*, 9 June, 1014–16.

SUMMERS, LAWRENCE H. (1986b). "Does the Stock Market Rationally Reflect Fundamental Values?" *Journal of Finance*, 41, July, 591–601.

SUMMERS, LAWRENCE, and CHRIS CARROLL (1987). "Why Is the U.S. Saving Rate So Low?" *Brookings Papers on Economic Activity*, 607–35.

SWEENEY, R. J. (1986). "Beating the Foreign Exchange Market." *Journal of Finance*, 41, 163–82.

TAJFEL, HENRI, and JOHN C. TURNER (1979). "An Integrative Theory of Intergroup Conflict." In W. Austin and S. Worchel, eds., *The Social Psychology of Intergroup Relations*. Montery, Calif.: Brooks/Cole, 33–47.

THALER, RICHARD H. (1980). "Toward a Positive Theory of Consumer Choice." *Journal of Economic Behavior and Organization*, 1, 39–60.

THALER, RICHARD H. (1981). "Some Empirical Evidence on Dynamic Inconsistency." *Economics Letters*, 8, 201–7.

THALER, RICHARD H. (1985). "Mental Accounting and Consumer Choice." *Marketing Science*, 4, Summer, 199–214.

THALER, RICHARD H. (1988). "The Ultimatum Game." *Journal of Economic Perspectives*, 2, Fall, 195–206.

THALER, RICHARD H., and ERIC JOHNSON (1990). "Gambling with the House Money and Trying to Break Even: Effects of Prior Outcomes on Risky Choice." *Management Science*, 36, June, 643–60.

THALER, RICHARD H., and HERSH M. SHEFRIN (1981). "An Economic Theory of Self-Control." *Journal of Political Economy*, 89, 392–410.

THOMPSON, REX (1978). "The Information Content of Discounts and Premiums on Closed-end Fund Shares." *Journal of Financial Economics*, 6.

TINIC, SEHA M., and RICHARD R. WEST (1984). "Risk and Return: January and the Rest of the Year." *Journal of Financial Economics*, 13, 561–74.

TURNER, JOHN C., and HOWARD GILES (1981). *Intergroup Behavior.* Chicago: University of Chicago Press.

TVERSKY, AMOS, and DANIEL KAHNEMAN (forthcoming). "Loss Aversion and Riskless Choice: A Reference Dependent Model." *Quarterly Journal of Economics*.

TVERSKY, AMOS, SHMUEL SATTATH, and PAUL SLOVIC (1988). "Contingent weighting in judgment and choice." *Psychological Review*, 95, July, 371–84.

TVERSKY, AMOS, PAUL SLOVIC, and DANIEL KAHNEMAN (1990). "The Causes of Preference Reversal." *American Economic Review*, 80, March.

TVERSKY, AMOS, and RICHARD H. THALER (1990). "Anomalies: Preference Reversals." *Journal of Economic Perspectives*, Spring, 4, 201–11 (reprinted here as Chapter 7).

VAN DE KRAGT, ALPHONS J. C., JOHN M. ORBELL, and ROBYN M. DAWES (1983). "The Minimal Contributing Set as a Solution to Public Goods Problems." *American Political Science Review*, 77, 112–22.

VAN DE KRAGT, ALPHONS J. C., JOHN M. ORBELL, and ROBYN M. DAWES, with SANFORD L. BRAVER and L. A. WILSON, II (1986). "Doing Well and Doing Good as Ways of Resolving Social Dilemmas." In H. Wilke, D. Messick, and C. Rutte, eds., *Psychology of Decision and Conflict*, Vol. 3, *Experimental Social Dilemmas*. Frankfurt am Main: Verlag Peter Lang, 177–203.

VENTI, STEVEN F., and DAVID A. WISE (1987). "Have IRAs Increased U.S. Saving?: Evidence from Consumer Expenditures Surveys." National Bureau of Economic Research, Working Paper #2217.

VENTI, STEVEN F., and DAVID A. WISE (1989). "But They Don't Want to Reduce Housing Equity." National Bureau of Economic Research, Working Paper #2859.

VERMAELEN, THEO, and MARC VERSTRINGE (1986). "Do Belgians Overreact?'' Working Paper, Catholic University of Louvain, Belgium, November.

VISCUSI, W. KIP, WESLEY A. MAGAT, and JOEL HUBER (1987). ''An Investigation of the Rationality of Consumer Valuations of Multiple Health Risks.'' *Rand Journal of Economics*, 18, 465-79.

WARSHAWSKY, MARK (1987). ''Sensitivity to Market Incentives: The Case of Policy Loans.'' *Review of Economics and Statistics*, 286-95.

WASON, P. C. (1968). ''Reasoning about a Rule.'' *Quarterly Journal of Experimental Psychology*, 20, 273-81.

WEINER, SHERYL, MAX BAZERMAN, and JOHN CARROLL (1987). ''An Evaluation of Learning in the Bilateral Winner's Curse.'' Unpublished manuscript, Kellogg School of Management, Northwestern University.

WEISENBERGER, A. (1960-1986). *Investment Companies Services*, Various years. New York: Warren, Gorham and Lamont.

WEISS, ANDREW (1980). ''Job Queues and Layoffs in Labor Markets with Flexible Wages.'' *Journal of Political Economy*, 88, June, 526-38.

WEISS, KATHLEEN (1989). ''The Post-Offering Price Performance of Closed-End Funds.'' *Financial Management*, Autumn, 57-67.

WEITZMAN, MARTIN (1965). ''Utility Analysis and Group Behavior: An Empirical Study.'' *Journal of Political Economy*, 73, 18-26.

WEST, KENNETH D. (1988). ''Bubbles, Fads and Stock Price Volatility Tests: A Partial Evaluation.'' *Journal of Finance*, 43, July, 639-55.

WILCOX, DAVID W. (1989). ''Social Security Benefits, Consumption Expenditure, and the Life Cycle Hypothesis.'' *Journal of Political Economy*, 97, 288-304.

WILLIAMS, JOHN B. (1956). *The Theory of Investment Value*. Amsterdam: North-Holland. (Reprint of 1938 edition.)

WILSON, ROBERT (1977). ''A Bidding Model of Perfect Competition.'' *Review of Economic Studies*, 44, 511-18.

WINSTON, GORDON (1980). ''Addiction and Backsliding.'' *Journal of Economic Behavior and Organization*, 1, December, 295-324.

YAARI, M., and MAYA BAR-HILLEL (1984). ''On Dividing Justly.'' *Social Choice and Welfare*, 1, 1-24.

YELLEN, JANET (1984). ''Efficiency Wage Models of Unemployment.'' *American Economic Review*, 74, 200-205.

ZAROWIN, PAUL (1988). ''Size, Seasonality, and Stock Market Overreaction.'' Working Paper, Graduate School of Business Administration, New York University, January.

ZELDES, STEPHEN P. (1989). ''Consumption and Liquidity Constraints: An Empirical Investigation.'' *Journal of Political Economy*, 97, 305-46.

ZIEMBA, WILLIAM T., SHELBY L. BRUMELLE, ANTOINE GAUTIER, and SANDRA L. SCHWARTZ (1986). *Dr. Z's 6/49 Lotto Guidebook.* Vancouver and Los Angeles: Dr. Z. Investments, Inc., June.

ZIEMBA, WILLIAM T., and DONALD B. HAUSCH (1986). *Betting at the Racetrack.* Vancouver and Los Angeles: Dr. Z. Investments, Inc.

ZIEMBA, WILLIAM T., and DONALD B. HAUSCH (1973). *Dr. Z's Beat the Racetrack.* New York: William Morrow, 1987.

ZWEIG, MARTIN E. (1973). ''An Investor Expectations Stock Price Predictive Model Using Closed-end Fund Premiums.'' *Journal of Finance,* 28, 67–87.

Index

225